T0408326

Dances with Sheep

Life only exists in relationship to other life.

Susan Aposhyan

Dances with Sheep

On RePairing the Human–Nature Condition in Felt Thinking and Moving Towards Wellbeing

Anna Dako
with foreword by Sondra Fraleigh

 **intellect**

Bristol, UK / Chicago, USA

First published in the UK in 2023 by
Intellect, The Mill, Parnall Road, Fishponds, Bristol, BS16 3JG, UK

First published in the USA in 2023 by
Intellect, The University of Chicago Press, 1427 E. 60th Street,
Chicago, IL 60637, USA

A catalogue record for this book is available from
the British Library.

Copy editor: MPS Limited
Cover designer: Tanya Montefusco
Cover image: Anna Dako
Production manager: Sophia Munyengeterwa
Typesetter: MPS Limited

Hardback ISBN 978-1-78938-693-6
ePDF ISBN 978-1-78938-694-3
ePUB ISBN 978-1-78938-695-0

To find out about all our publications, please visit our website.
There you can subscribe to our e-newsletter, browse or download our current
catalogue and buy any titles that are in print.

www.intellectbooks.com

This is a peer-reviewed publication.

Contents

Foreword:
Dancing with Sheep and Paradox

Sondra Fraleigh
30 September 2021

It is a great pleasure to invite readers to Anna Dako's feast for thinking somatic sense and sensitivity in this book. I marvel at what she accomplishes here with her comprehensive engagement of the natural world and well-studied view of human nature. I have witnessed this book mature over time, first with Dako's doctoral work so extensively based on biological sciences and analysis of the human in culture and philosophy.

Is the book really about dancing with sheep? Yes, quite literally, but more about what the dancing, the sheep and the land have to teach us about ourselves and our responsibility to all life. When I first read Dako's title, I laughed, but then I was intrigued. What would the author make of dancing with sheep, and why would it interest her as a topic of study to share with others? I hoped the dissertation would become a book and said I would buy it.

I confess to reading new work with a phenomenological orientation toward nondualism. Thus, I endeavour to find evidence of body/mind bifurcation in Dako's position, but my search is like looking for a needle in a haystack. Dako writes through a unified embodied feeling for relationships, always led by ecological urgency. Still, she problematizes nature and body. This work is original, heartfelt and committed to its purpose of explaining life through embodied relationships.

It isn't often I encounter such fully developed practice research. In this case, I appreciate how *Dances with Sheep* moves with experience and intellect alike. It is also historical and cultural, not splitting these apart, even as it acknowledges unique aspects and differences of these bodies of knowledge. Intricacies of moving with receptivity and sensuous co-presence in physical time – ontologies of where and when, in and out, now and then, the temporal and the infinite – inform the book's pages, while surprising stories in sensuous receptivity breathe life into them.

At one time in the development of this book, Anna and I had long e-mail discussions about felt thinking. We finally realized how we might state the issue of feeling and thinking in movement with economy. Now I see how the issue explodes conceptually and in practice. I learn as I dance with sheep in this beautiful book. It convinces me to take time to dance in nature, as nature, moving with other animals and creatures, reading in and out of Anna's dance, feeling in tandem with those influenced by her work.

I applaud this book and its eco-soma commitments. It piques my reflection on what it takes to live a full family life while writing, researching and staying with the difficulty over time. I also know how much effort it takes to study effortlessness and let it be (like a natural makeup look). Yet, in the paradoxical body, there is always enough to share in somatic reserves and extensions. The friction makes it so.

Now! Shall we dance with the sheep and trees and crawl over fences like happy children who know how to play creatively? The thought-filled play of Anna Dako's book is a feast to be shared and savored through dancing – moving towards wellbeing wherever you are – with adversity and joy.

Acknowledgements

Dances with Sheep has definitely been a very rich and most adventurous few years in my personal journey as a practitioner researcher. Having moved homes, internationally, many times before, another move to Scotland seemed like the craziest thing to do. Yet, chasing my dreams to keep working outdoors and moving with the natural world around, I couldn't have pictured a better place for my work to unfold and bear fruit.

I would then like to thank here all the hills, valleys, rivers, lochs, forests and animals of the local Scottish landscapes, so rich and so alive, including all the colours and flavours of the famous Scottish weather that I encountered and danced with on this journey. Thank you for welcoming me.

Taking this opportunity to express my further gratitude, I would also like to thank a strong handful of people who supported this pioneering work in expressive writing in its original format as a doctoral thesis and in earlier years guiding me onto this path.

I would like to thank my wonderful teachers, Sondra Fraleigh for inspiring me with her work over the years and for her most nourishing support for mine, Penny Collinson for 'taking me home' in somatic movement experience during the intense years of my time at the University of Central Lancashire, and Andrea Olsen for helping me connect many threads of my moving thoughts with her own teachings.

I would like to thank Dr Salma Siddique for making this work as an academic project possible and for her personal support and trust in the value of the experiential work within therapeutic education at the University of Aberdeen. I am also grateful for being invited to join and participate in the concluding year of Prof Tim Ingold's *Knowing from the Inside* project that took place at the Department of Anthropology and to all the people I had the pleasure to meet and exchange with throughout its duration. And I would like to include here all the warm-hearted and most supporting staff at the University's Multi-Faith Chaplaincy where majority of the indoor movement work took shape. I feel I learned a lot there about where and how the work I am presenting here belongs.

I would like to thank, for wonderful supervision support, Dr Elizabeth Curtis from the University of Aberdeen and Prof Vicky Karkou from Edge Hill University, as they offered me both guided and grounding direction on the work's way to completion. Like all challenging journeys, this one definitely found their expertise and applicable advice absolutely indispensable. Thank you kindly.

Also, this work would not have been possible without my dear movers: Grace Archer, Gulliver Brodbeck, Kelly Suleman, Martina Polleros, Marta Bury, Dr Sarah Luczaj, Valeria Lembo and Jack Wylie, who did all the nimble work with the camera for us. I would like to thank them from the bottom of my heart simply for opening theirs and for offering their best to the work and the time shared. My thanks here also go to all my clients and students over the years, who strengthened the principles of this work through their own trust in outdoor movement explorations.

Last but not least, I owe endless gratitude to Ronald Dako, not only for creating conditions for me to work and bearing with all the challenges brought onto our family life by such intensive times, but most importantly for being the 'rock' in all this. Our shared journey is an amazing legacy we keep 'being on the move' with. Thank you, wholeheartedly.

And to round up, I see this work as a beautiful continuation of my ongoing journey as a writing mum, multitasking and weaving priorities, every single day. And I couldn't be more proud to say that the most precious insights within my work always come from this most nourishing, every-day home life, as I watch the kids grow. Thank you Noemi, Nantai and Nolen, you are my light and endless inspiration. Always.

Summary

With human nature being standardly defined as ways of thinking, feeling and acting, the contemporary discourse on the topic reveals a primary emphasis on thinking, i.e. mental processes, as the essence of being human. This observed prioritization of cognitive activity over the lived experience, and which Merleau-Ponty calls 'disembodied scientification' (Merleau-Ponty and Edi 1964) creates and re-enforces the commonly visible boundaries between the human and the natural world and forges many conceptual contradictions as well as prevailing objectification of the natural world as mere resource to humankind.

In this book, I argue that the operational attitude towards Nature presupposes its existential passivity and renders it barely contextual to our own wellbeing. Next to that, I also propose that personal engagement and storied narrative offers more valid, subjective depth to how one can understand human nature and that the importance of deepening one's comprehension of the *relational interconnectedness* with the living world around and caring for that relationship in everyday life has never been more urgent.

And while the currently opportunistic relation to Nature resides primarily within mental attitudes toward human nature that prioritize what we *think* over what we *feel*, *somatic sensitivity*, where somatic means to study the self from the perspective of one's lived experience encompassing the dimensions of body, psyche and spirit (Hanna 1986), emphasizes our inborn ability for *internal perception* and offers help in opening and widening our embodied capacities to engage with the world in 'movements made special through care' (Fraleigh 2015: xx).

The mindful practices of somatic *felt thinking*, that sprang from this intuitive, practice-based inquiry as its methodological grounding, develop here into a holistic practice offered as a way of re-connecting with the ecological depths of the self and which value internal sensations, emotions and imaginings as integral part of being human in a 'more-than-human' world (Abram 1996).

Dances with Sheep presents then the scope of experiential load shaped by felt thinking about human nature while moving in/with Nature and elaborates on such processes in relation to the movers' overall wellbeing. It covers creative journeys of opening up to the living agency of Nature itself through the emergent three phases of experiential relatedness and its dimensionality in embodied experience of the self as analogous to the dynamics of embryological layers formation, namely its ectodermic attentiveness, its mesodermic connectivity and its endodermic intensity. The experiential depths also provide different time/space contexts for the embodied comprehension of the self that expands on the pre-phenomenological heritage of thought in practice.

The first phase of experiential flux connects the movers to the natural environment as self through *sensual presence* in physical time of inward and outward listening. The second phase offers co-creating engagement with the natural world through *experiential responsiveness* in psychological time of animating. And the final stage of becoming the Nature/Self through *insightful intuiting* in primordial sense of relatedness takes the movers to the most meaningful extent of experience by deepening one's sense of being and belonging.

Laid out as a thorough interpretation of practice, the book presents its original contribution to eco-phenomenology with its ontological principle of embodied relationality in *towards* and *away from* movement as a primal gateway to well-being and its creative inter-constitution.

It also constructs a cyclical paradigm for ecological felt thinking grounded in unifying depths of experience of 'other' within the self and provides a proper look at contextualising it theory.

Supported by wide considerations of ontological co-creation in Nature the volume concludes that felt thinking with Nature, as experiential reflexivity practice guided by *being with* Nature in contemplative movement, and a practice-based method of self-inquiry, can path a more ecologically mindful way for an inclusive understanding of human nature/Nature relationship as Nature/Self. It also promotes a more intuitive, movement-guided alertness to modes of 'being well' with self/other in broader life contexts that weave both, the creative and the caring together.

Figures

Terminology

Nature (with capital 'N') – referring to the living Earth;

nature (with small 'n') – referring to 'the essence' or 'core quality';

natural – referring to being 'in agreement with the way of Nature';

self – referring to a person's essential being accessible through reflexive perspective;

Nature/Self – referring to an ecologically-widened comprehension of the self as Nature;

earth (with small 'e') – referring to 'the ground', 'soil' or one of the 'classical elements';

Earth (with capital 'E') – referring to 'planet Earth';

Life (with capital 'L') – referring to 'all life on Earth';

unless used differently in quotations.

Preface

The subject of this book arises primarily from my wonderings about human nature. Looking at how the living world is always there with me in all my daily thoughts, I often wonder about being labelled as belonging to the human world only, while within my practice-based work I continually strife for a more ecologically inclusive self-understanding.

I have also been wondering why in western philosophical thought in general, when talking about human nature as human essence, there is hardly any relation to Nature as our living environment mentioned or considered, almost as if the human race were an alien species that happened to occupy planet Earth.

So, living in the world swept by the environmental crisis of today, my motivation for a more heart-felt comprehension of human nature in its 'lived' dimensions invited me to embark on my own creative journey, as a somatic movement practitioner. It invited me to re-discover the role of feeling, and somatic sensitivity, in reflecting on the human condition in a more embodied and more environmentally inclusive experience of the self in movement.

I have thus been interested in responsive listening through the prism of movement itself, only to re-discover that the very essence of my experience of selfhood lives in being connected to ongoing change in Nature as a continuously re-creative ontology itself, and my deeply felt, primal world of movement.

And, looking back, I would also like to consider this process a fruitful attempt at rewriting some of the negative narratives behind sensitivity itself, as well as at expanding on what being somatically sensitive can offer to current perspectives on human kind.

Now, before I realized the paradigmatic structure to my own movement experiences, I set the written work off with critical verifications of most current perspectives on human condition and wellbeing offered by various thinkers within eco-phenomenology and ecological psychology. While developing the practical depths of the process, I saw this enterprise as an opportunity to advance the multiple perspectives that the phenomenological method seemed to have been offering.

I also envisaged it as a thorough continuation of heuristic research where somatic work could offer its more embodied depths of study.

Yet, having indeed dived deep into the experiential and highly intuitive journey of somatic work with movement and creative expression, I have gathered so many enlightening and transformative insights coming from movement practice itself that the wealth of those experiences transformed slowly into a mature practice of self-discovery.

It is a practice guided by its emergent three dynamics of engagement that comes about as experiential transitioning through embodied flux of relatedness, as I call it, and which I have been able to awaken and embody in free movement. It is the practice that has shaped from being a methodological tool of voicing movement only to later become a method of felt thinking in movement as a way of connecting the psycho-somatic functioning on both conscious and subconscious levels of being.

Having said that, realizing the intrinsic and deeply felt value of such an enriching practice itself, the difficulty of putting it all in writing and contextualizing in terms that go beyond somatic literature exceeded my expectations. Still, connecting the experiential, somatic way of understanding movement with more established philosophical schools of thought has been the ultimate goal of this undertaking. Eventually, while progressing on the path of linear advancement in scholarly sense, the process itself brought many sideway turns only to divert me onto the path of re-discovery of its pre-phenomenological roots.

The process took me back beyond the schools of phenomenology, process philosophy or existentialism, mainly to the cross-disciplinary, creative practice-based scholarship of Bergsonian heritage. I could then relate my own discoveries of the principle of 'towards and away from movement', followed by the three phases of qualitative deepening while listening to/in/with movement and responding to/in/with movement in felt thinking, especially in its relation to experiences of time as creative self.

I would then wish the work presented here is viewed as an authentic journey of a practitioner–researcher. The journey that while being shaped by ongoing strife for more insight into the questions asked has also shaped itself by ongoing reshaping of the questions as well, and eventually, by incorporating them into the practice.

Also, in sharing this work, alluding to meaning making as a fluid activity, where 'meaning refashions itself at the risk of destroying itself' (Hanna 1962: 143), as Maurice Merleau-Ponty said while reflecting on Bergson's work, I would like to care for giving time and space to finding different meanings of the experiential content that perhaps are not explicit enough in my own conclusive thoughts coming out of this journey, or the imagery included, but which resonate with reader's individual ways of relating.

The density or complexity of the experiential material offered in this book could then be further recognized, as both a presented difficulty of finding the reader's own way through the experiential part of this written work, but also as an opportunity for personal meaning making.

In any case, thank you for letting me be part of that journey by attending to this book. The chances are, it is a real reflection of the complexities of 'being' itself, and of the fact that the nature of 'being human' needs constant effort of discovery and not, as once thought, a singular or clearly applicable conclusion. It is also an invitation, as Bergson would say, to stop flying above perception, but to penetrate it, within ourselves as living Nature.

It is important for me to acknowledge that the mentioned ongoingness of reflective processes on the subject of Self as Nature relates to connecting my research on Bergson's life philosophy to the work of one of the somatic work's pioneers, Thomas Hanna. The suggested circularity here lies then in beginning this practice-based writing process with Hanna's definition of somatics from 1976, and whose quotation on the role of somatic education opens an experiential journey for many somatic practitioners in training and rounding it up with Hanna's book on Bergsonian heritage from 1962 in my hand.

It is a great finale for me to realize again how 'moving backwards', only to make another emergent move onwards can be valued as the biggest stepping stone and an insightful recap on life's onward journeys. And I definitely connect such 'moving backwards' to its role in re-finding balance as the main principle of wellbeing too.

More importantly though, by being revisited in my writing processes, Hanna's definition of somatics, and somatic movement experience, has also seen an occasion for renewed expansion, thanks to Sondra Fraleigh's most welcome annotation to this work. She helps us understand that somatic experience does not only lie in our internal perception of the self but also in many inclusive ways of connecting with ourselves through connecting to others as the unity of soma and psyche (Fraleigh 2015). This work is indeed all about re-defining ourselves as an ongoing, all-inclusive relationship, made up of both inner and outer worlds and landscapes, always different, always the same.

I would like to note that the restorative effects of every movement session performed in this process have been absolutely astounding and that my ongoing motivation to pursue this work further, and deeper, has come from my personal awe for wisdom implicit in movement as life philosophy per se, and which I feel we all, human beings, should tap into and live by more.

Being guided by movement within and around ourselves is what steers and shapes this work. By sharing developments of felt thinking here, in its expressive writing formats, I am also hopeful that it can serve as a guide to an everyday self-care practice that will keep springing, ever-changeably, from such wisdom implicit in omnipresent movement of life. Finally, I also hope that it can facilitate a more inclusive and mutually supportive relationship with the Earth that, in time, can help us to become our better selves.

Now, the work presented in this volume comes in three sections that reflect the pre-practice stage of the research, its practice-based reflection stage and the final post-practice stage.

In Section One, I present an introductory scope of relevant references that create the motivational context to the practical work undertaken, and the work's methodological groundings. I also introduce a thorough overview of the current contexts to the theme of human nature in relation to the natural world and its direct relation to the issues of wellbeing faced by many modern societies.

I then move to grounding the theme in its relevance within movement-based work and explain why attending to contemplative movement as methodology offers a more embodied way of looking at the problem and for finding practical solutions within it. Here I also bring the reader's attention to concepts of kinaesthetic awareness and somatic sensitivity and introduce the intrinsic value of subjectively sensed feelings and intuitions as a way for overall wellbeing improvement as an ongoing dialogue within self-care practices.

Next, I introduce an overview of how such relational awareness to 'feeling well' shapes itself through a more historical look at the concepts of Self and Other within the European, and later the North-American geospheres. It is also where I suggest that the common understanding of human condition has been widely influenced by its cultural and mainly anthropocentric contexts, with not enough emphasis being placed on the individual comprehension of such condition as a living being like all other. The chapter also introduces reasoning for why the contexts of the natural world have been practically absent in literature on human nature.

Then, I introduce a more detailed summary of different therapeutic and philosophical approaches that concern a more inclusive way of working with human nature, in relation to Nature and in relation to wellbeing. I also shape further grounding for why working with movement offers an open pathway to questions about the ontological connection between the human and the natural world.

Next, I present the theme's ecological contexts, mainly in somatic and dance research literature and practices, and which contextualizes the interdependence of feeling, thinking and acting processes as present in Nature and which one can attend to through the somatic experience of the self.

I further describe somatic movement experience of felt thinking as a self-inquiry method based on *in-search*, furthering the reader's understanding about the internal focus presented in the experiential material gathered and its intimate value.

I then introduce a detailed reflection upon the stretch of individual practice that shaped the circular methodology of the work and clarify all the journeys that the questions asked throughout this process have made.

Finally, I round up the section with elaborations on felt thinking and languaging the experiential content and introduce the practice-emergent themes as phases of felt thinking and connect the three emergent themes with somatic processes of germ formation and its ectodermic, mesodermic and endodermic dynamics.

Section Two comprises of experiential descriptions of the three phases of felt thinking practice, with each phase being introduced and interpreted through the prism of my own experiences first, and then contextualized within the experiences of other movers.

Phase I focuses on pathways for *connectivity* through experiences of both Nature and self in time and space through listening, sensing, pacing, tuning into and being with. It is the phase in which the experiential content is shaped by open questions of *Where* and *When*. It is the phase where my own and other movers' *sensual presence* comes to the fore of the study in its ectodermic relevance.

Phase II focuses on pathways for *co-creation* through experiences of both Nature and self in subjectively lived exchanges through opening, experiencing, imagining and embodying. It is the phase in which the experiential content is shaped by animating questions of *What* and *Who*, and where my own and my fellow movers' *agency* together with the *agency of Nature* itself in its mesodermic dynamic is being attended to.

Finally, Phase III focuses on pathways for deeper *insights and intuitions* about the ontological relation between Nature and self. A phase attended to as a continuation of the other two and which includes experiential processes of full engagement, of letting go, and of embodied intuiting and transforming. It is the phase in which the experiential content is shaped by motivational questions of *Why* and *How*, and where the movers' rediscovering of 'the natural' within our/themselves happens in its relevance to the endodermic, deepest intensity of experience and where a more inclusive belonging to the ontological and the primordial time is found.

In Section Three, I then offer a thorough contextualization of the experiences in felt thinking. The section starts with elucidating all the findings brought by experiences of 'the felt' and how the process itself has shaped into a well-rounded practice of felt thinking in movement.

I then discuss and offer more review on how the practice of felt thinking fits within its broader understanding of philosophical and psychological theory. In a selection of sub-sections, I present its relevance with both somatic and Bergsonian lineage of thought and in its further relation to the practical, philosophical and cultural implications. I also draw its relevance to the ecologically grounded concepts of temporality and circularity, of Nature as Wholeness, and concepts of philosophy grounded in movement as ontology of being.

I conclude that felt thinking in movement presents an inclusive way of re-discovery of the living connection between Nature and self, as well as a way of finding deeper meanings in our human experience as reflected in our wellbeing condition.

I also resolve that the experiential travelling through in-search and out-search, following the three phases of somatic movement experience as self-care, brings to fore the ontological principle of moving *towards* and *away from* movement being relational, thus caring, in the first place. It is in the endless possibilities (or dynamics) of movement itself, which bypass all the dualistic reasoning that the real meaning of being can be found, ongoingly, and in ever more accessible ways to all beings.

Read more about the work's continuations and trainings offered within the online presence of my practice at Dunami – Movement | Arts | Wellbeing: www.dunami-somatics.com.

SECTION ONE

OPENINGS AND CONTEXTS

Introduction:
Contemplating Ecological
Belonging in Somatic Felt Thinking

FIGURE I.1: *Felt Thinking in Movement*, Scotstown Nature Reserve, Aberdeen.

I am treading gently through the grass. I just stepped off a walking path and onto a mire. The grass is dense and somewhat integrated in its many protective ways. Every step makes me feel like a trespasser, so I slow down, also because I feel its hostility sharpens with directional motivation of each of my steps taken – forward.

I have to give it up. I cannot just cut through. It is really spiky and hurtful. The grass is full of prickly-sow thistles.

And so eventually, I do stop. I have grown in respect already. This weedy grassland is at home here, I am the odd one out. I need to find a place for myself, quick. I cannot just roam about.

There, an inviting tree, a few steps away, surrounded by a softer patch of pasture. A few quicker leaps get me there, and another one yet lands me safely on its low and huggable trunk. The cool temperature of the tree invites me to settle and to share my own warmth. The smooth surface of the bark feels so delightful. I hug and tuck myself onto it, and the tree's two main branches create a cradled space for me to feel into and start taking my time a bit more.

When meeting a tree in such open experience, what comes to me first is the nudging consciousness of my own weight and how the support of the surfaces of the tree makes me experience my weight differently. I feel how much work it is for the tree to keep me on. I have to spread my weight onto limited surfaces that twist my skin and press against my bones. I try to hang rested on my chest and with hands down too, my legs stretched about, learning a different relationship to gravity. And I find some amazing curves in stretching backwards while I am lifting my feet up into the air, letting my weight say hello to the branches above my head as well. 'Can you hold me?', I ask them silently, while I swiftly browse the younger offshoots, in their slimmer bits.

The density of the branches in my grip communicates well. It feels straightforward and safe. Its flexibility does correlate to its strengths in handling my weight. Soon, the many twists and lifts I do make me want to take my shoes off and meet the bark with the grip of my feet too. Now, it feels like home. I feel I can offer some playfulness to the tree, while being safely lifted from the hostile ground and nestled by this young, friendly tree, stretched horizontally just above the spiky green lands. And I hope the tree feels alike, in this peaceful, if only for a little while, symbiosis.

I close my eyes and stretch slowly on my front, arched a little bit upwards. Skin to skin with the tree. Cheek to bark. The tree's stillness, and it being placed in this particular spot, makes me feel like I'm gliding. I'm gliding attuned to its own slow rhythms of growth. And I sense this growth so palpably present in the complexity of its outgrown smaller branches, the twigs and the deeply green and fresh foliage. I see all possible dynamics of its steady movement of 'reaching out to the sun' in the endless amount of leaves. So active in today's gentle breeze, catching the sun's countless reflections. Making me look so still now, so simple, with my two arms and two legs only.

The number of my fingers and toes doesn't add much to match the tree's dynamic, I must admit. Perhaps my loose hair …

Anyway, it all comes down to being so aware of my own presence felt-in-weight here. I don't feel so heavy or needing so much support on the ground. I suppose it is easy to take it for granted, many times, as the ground is naturally always there, always so spread out and cushioned by footwear too, on daily walks, unlike this one.

So, I am thankful for this reminder about the gravitational support that I constantly require and that this ongoing relationship with Earth's pull is such a living and changeable process.

My movement habits make it easier to cope with this relationship every day, they sustain my shape, of course. Yet, the more I take the ground for granted the less I realize how it is thanks to the Earth's pull that I am able to create every push away from it, or a reach-out, as an individual response, even if it's just that conscious lifting of my foot, off the ground, slowed down to the minimum, in full attention.

I experience it as an amazing exchange created in this body–earth relationship of towards and away from movement. And I know my thinking also emerges from this exchange as creative improvisation, guided by sensations and feelings, I only need to free it up from any limiting purposes …

We, living beings, walk on the ground every single day, yet we don't give it much thought in experiential terms, do we?

How often do we dance in response to movement present in a tree like this one? Or walk in tune with the singing birds? Do we ever try to exchange a thought with the clouds above our busy heads? Or get all fuzzed-up muddy rushing barefoot down the nearby grassy slopes?

Are we too grown up for all that?

To me, creative attunement with the living environment around is undoubtedly inexhaustible, as life itself, always on the move, always changing.

And so, following this first description of my experiences outdoors, I would like to now introduce the three steps of experiential immersion as creative methodology of felt thinking as an eco-somatic practice and discuss multiple entry points into an ecological connectivity, like one just described, in movement and reflection.

And I would like to do it guided by a few more questions, starting with: What does it mean to feel think?

To put it simply, to feel think is to wonder about 'the flow of things', every day, solely by allowing some time and space to listen and contemplate, whole-bodily, nourished by open landscapes of self, yet shared with all other life, discovery.

And how can we let the natural environment speak through movement and creative expression to help us learn about the felt qualities of the living, versatile landscapes and the vivid wildlife all around in more engaged and embodied ways?

To me, felt thinking in somatic movement experience of the 'self' addresses just such wondering. And I dive into it as a deep self-inquiry practice that brings the lived connections between Nature and the Self to the fore and which offers new insights on how we are in the world and how to remedy multiple imbalances through experiential in-search, out-search and connecting it all – insightful intuiting.

After all, contemplating relationality in movement is a very intuitive, imaginal, spontaneous and improvisational activity that involves all the sensual acuteness, kinaesthetic and proprioceptive awareness, embodied presence and a very open attitude towards listening, receiving and being with whatever is, internally, externally, always transitioning. It is based on practising one's ability to move that emerges from inner sensing and the visceral phenomena, as well as staying responsive to the external stimuli of the space or landscape, where movement shapes itself as a living conversation, and a meeting ground between what is and what comes into being, at any given moment.

In practising felt thinking, preferably outdoors, I am then able to bring all the living and wellbeing-enriching aspects of the natural environment to my awareness and ponder over their deeper meaning as experienced in ongoingly moving sensations. More importantly though, I am also discovering how to give the experience its voice, or its many voices, and how to build a creative dialogue between the conscious observation and the intuitive responses that shape in relation to the landscape's qualities. Last but not least, it also helps me grow as the environmentally inclusive 'whole self'.

Now, what would that look like, in practice? And how is felt thinking different than thinking itself?

Somatic felt thinking starts with being mindful about Life's all-inclusiveness, and our personal belonging within it. We are the offspring of this Earth after all, and felt thinking is about giving this experience a voice that can speak for both our biological historicity as a species on Earth and our futurity. All of this is merged into the openness of the experience of 'the now' as movement per se, in free flow sounding, singing and embodied expression.

Felt thinking and voicing the experience is also about using the language as an implicit, expressive and creative process and not primarily as an explicit communication tool. All deterministic thinking alike needs to merge free into improvised movement exploration.

Thoughts themselves become the endless experience of movement, acknowledged in the reflexive mode of 'being with' them, as they emerge, transition and merge again. The 'Now' feels responsive and alive. All is movement.

As a reflective practitioner, throughout the years of practising felt thinking with the natural world around me, and in many different, shared contexts of movement experience, I have come to observe and distinguish three main stages or three phases of the practice. My ongoingly reinforced conviction, and realization really, has been that the experienced movement engagements differ in their experiential depths, as much as they differ in the visible dynamics of movement patterns. Consequently, whenever I practise free movement in felt thinking, I can feel and distinguish three different types of connectivity to myself and the environment taking place, as reflected in movement patterns and forms.

Let us take an initial look at those dynamics now.

During the initial phase of free movement engagement, there is a noticed tendency for wide-spread, open armed, inquisitive encounters happening. The physical expression during this initial stage appears as mainly horizontal in patterns, following inclinations for sensual encounters through vision, smell, touch and a willingness to meet and reach out.

FIGURE I.2: *Felt Thinking in Movement* – Phase One, Drumoak Woods, Aberdeenshire.

During the following phase of movement engagement, a visible tendency for more dynamic encounters with the sensed dichotomies of experience takes over. The physical encounters deepen in psychological meaning creating a new dimension of relating through giving and receiving in experiential exchange. Multidimensional patterns of expression in movement peak at this stage as well.

FIGURE I.3: *Felt Thinking in Movement* – Phase Two, Drumoak Woods, Aberdeenshire.

Finally, during the third phase of movement engagement, following the often exhausting exchange of Phase Two, a more vertical dynamic observable in movement emerges. Visible reaching up with hands or the whole body stretches happen

FIGURE I.4: *Felt Thinking in Movement* – Phase Three, Drumoak Woods, Aberdeenshire.

which reveals strong connectivity between the grounded, the earthy and the more metaphysical, spiritual and soulful depths of experience.

Throughout these movement phases, of remarkable notice are also the changes happening in the audible experience of movement, where the breath changes into sounds and sounds change into free flow expression in words, lived narratives and melodies.

Those phases of reflexive felt thinking and their unusually qualitative content have their wider philosophical and theoretical relevance worth bringing up here. In my opinion, alluding to somatic experience as free movement improvisation, the creatively voiced content that comes through in felt thinking out loud, can be seen as a potentially new way, or new depth of contemplative, visceral thinking, away from habits of only mental, i.e. conscious processing. This voiced content offers experientially valid connections to wider contexts of life in general, human or 'more-than-human' (Abram 1996), and its creative ways.

Drawing from Bergson's way of practising philosophy, in his book *Thinking Beyond The Human Condition*, Keith Ansell-Pearson writes that

> it is not so much that we are caught up in an existential predicament when the appeal is made to think beyond the human condition; it is rather that the restriction of philosophy to the human condition fails to appreciate the extent to which we are not simply creatures of habit and automatism but are also creatures involved in a creative evolution of becoming.
>
> (2018: 5)

Additionally, our habits of thought 'prevent us from recognizing our own creative conditions of existence and restrict the domain of praxis to social utility' (Ansell-Pearson 2018: 17).

The task of making any progress in the direction of thinking out of habit then, if we think of phenomenological philosophy as an affair of sensual perception, is 'not to leave the human behind but rather to broaden the horizon of our experience of life' (Ansell-Pearson 2018: 5), as somatic felt thinking suggests, and think beyond our customary images of matter, as Bergson (Bergson et al. 2007) too proposes. In *Creative Evolution* (Bergson et al. 2007), Bergson reminds that evolution involves 'sympathetic communication' and 'reciprocal implication and interpenetration' which to me, re-affirms working with free movement expression in felt thinking even more, including its metaphysical dimensions.

The way in which I understand the metaphysical inquiry is that it is first and foremost grounded in bodily experience which then expands beyond to meet our multiperspectival reasoning in a looping and interactive way.

What is also important to point out here is that what is often seen or understood as the nature of human belonging is but a simplification or generalization of many cultural tendencies of action which hardly ever have a chance to speak for themselves. And I agree here with what Eugene Gendlin proposes, which is that

> human nature, living bodies, and reality (should) be thought of neither as a separately given order nor as simply lacking in any order but an order that is carried forward by the variety of livings we observe, as well as in many other ways that have never as yet happened.
>
> (1993: 6)

Also, in his 'Introduction' to *Metaphysics* (1912), Bergson expands on the central role of intuition when thinking about self as time and he concludes that the true purpose of knowledge is to know things deeply, to touch the inner essence of things via a form of empathy. For people like myself, living with highly myopic vision, invitation to the sensuous is always open. To feel think, I don't necessarily need to close my eyes. The ongoing practice and experiences outdoors transition seamlessly in direction of kinaesthetic dialoguing guided by open anticipation for emergent sound, touch, feelings and sensations and away from any judgemental thoughts.

Cultural prioritizing of visual experiences does limit the activity of other senses. And so, as I now reflect, had I been seeing the world perfectly with my eyes … I might have never become a mover whose creation thrives on the magical mysteries of the unseen. Undeniably, the world sensed in my experience of open movement does widen up in its many ways of meaning-making and relating. And I believe that there are endless doorways to the sensuous, dependent on an individual take, once we soften the priority of vision.

Again then, I am exploring felt thinking in movement as opening up to new possibilities of relation to ourselves as living beings, and the three stages or the three dynamics of engagement, in experiential transitioning through the embodied flux of relatedness, reveal to me yet more depths in experiential qualities that I am able to awaken and embody in free movement. Those new depths correspond to what Bonnie Bainbridge Cohen (Cohen et al. 2012) calls the somatically sensed cellular levels of agency, attending to which offers many ways of overcoming the conceptual dichotomies of self and other. Engaged in practice, such deep awareness finds its immediate correlation to the perception of the self as ongoing, both becoming and differentiation in the experiential realities of time and space.

What might that mean though?

In her experiential guide on *Body and Earth*, Andrea Olsen (2002) reminds that at the advanced level of every discipline, there are more questions than answers. I couldn't agree more. Yet, interestingly enough, wondering in movement guided by open questions of relation becomes an easier way for me to engage in felt thinking.

The questions that guide the movement journeys, go in complementary pairs of 'Where and When', 'Who and What' and 'Why and How' does the free movement belong?

Experientially then, the first phase of felt thinking opens up pathways for connectivity through experiences of relational 'out-search' through listening, sensing, pacing, tuning into and being with. It is the phase in which the experiential content is shaped by open wonderings about Where and When, as the mover's sensual presence comes to the fore of the self-inquiry in its ectodermic relatedness thanks to the peripheral nervous system activation.

 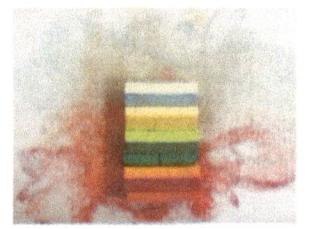 

FIGURE I.5: *Felt Thinking in Creative Arts Practice* – Phase One: Ectodermic Relatedness.

Phase Two opens up pathways for more animated co-creation through movement experiences in lived exchange, of engaging, remembering, imagining and embodying. It is the phase in which the experiential content is shaped by questions of What and Who, and where the mover's agency together with the agency of the natural world around in its mesodermic dynamic is being attended to in more psycho-physical engagement.

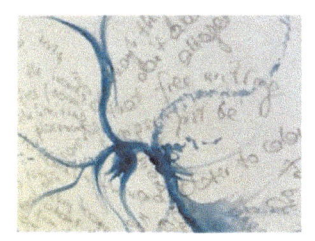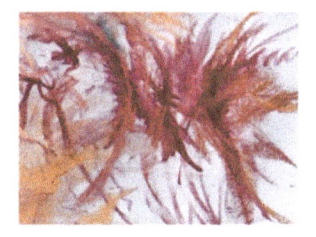

FIGURE I.6: *Felt Thinking in Creative Arts Practice* – Phase Two: Mesodermic Dynamism.

Finally, Phase Three opens up pathways for deeper insights and intuitions about the ontological co-relation between Nature and the self. A phase attended to as a curious continuation of the other two and which includes experiential processes of letting go, of embodied intuiting and inner shifts. It is the phase in which the experiential content is shaped by 'in-search' merged into 'out-search' guided by Why and How questions as the mover rediscovers 'the natural' within themselves in relation to the endodermic, deepest intensity of experience, where a more inclusive belonging to the primordial 'time as self' is found.

FIGURE I.7: *Felt Thinking in Creative Arts Practice* – Phase Three: Endodermic Intensity.

Thus, this experiential transitioning through embodied flux of relatedness to self and other is understood here as two fold – through the metaphorical lens of embryological development of ectoderm, mesoderm and endoderm and their dynamic activity patterns observable in movement but also through the corresponding questions that attending to those layers of experience seem to be addressing, and which relate the mover to different realities of time/space experience.

The movement dynamics, as observed in my practice of felt thinking over the years, do show grounding similarities to the dynamics of germ formation, as the experience of free movement travels from the outer layers of the skin and the nervous system on the horizontal plane, through the muscular and the bone-felt multi-dimensional patterns, and finally, onto the deepest, internal organs and cellular levels of experience that become externalized in more vertical forms and engagements, guided by all-inclusive gut feeling and intuition.

And I like to describe that journey by three important words: receptivity, responsiveness and responsibility.

Working with experiential levels of (1) ectoderm, an outer germ layer of an embryo that gives rise to the skin, retina, brain, spinal cord motor neurones, peripheral nervous system, etc. the questions of Where and When create a direct link to the physical time of experience in receptivity.

Working with experiential levels of (2) mesoderm, the layer that gives rise to muscle, blood, bone, connective tissue, etc. the questions of Who and What create a direct link to the psychological time of experience in responsiveness.

Working with experiential depths of (3) endoderm layer, the layer that gives rise to the digestive track, liver, bladder, the respiratory system, etc. the questions of Why and How create a direct link to, what I call, primordial or ontogenetic time of experience as the sensed integrity in cyclical experience of belonging and responsibility becomes self-explanatory.

To me, felt thinking in movement presents an integrative way of re-discovery of the existential connection between Nature and the Self and a way of finding deeper meanings in our human experience as reflected in our co-living condition. I also suggest that the experiential travelling from the objective, physical time and its ectodermic relatedness onto the subjective, psychological time and its mesodermic dynamism, and finally, onto the primordial time and its endodermic insights, brings to the fore the caring principle of life as relational, in towards and away from movement, and as an ontological principle of all movement.

Like in breath. On an inhale, the movement embraces you moving towards yourself and away from the world, and, on an exhale, it embraces you moving away from yourself and towards the world. One movement in its endless creativity and omni-directionality of Life's relational in-between-ness.

To me then, it is in the endless possibilities hidden within this unifying movement itself, which bypass all the dualistic reasoning about what is 'in' (or internal) and what is 'out' (or external), that the real meaning of being can be found, ongoingly, and in ever accessible to all beings ways.

The conscious mind feels as if coming from its attachment to the temporal, as a survival tool. But the real skill in living a meaningful life, as it shapes itself in my experience of belonging in movement, is to stay close to the relationship between the temporal/conscious and the infinite/unconscious realms and in keeping that 'back and forth' or the 'towards and away from' movement exchange open and permeable.

We, living beings, all participate in and are part of that dancing dynamic of creating and being created at the same time. One cannot be one thing without potentially being its opposite other, just like our skin is both a containing home and a protective limitation.

My reflection here is that by following the tangibility of things only, even in naming phenomena, we create false divisions and contradictions. Our constant effort to rationalize experience takes away from the depths of the informal layers in natural connectivity with the living world around, the connectivity that we do develop if we follow the felt cues that life's creative processes store and make available to us.

If life is indeed so relational and refreshingly malleable, as I sense it is, it is the patterns of movement, perceived as constant entities, that bring us support and comfort. As I continue my practice, I begin to see the elements of Nature as patterns of movement too, created by different time/spaces of the Earth's becoming. And walking barefoot on the moss confirms those thoughts to me, as I hear myself say:

Perhaps there was a time, the time that didn't know the Sun …,
Perhaps the Sun was not born yet.
And perhaps the Earth, as we call it now, comes from those times …
Darkness feels much older than the light …
I am lying down […]
With my eyes tightly closed
Experiencing the cold breath in
Through my mouth
And the warmth …
When I exhale
All my senses seem to work much sharper in the dark
They come from that realm
But, they were created to meet
The light of the outside world …
To soften the meeting grounds
To be gentle
To make friends
To protect the dark
(And) To feed the eternal darkness too
They are both the offspring and the breadwinners
The expressions of ultimate being
And the receptors 'of' and 'for' all the current states
(Breathing …)
The push and the pull
And their creative dance
No wonder the Earth is round

Or roundish, at least
As that is its grounding balance
Between the push and the pull
The forward and the backward
That creates togetherness
And support for each other.

(Moving Thoughts Journal, Felt Thinking in Movement –
audio transcript, August 2017)

As felt in this experience, movement itself then indicates that we embody the deepest levels of relation to the widest sense of Life possible and that within that movement lies an opening to something beyond it all, the eternal and infinite creative force we, living beings, all take part in, both consciously and unconsciously.

I live through time as much as time lives through me, just like my movement is not separate from me, and yet I give it its form, which I can look back at, in reflection.

Through my ongoing practice, I get reminded that a significant part of being human resides in ongoing wondering about where and how we belong, and that perhaps, we should be open to such wonderings without, or beyond words, in responsive listening in expressive movement. Wondering about the self and the world could then be understood and practised more as 'being with' and less as making sense of something external to ourselves for cognitive understanding only.

By practising that in felt thinking, we can enrich our embodied comprehension of co-existence, as children learn about life in full engagement, and indeed engage with the world, as Sondra Fraleigh writes, 'in movements made special through care' (2015: xx). Moving flexibility between the smallest and the largest contexts of any question gives us an opportunity to grow alongside the work and comprehend its depths, not only understand or organize its contents for further use, utility or reproduction.

The bodily ways of being, filled with creative, life giving energy and movement can be seen as the source of our creative expression, whether translated into colours and shapes through the manual handwork, into words in creative writing, sounds picked up in singing or expressed in physical movement per se. This rendering of patterns, tones, pigments, movement spaces and words, as Barry Lopez (2014) reminds us, is the essence of our creative nature and in this sense, art acts upon us and lives through us like Nature does, through mindful improvisation. When we are in an elevated state of our creative nature, we encounter something inexplicable – the mystery of life itself.

Lopez gracefully points out that our usual two responses to such an encounter are: analysis or awe, and that it is about time, considering the urgency of times that we live in, that we stop referring to our taught tendency for analysis of 'other' and instead choose to be in awe and by doing so become the part of the inexplicable. Moral order, rephrasing Lopez, is deep in our tissues, and exposure to Nature or art reflects upon our own humanity as much as it reflects upon how we really want to be or become.

Our physical bodies are made of all the same elements as the Earth itself, developed over the course of the history of our planet. Conrad too writes that 'abhorrence to the "body" leads to vast realms of ignorance' and that 'sensation is not just the messenger of pain, discomfort, and other emotions but is the link to an extraordinary aesthetic landscape that is our birthright' (2007: xxiii–xxiv). Fraleigh adds that 'soma would simply be a floating unconnected sensation of self if we were not aware of others as also constituting consciousness of self' (2015: 42). Along this line of somatic thinking about ourselves as living landscapes, Romanyshyn (2018) too connects our understanding of who we are in relation to Nature as an intertwining and soulful dance of Nature as the psyche, which 'makes itself through the world', not as a thing, but as a living relation to the world in motion.

Indeed, our thoughts are moving, they can wander off, tumult, collect randomly or fade away with different levels of relating awareness. Our emotions rise, collect, overwhelm or show their tempted side as they flow softly with different points of referential concerns. Our physical sensations can also impinge and change intensity in relation to different stimuli. Our awareness itself is fluid and on the move constantly too, taking us through shifts of attention and endless forms of tactile life engagements. The way our functional life within our own skin happens for us every millisecond is absolutely phenomenal, with billions of intelligent cells that just carry life processes forward with ever continuous internal movements driven by implicit intelligence.

Only a deep engagement in movement experience can give us a more holistic sense of what the nature of being movement really is. We are, after all, movement (Dako 2014) and what we conceive of 'the body' is a moving phenomenon as well, and so is our primal world. It is important to see the value in life as not only something we strive for or constantly move towards but also something we are all born with and that what is currently needed, as Michael Yellow Bird reminds, is to 'go back to what we know' (2014: n.pag.) in search for a deeper connection with the living Earth.

As a practitioner then, I argue that somatic experience of felt thinking as a form of contemplative practice can be a living act of such reconnection and a way of dipping into our primal resources for restoration that come from being one with Nature. Creativity resides not in specified talents but in every breath we exchange and every heartbeat we chose to pay attention to.

The practice of felt thinking reminds us that the living dynamic we embody is not only productive but first and foremost receptive. And that both receptivity, i.e. an ability to listen whole-bodily, and productivity embrace each other in the living dynamic of life and co-create ongoingly.

Every stage of the process described here, transitioning from the mover's sensuous presence onto experiential responsiveness and then onto insightful intuiting, is not separate from another. They permeate and enable one another. Feeling and thinking are both movement-based experiences and in felt thinking we can help ourselves to translate them into deeply informed action, in a very authentic and mindful way.

In a personalized form of self-care, practising felt thinking can take as little as three deep breaths or as long as days of inexhaustible explorations. An opportunity to revive what's most important in embodied kinship experience. Depending on what one can attend to on a day, free movement of felt thinking never fails to offer a thorough enlivenment of the psycho-somatic functioning while reconnecting the mover to the deeper meaning of livelihood we participate in, and thanks to which we live and breathe.

In felt thinking, breath itself feels as if yearning to trust and follow the movement. On an inhale, it becomes part of me. And on each exhale, it continuously wants to be part of other things.

So what does it mean to feel think again?

My rounding up summary to this introduction here would be an invitation really, to move with that question for a while, letting it sink in for longer, getting to feel its whereabouts and possible re-shapings. Letting the answer(s) emerge slowly, not necessarily as a bounce back or a definitive so and so, but as an opening onto a new journey. Again and again. As I experience in the felt movement of thoughts and co-lived sensations, the aural, the tactile, the visual and the intuitive – is the true way of Nature/Self – to trust the emotive ongoingness of change in its primal creativity while it seeds and nourishes our ever-evolving belonging.

1

From Living Practices to Practising Life: A Bitter Pill to Swallow

We live in times of great shifts in human history. The times when humanity, having secured its planetary presence, is now shaping not only its own future but the long-term future of all life on Earth. What we, as human beings, think, how we feel and how we act upon our daily life influence this delicate relationship and interdependence between the Earth and its habitants in more and more severe ways. By now, the consequences of human ways of life and its consumerist economies become more and more irreversible, in both human and Earth's wellbeing and functional vitality.

Looking back, considering the widespread advancements of European heritage throughout generations, western societies did get used to living with natural resources available in abundance. As well as living to prove both the personal and the professional success in life, often without minding the side effects of such a lifestyle and the severe imbalances it causes.

What are the reasons for humankind's development in this direction? Is instrumental wrongdoing, including large-scale deforestation, destructive irrigation of cropland, chemical pollution or putting more and more asphalt on wild land, part of human nature? And how can we better comprehend and develop the full potential for 'being natural' in how we inhabit planet Earth, and for living in tune with and not against Nature?

For the last couple of hundreds of years, or at least since traditionally practised sensation-based Aristotelian philosophy gave way to more scientific modes of mechanical discovery in the seventeenth century, the mainstream ways of thinking and comprehending our human condition have been stuck in multiple dualistic paradoxes of seemingly clashing realities. Body–Mind, Culture–Nature, Self–Other, Psyche–Matter, Human–Non Human or Man-made vs. Natural are but a few of the most recognized examples amongst many other dualistic distinctions that still remain in wide use today.

Following some of the most dominant anthropocentric traditions of the West, both in philosophy and Christian theology, what has been commonly assumed, as Theodor Roszak points out, is that by nature, 'human beings exist in total alienation from the natural environment' (2010: n.pag.), and that by abstracting ourselves from it we are able to see and study both ourselves and the natural world more rationally.

The resulting effect of such paradigms is that the philosophical body of work on human nature has seen countless contributions, yet there are practically no studies done which combine the theme of human nature with that of Nature itself. The main focus of the philosophical work so far has been predominantly placed on reflecting upon living in human societies, thus leaving the natural world as a less important, or practically irrelevant context.

Interestingly enough, this exclusive approach within western humanities carries on its dualistic outlook even further as the majority of modern studies on human nature are not only predominantly written from a dissociated Nature perspective, but also from a 'disembodied self' perspective, which primarily, was supposed to secure an objective view on the subject. That applies to the widely performed empirical and so observational inquiry upon cognitive, affective and behavioural components of the subject of human condition and which, in my opinion, does not reveal any truly meaningful, from subjectively lived experience, perspective.

Over time though, the growing obsession about this quantitative 'knowledge of' obtained through often patronizing, rational scrutiny has caused a severe damage to the quality of our, both human and humane 'being with' the natural environment and that includes our ability of being with ourselves and knowing our own nature as well. 'What on earth are we doing?' asks Deborah Winter in her book *The Psychology of Environmental Problems* (Winter et al. 2004).

Our inborn intellect and love for discovery can be easily identified as distinctive qualities of humankind. But why, all along, have we forgotten to be part of our own learning process by excluding ourselves from the first-hand experience of feeling inseparable from the environment which we come from? Or to attend to the less formal and subtler ways of connecting with both ourselves and the world?

After Theodor Roszak coined the term 'ecopsychology' in his book *The Voice of the Earth* (1992), the developing field of ecological psychology is slowly beginning to open such wonderings further. In addition, the unprecedented discussion between the United Kingdom's parliamentary committee and David Attenborough (News 2019), as an expert in natural history and environmental research, held to offer support and advice on issues of climate change, reveals how pressing the condition of the world's natural environment and what our place in it really is.

It is sad to admit that as co-creators of the current, ecologically daunting realities, humankind has been visibly lacking an ability to co-exist in the living world around us in a healthy and balanced way, without creating alienating conditions for objectifying knowledge or without losing the sense of belonging in Life in a wider than 'human world' context. Emily Conrad writes too that 'our lack of active identification with the miraculous flow of life and the creatures that have spawned us is reflected in our surrounding spoilage, which demonstrates our disregard for the life that engendered us' (2007: xxii).

One simple explanation to such a state of affairs is that, psychologically, in any relationship, it is always easier to focus on self-benefit first, and consequently handle such a relationship by distancing ourselves from it, emotionally. After all, western civilization has been very successful in creating interdependent chains of specified professions where vocational separateness limits the possibilities for personal contact or emotional bonding. The free market filled with imported and processed foods and goods can serve as one of many examples, whilst the capitalistically oriented international business relationships that hardly call for a person to person contact, as yet another.

Lester Brown, one of the world's most authoritative voices on planetary well-being, also shares his firm opinion that 'socialism collapsed because it couldn't tell the economic truth. Capitalism may collapse because it couldn't tell the ecological truth' (Brown and Brown 2008: 267).

In this process of maturing as a civilization, it is important to realize that aspiring to skill, reason and a rational attitude towards the known cannot be happening at all costs. Reflecting on social functioning organized around 'owning of capital', the free interrelation and the versatile but respectful co-existence have been replaced much too eagerly with power-based interdependences, working hierarchies and confrontational dominion. Next to that, our naturally helpful curiosity, love of wisdom and physical resourcefulness as humankind's best facets do also get corrupted by social conditioning or far-fetched ambitions in making our lives ever easier, in survival terms, as well as more successful, be it socially or economically.

Noticeably, the virtualities of modern life seem to offer us ever upgraded alternatives to the naturally embodied phenomena. So we continue living tuned to technological advancements and top-down thinking strategies, keeping ourselves preoccupied with producing things like high-tech seamless footwear, instead of enjoying a simple barefoot walk on the grass, at least from time to time.

In a way then, outsmarting Nature has become human life's purpose. At the same time, we often neglect the many kinds and versatility of human intelligence, and stick to inborn instincts as off-record behavioural hints only.

In his book *Wholeness and the Implicate Order*, David Bohm advises about the theoretical assumptions that are regularly made about life. He says that:

> [I]n scientific research, a great deal of our thinking is in terms of theories. The word 'theory' derives from the Greek 'theoria', which has the same root as 'theatre', a word meaning 'to view' or 'to make a spectacle'. Thus, it might be said that a theory

is primarily a form of insight, i.e. a way of looking at the world, and not a form of knowledge of how the world is.

(Bohm 1980: 4)

Further still, with no intention to overgeneralize but simply to mention the observed societal tendencies, I often notice that driven by such societal theatrics of success and progress, fed by analytical attitudes of corporate functioning and mediated truths, we steadily degrade our sensual and ecological literacy and impair our naturally embodied and multi-layered relationship with other living species. Often too, for many, regularly sharp-cut with our culturally dominating contexts of determinism and ever more artificial needs and wants, life might become a lonely treasure-hunt journey equipped with tunnel vision and no real soulmates 'out there'.

How often do I look forward to things, assuming the linear patterns for life developments and single answers to the questions asked, instead of opening the senses to what the subtle weather changes indicate and staying open to change? A question worth asking. Life is too short, we often say, let's make the most of it. And most of the time, we do indeed – use our life, instead of living it. Why is it always easier to emotionally detach ourselves from both ourselves and the multiple rhythms of the living environment around and handle a sudden change only when it is well foreseen and performed with mental preparedness? Why do we not allow life to speak for itself? Well, life can be too uncontrollable, too unlike what humankind wants it to be.

But in such a well-controlled environment of industrial dominion, we often live an artificially assumed rhythm, created and constantly stirred up by an accumulation of individuals trying to win a race, living under the illusion of running for a goal, and that achieving it is always just two steps away. We just need to get there, right? And while 'waiting for Godot', we think our rational mind will take us there and that the body has to be kept strong only to allow for the next step to be taken. We keep following the head. And yet, when we do, we seem more and more confused about the balance of individuality and collectivity of the world around.

Having grown up in such contexts to everyday life, as I have, oriented too much around personal achievement, the most important point seems to be missing, that 'life exists only in relation to other life' (Aposhyan 1999).

As human beings, we definitely are social creatures, yet we are not deprived of wider life contexts. It is impossible to live a truly meaningful life while being the only context to it, and by continuing to use the word 'others' as referring to human beings only, and not to any other being, plant or animal, that lives, shares air and enables our existence as humankind on the Earth. My feeling here is that we also tend to forget that our now dominating skill, i.e. language, developed from the 'practising life' bodily gestures (Abram 1996; Sheets-Johnstone 1990; Lakoff and Johnson 1999) and that we should focus on expanding that skill to share life experiences and not to act as an independent judge to all life on Earth, which is so often the case.

Looking back at over 25 centuries of western civilization, with the written cultural heritage of Greek, Roman, Jewish, Celtic, Germanic, Slavic and other ethnic and linguistic groups, and the hugely influential impact of Christian culture, are we happy with our intellectual development? Are we proud to live life as the world's oppressor? Most importantly, are we, human beings, living so according to or against our human nature?

The answers to such questions are obviously not simple. It is generally very harmful to judge within good or bad categories only. But what can be observed is the tendency of moving towards the positive change or away from it. As a westerner, and, more importantly, as a practising somatic movement educator and therapist working with world-wide life-affirming traditions, I have been living alongside this civilizational transition from living life to treating life as a performance, and I have seen its effects on health and life-long wellbeing of life on Earth.

It is quite visible that due to living alongside alienating concepts of our own humankind we are now facing the result from its real psychological split and the poor condition accompanied by a devastating state of misuse in our natural habitats. Because our civilization has been developing in this direction for many centuries, it currently does appear almost impossible to believe that such a disembodied, machinist mindset will ever change.

Similarly to the experiential philosophies of antiquity that have transformed into the leading ways of scientific inquiry, our true love for wisdom, i.e. philosophy of life, has been giving ways to the performative and computational functions that constantly speed up our natural pace and revolve around competition. In her book *Natural Intelligence*, Susan Aposhyan also writes:

> We learned to view our body as an inarticulate machine that we should spend as little time as possible maintaining. And we were taught to keep it as still as possible. These are the denials of body with which we have been unconsciously indoctrinated.
>
> (1999: ix)

As a result, for many, life ends up being simplified to following beaten paths, proper or wrong addresses, formal communication etiquettes, standardized criteria, bank account numbers, performed and ticked task lists, coffee breaks and quick-fix remedies. We fall asleep double-checking on the usefulness of the day, instead of following life as it unfolds for us.

What is not noticed is that the constant going forward with our lives will, at some point, have to be balanced and counter-acted by going backwards, sideways, and the other awkward ways, or at least by stopping for a while to consciously exchange some air and touch the ground beneath our feet. In times of rapid change like these, we have to develop new ways of understanding the dynamics of change itself, as naturally, we are a part of the ongoing change in Nature all the time.

Through the lens of depth psychology, Stephen Aizenstat writes that:

> [H]uman behaviour is rooted most deeply in nature's intentions (and) that our actions are fundamentally expressions of nature's desire. The rhythms of nature underpin all of human interaction: religious traditions, economic systems, cultural and political organisation. When these human forms betray the natural psychic pulse, people and societies get sick; nature is exploited; and entire species are threatened.
>
> (2003: 2)

Eventually, the urgency of balancing our natural rhythms cannot be denied anymore. And until we realize some bigger truths about life and ourselves in it, and that we cannot carry on without some necessary changes, like creating a bigger space for Life itself in our body–minds and in our hearts too, we will continue living in an 'unhealthy' society. Human life, as Life in general for that matter, does escape our artificially created methods of studying or controlling it anyhow. The moment we realize that our life, just like our living bodies, is attuned to the constant change in the universe, we may start re-defining our natural pace in it and feel we live attuned to our own nature again.

As an important observation, Theodor Roszak brings forth that, as opposed to our modern western psychology and psychiatry attending to patients as individuals in an assuringly alien universe, in traditional societies and in ancient traditions of spiritual healing, it has been understood that

> sanity and madness have to be defined, always, in relationship to the natural habitat, and that, indeed, to a larger extend, madness is understood to be an imbalance between an individual and the natural environment or between the entire tribe or people and the natural environment.
>
> (2010: n.pag.)

Striking as it sounds, Roszak continues with the fact that the whole social system or the entire culture, perhaps like Euro-American societies, might become a victim of what Freud called 'collusive madness' (Roszak 2010) that creates a difficult baseline for any effective healing. He states that we cannot help each other if we are all involved in the same context of performance-based life theatrics.

To me though, as a practitioner, it is through the opening to the wider practices of life outside humankind that the developing fields of somatics, depth-psychology, eco-psychology and eco-phenomenology can offer some complementary insights into the overly quantitative ways of living a life. We have to face the fact that many of the problems of modern life, as Jung reminds us in his book *Undiscovered Self* (Jung 1958), are caused by man's progressive alienation from his instinctual foundation and seek reasons for such developments within ourselves.

The observations described here about how we, in the West, go about our lives and how we cohabit and familiarize ourselves with life itself, create the context for my work as a somatic movement educator. But more importantly still, they create the context for me as a living being co-habiting planet Earth.

In the following section, I will offer a substantial overview of the philosophical thought developments and the later psychological and other interdisciplinary extensions on the subject of human condition that present relatedness to the therapeutic outlook on human nature. By promoting the view that real, living knowledge must be grounded in our ability of experiential 'being with' the world, I will be looking for ways to complement and enrich the current perspectives on human life and wellbeing within the developing fields of somatic psychology and eco-psychology. I will also pay special attention to the shaping perspectives on the sense of self, environmental responsibility and the living relationship with the Earth.

2

Moving towards Wellbeing:
On Change and Continuity in
'Being with' Experience

As mentioned already, the academic body of work on human condition is voluminous, and the chronological scale of publications on the subject stretches from antique times of Greek and Roman empires to globally relevant 'nowadays'. This ever-present subject of common interest entails a lot of entry points to possible answers, as well as a lot of questions that remain unanswered.

Wondering about human nature, when we actually mean the 'essence' of being human is one of the possible ways of looking at the subject in its philosophical take. It can either mean looking for the most unique things that distinguish us from the wider, wild contexts of Nature 'out there' or looking for the most universal characteristics that all people share but which similarly shape human species as separate from its original contexts of co-existing in Nature. In a more recent sense, human nature has also been described as a pervasive concept, the one that 'most of us use to justify our own behaviour as well as that of others' (Wrightsman 1992: 4), and generally used as a blaming excuse for thoughtless or carnal action.

Other ways of deliberating upon human nature focus on the word 'nature' itself, and relate directly to our biology and the study of our human, innate traits within environmental and/or societal structures and are known best within the culture–nature, or nature–nurture debate which connects an array of academic disciplines within humanities and social sciences. Even though, in this take, there is a common agreement on human nature being a good combination of both innate traits and cultural shaping(s), which can now be unanimously considered as being a 'biocultural trait' (Prinz 2012), the problem of studying human nature in contextual opposition to Nature itself is still very present.

The up-to-date studies on what it means to be human dwell then on a long-lasting enterprise of demarcation, separation and alienation of humankind from any other living kind, and revolve around the context of anthropocentric tradition of trying to conceptually understand ourselves and the world we live in through notions we create, or rather make up, by ourselves.

The above-described problem of alienation, both from our own bodies and from the body of Nature, might then be connected to a culturally evolved focus on the rational ways of conquering the elements of Nature with no attention paid to the subtleties of the instinctual levels of being alive, thanks to and together with Nature. It is a complex problem that our modern societies are currently facing, as described already in the previous section. Additionally, as I argue here, its complexity calls for an in-depth, transformative shift in our dominating mindset which has, up until now, been driven primarily by modes of technical rationality.

As observed on multiple occasions in the written work by many somatic practitioners (Aposhyan 1999; Hartley 2004; Chodorow 1991; McHugh 2016; Whatley et al. 2015, to name a few), what should be a naturally fluid connection between the internal and external functioning is alarmingly distorted by modern ways of living and being, and this is precisely what felt thinking methodology is meant to address in an active and reflective way alongside proposing ways to work through such condition. It is of crucial importance to notice that our global circumstances require a devoted participation in practices which can develop new and unique competences, which are complex enough to handle the requirements of the present state of affairs, ecologically speaking, and which can revive liveliness and passion for the nature of being human in its full sense.

I will share my own example here. When I think about motion in general, without trying to attend to the thought in embodied feeling, I immediately tend to follow the pre-set definitions once taught at school during physics class and which describe motion as a change of position of an object over time, following the laws of physics, and usually relating to the external world of man-made 'moving objects'. Consequently, my associations within the material world of physics are mostly those of displacement and distance. Those, often imposed concepts of movement, based on the linear, mechanistic use of force and caused displacement, definitely shape the way I can see many people relate to the world around.

At the same time, within the contexts of contemporarily versatile societies, progressing from organizational, single-channelled power relations to ever more complex interrelationality and heterogeneous co-living, I then ask:

How can embodied experience of the natural world help us in bringing up, feeling into and comprehending the essence of being human while restoring the well-balanced connection between the self and Nature? And,

How can our embodied focus on movement as the source of all experience redefine our comprehension of our creative Nature/Self with its effects on overall wellbeing?

Within my current involvement in somatic therapy work, I have experienced that the non-judgemental attending to our own internal 'being in movement' teaches us about the natural rhythms of change and the different frequencies of being that offer ways for immediate reconnection with the living world around and our own instinctual nature. Minding our wellbeing through attending to movement is a very basic yet most nourishing practice that grows one's connection to the living environment and to which we should invite others too, to share both our energy, and our potentials that naturally thrive in being alive together.

All because an ability of 'being' does not only mean co-existing but rather, co-creating in a worldly sense. When I am able to attend to those basic impulses and instinctual drives for acting from the expanded natural-self perspective, I am able to relate to the wider Life context that we share this true world of interwoven movement with, be it a bird, or a tree, or the sight of a mountain covered by evening sunlight.

I connect to the knowledge that we continuously grow into simply by conscious 'being with' self/other in a cyclical and interdependent dynamics pattern. To appreciate this integral wisdom in an introductory way here, an expert on world-wide sustainability movement, Karl-Henrik Robèrt writes:

> The basic structures and functions of our bodies are nearly identical to those of eagles and seals, all the way down to the molecular level. It is very clear that, from a biological standpoint, we are not the masters of nature, nor even its caretakers. We are part of nature. It also happens that nearly all of our natural resources have been created by cells. Over billions of years, a toxic stew of inorganic compounds has been transformed by cells into mineral deposits, forests, fish, soil, breathable air and water as the very foundation of our economy and of our healthy existence. With sunlight as the sole energy supply, those natural resources have been created in growing, self-sustaining cycles – the 'waste' from one species providing nutrition for another. The only processes that we can rely on indefinitely are cyclical; all linear processes must eventually come to an end.
>
> (1996: n.pag.)

Now, I often hear that if we are okay on the functional level, we are fine, healthwise. But when given an opportunity to engage in somatic movement reflection, it is quite obvious that if you listen closely, our physical body is not just a reflection of how it functions. Having all organs healthy and no visible symptoms of any disease does not mean wellbeing, as wellbeing is not a condition stored within our physiological boundaries only.

Our soma is a living orchestra of all the subtle and interacting balances or imbalances that communicate a lot about our emotional condition, our spiritual strength, cognitive habits and sensual soundness based on our current life experience. Without these subtle levels attended to, it is possible to function – yes, but without making the most of our given potential. The concepts of trust in life itself, connection to the ground and support through reciprocity in somatic work refer directly to our psycho-somatic being well with the world, which very often resonates internally on multiple frequencies.

When faced with the loss of that 'being well with' relationship, it is not often easy to pinpoint one cause. Even our mood is not something we simply wake up with but a subtle inner attitude that constantly changes in relation to our immediate realities. A close listening into, and awakening of our internal sensitivities that guide our movement through life is a delicate play of picking up the subtle, often indirect, clues and echoes.

If we remember we are not just a head attached to a functional vehicle, but a united and responsive combination of trillions of intelligent cells, we can then enter that 'organic source of intelligence' (Aposhyan 1999). And if we, following Darwinian theory of evolution, assume that human psyche, which, etymologically, derives from the old Greek term *psychein* meaning 'to breathe' or 'to blow', must have evolved out of thousands of years of evolutionary development on Earth, it is then reasonable to assume that it does connect in intimate and most significant ways with the natural environment out of which we evolved and with which we have to establish a real and open relationship.

Again then, wellbeing is not just functioning, but an on-going process of active exchange, the embracing of our vitality and potentials that we realize and make real every single day.

It is dependent on our ability to attend to the often intuitive levels of what can be called 'nebulous knowing' (Tougas 2013) and which is difficult to describe in words but which can be followed with attentive embodied listening on both internal and external levels. As we are born with different dynamic potentials, it is crucial to be able to tune to them in a right, individual way so that they can serve us well and be a platform for self-development and health. Put in a nutshell, if we constantly fail to give ourselves the time for such attentive listening, and to what feels right both internally and in agreement with our environment, we will keep creating artificial reasons for harmful comparisons and by so doing we keep creating new reasons for domination and alienation.

The movement practice developed in felt thinking reminds me that Nature is what mobilizes, propels and sets in motion every single aspect of our embodied lives. Our human nature, like Nature itself, is the nature of change, and not of any stable quality in a linear progress of life as we tend to think. It is moving through life as living Earth and as us, beings, moving along and being a living part of its/our constant change. Nature is movement and movement is Nature.

Without following Maxine Sheets-Johnstone's more theoretical elaborations on movement too closely here, what resonates with the somatic, more practice-based approach is her reference to the work of Algis Mickunas (1974), that movement, i.e. our kinaesthetic awareness is our basic sense and 'perceptual organ' of time and space and that our 'kinaesthetic consciousness is the basis for all perception' (Sheets-Johnstone 2011: 145).

Indeed, by attending to movement in the somatic experience, we are able to tap into the many different dimensions of our spatio-temporality and into how we can feel connected to time unfolding in different ways within ourselves as opposed to managing it as an external context to daily life. In fact, time has always been one of the basic categories by the help of which human beings have been making sense of the world in their ways of controlling reality.

Yet, as attending to movement means attending to stillness too, it is the experience of stillness or slowness at least, for example in the already described experience of the breath, that widens our awareness of movement and our traditional awareness of the present moment as supported by the internal processes of ongoing change.

Again, movement and stillness are in conceptual language considered as opposites, leaving little room for understanding 'absence' as a process itself. The way I understand it somatically though (Dako 2015a) is that stillness is where movement comes from and where it is heading towards. It is both the beginning and the extension of movement and what makes movement possible as the process of ongoing continuity.

If we pay too much attention to the fast, usually most engaging movement, as we have as a civilization, we will risk losing sight of its roots and hit the stage of exhaustion. It is then through the realization of this natural continuity of intertwined rhythms, through the natural developments of life-sustaining motion, that we are able to move beyond restrictions in physical movement, and life as such, and start living in an embrace with the responsively changing world. The method of felt thinking in movement is to help just that while being a simple self-care practice as well.

Additionally, I will also propose later that such embodied relationality-based approaches should become a more common standard in the growing educational research, and its more and more interdisciplinary scopes of relevance. But now, let us look back again, at a selection of both historical and cultural contexts of relationality, just so we can move towards a more experiential understanding of the processes of felt thinking.

3

Historical and Cultural Contexts of Relationality: On Otherness and Interconnectedness in Movement Experience

Since the onset of western thought, from the times of the Greek and later Greco-Roman empires, there has been an obvious interest in both philosophical and cultural debate on what it means to be human as based on ever-present wonder over the shared human condition but also over human diversity. Such interest has been driven both by internal observation of everyday life in societal realities as well as external contexts of conquest and expansion. Since the recorded, i.e. written knowledge can be seen as a high-end privilege of most powerful nations throughout time, the mainstream and most prevailing conceptions upon the subject of human nature have been obviously shaped amongst the most developed or civilized societies of the West, i.e. within European, and later, the North-American geospheres, and within their socio and psycho-historical traditions.

As the history of human expansion has made a full circle, literally, with its omnipotent presence influence on the whole planet, I would like to argue that all up-to-date written work on human nature written in culturally specific contexts of its authors calls for a current, wider-reaching update. It calls for an update that does not only reside within an anthropocentric tradition of thought but one that extends its view over the intercultural horizons and which presents an integrative view of people in the immediate, living context of the globally viewed, natural environment.

In my opinion then, the written discourse calls for a post-colonial update on human nature which, paradoxically, in the current environmental situation of misuse and disintegration, while following the circular pattern of life itself, takes us back to revisit our roots, i.e. 'our primal origins', where primal means the central, the fundamental, and the original, and not the primitive, in its colonial, mainly pejorative sense. It takes us back to restudying our ontological basics, i.e. our being in movement and the evolving from that primordial motion relationship to the living Earth.

It is perhaps important to notice that because each culture develops methods for knowing the world in consistency with its assumptions about reality, any new relational shifts in social connection to the natural environment will mirror and go together with new understandings of human nature and new conceptual frameworks within which such understandings hold valid. Like the concept of 'culture' itself, which, in fact, has been initially used interchangeably with that of 'civilization' and used as an opposite to what was understood as 'barbarity', i.e. living outside civilization, and which underwent a thorough transformation over time (Jahoda 1992: 4).

To continue tracing its interesting change in usage, the most sudden transformation in world-view upon 'culture', as Jahoda writes happened around mid twentieth century, during times of intensive intercultural dialogue, when 'the normative ideal had given way to recognition that cultures or civilisations can vary in time and space' (1992: 4). Eventually, the normative viewing of culture as high-end privilege to seeing it through the anthropological lens, as a way of living, took over, and cultural relativism remained a prevailing view within natural sciences and humanities ever since. Having said that, let us not forget that 'culture', as any other word or concept, is being used daily in a multiplicity of other contexts dependent on the individual meaning and referring to specifically varied sets of phenomena.

Historically though, we have now arrived at what can be called a 'beyond anthropological' stage, the stage which opens up to different relationships with what used to fall under a non-western 'otherness' in scholarly discourse, both culturally and ecologically. The contextual 'otherness' that all new knowledge about different living environments used to fit into, and which surpasses its previous relations to many historical developments.

To give it a quick overview, as chronicled by Bernard McGrane, it has developed from the cultural phenomena starting with the Christian ideology of sin and demonology, then the Enlightenment discrimination of ignorance and superstition, and later, from the nineteenth century's authoritative paradigms of 'cultural difference' (McGrane 1989). Along with the mechanization of Nature during the Enlightenment period came calls for its control and so the scientific revolution of the sixteenth and the seventeenth centuries was practically born from the gender bias-based argument that Nature, seen as the feminine, can and should be controlled, as ecological psychologist Deborah DuNann Winter describes in more detail in her chapter on 'The "nature" of western thought' (1996: 25–61).

With the civilizational and environmental changes at hand, and by keeping in mind that the conceptual framework of studying human nature developed mainly in contextual opposition to the natural world (Roszak 2011; Winter 1996), such developmental shifts in the concepts of 'culture' and 'other' can be easily viewed as corresponding to that of 'human nature' itself, where the 'human' aspect of this binding concept stands for the civilized dimension of life in the context of the animalistic other. And where the historically visible, conceptual shifts between using the concept in its singular form, meaning one, universally shared human nature or plural form, assuming multiplicity of human natures, can be seen as dynamic shifts of reconceptualization and as live responses to contextual changes at hand, which have been taking place throughout the history of anthropological inquiry.

As what we mean always depends on the context we refer to, the presence or the absence of the natural environment as a contextual base for thinking about human nature makes all the difference between seeing it as singular or plural. Similarly to deliberations on culture(s), if we exclude Nature as context, thus rendering it irrelevant, we assume the plural meaning of human nature and mean the many (human) natures, and if we include the context of Nature as 'the other' we mean human nature as the unique human experience.

Having realized the urgent need to rebuild our own relation and place on Earth not in contrast but in interconnection with the natural world, we can no longer afford such ignorant attitudes or hierarchical thinking. With all due respect for cultures older than the western one, and the many ancient and indigenous traditions of ancestral wisdom which, unlike the West, have never lost their life-affirming connection to the Earth and its living environments, it has never been more important to think and live inclusively and ask ourselves again: how is our nature different from, or other to, the Nature itself? And is it, at all?

To back such questions up with an overused reference to Man's unmatched capacity of the human mind at work is perhaps not the most desirable answer assuming this human mind of ours, did not help us consider, culturally, that like Nature itself the nature of human beings is grounded in change as well. We are, after all, masters of bringing change into the world, and we often applaud such presumably altruistic actions as driven by the slogan 'to make a change'.

The only difference which prematurely yields Nature as less capable in the visibility of 'change making' is the different time frame and the cyclical dynamic within which its changes take place.

We, human beings, are the masters of immediate, fast-paced and progressively linear change, often unable to comprehend Nature in that sense, as it operates within much larger time frames that circulate rather than progress. Being so, Nature simply becomes obsolete to the human life span perspective, and becomes the less relevant and easier to manipulate for us 'other'. This slow, in human terms, speed of ongoing change happening in Nature is often overlooked, or simply considered as contextual stillness. On such a straight line of conceptual simplification, 'stillness' takes us straight to 'weak', or 'unable', and thus rendering Nature easy to dominate, or make contextually irrelevant.

The grounding fact that Nature makes all change within our human world possible is hardly mentioned or recognized at all, at least not in the educational system I have been through until adolescence.

Interestingly enough, it is important to notice that the ecological inevitability of a switch to the environmental, i.e. larger than simply anthropocentric context of our deliberations over the subject of human nature, introduces significant changes to the debate over a long-standing conflict between culture and nature and makes such a dualistic distinction obsolete.

I would like to propose that, in the all-embracing context of Nature, should we eventually take Nature into account, the concept of human nature, becomes practically synonymous with that of human culture, assuming we stay aware of the depth and multiplicity of meanings within the term itself. In that sense then, all innate aspects of human nature can always be seen as being a part of the world-wide culture of being human, or of our human being/living in the world, and never separate from our biological or rather our ecological existence. And it is also why all the post-modern associations about culture previously linked to seeing it, through the prism of cultural or theological theory, as mapped systems of live discourses, change significantly and become a more dynamic picture of multiple interrelations and living connections understood in a more phenomenological way within the contexts of flora and fauna.

Further still, alluding to an earlier point about movement and stillness, in his talk on 'Changing epistemologies and life' delivered during a symposium on *On the Expression of Difference and the Language of Similarity* (2016), Tim Ingold takes us through his thinking on the current role of anthropology in amending its previous fixation on cultural diversity by seeking ways of bringing difference and sameness together. This appeal to plurality is misguided, he says, 'not only wrong in principle [...], but it also leaves us powerless to oppose those hegemonic constructions of the global predicament, more often than not, bolstered by big science, data analytics, mass inequality, disenfranchisement and deprivation' (Ingold 2016: n.pag.), and that when thinking in terms of cultures, it has actually been 'sameness' that has been dividing people, not the difference, as we tend to think.

How many times, Ingold asks, 'have we attempted to define human nature in terms of the common possession of this or that attribute' (2016: n.pag.), innate capacities or behavioural traits like rituals, language, symbolic thought, and so on. In a way echoing somatic attention to the compatibility of the opposites, while referring to the work of Heather Menzies (2014) and Alain Badiou (2010), respectively, Ingold makes a case for looking at commoning and differentiation as two parts of the same coin, i.e. the social life, and the world of the ever emergent difference created by generative processes of life and defined by co-participation in the universe of relations.

In such a world the 'commoning is not inhibited to human inhabitants nor is it just about the world, rather it is the world – a world of beings that immersed in life are continually answering and answerable to one another' (Ingold 2016: n.pag.), and where

> the common, is not to regress to the set of baseline attributes with which all the participants are endowed to begin with, but which entails attentive stretch whereby every participant casts their experience forward in ways that can answer to the experience of others.
>
> (n.pag.)

With an individual focus on the phenomenological experience of interdependent change and movement itself, it is possible to move beyond the culturally shaped creation myths too, as Emilie Conrad points out. As such myths, like the western one, based mainly on dualistic Christian traditions of Man and nature, form our basic reality and which have 'insidiously shaped the foundational movement of our social thought and to very large degree our bodies' (Conrad 2007: xxviii) too.

Thus this western linear view of the universe lives in the hierarchical spatial ordering of our physical belonging to the Earth as well, as created upon the vertical line, and the vertical concept of reality. Yet, speaking from experience, my attention to movement and somatic experience proposed here as a living resource for life developments bears a strong potential for reconnecting us with the very sense of a more complex dynamic taking place which shapes us as a living species happening every single moment. It also puts in perspective all, often very harmful, simplifications of social or cultural reasoning.

I would also like to see it as a very individual way of accessing what Conrad describes as an unfolding process in itself, shaped by 'billions of years of intelligence that is spiralled into the very swirl of our embryonic coil' (2007: xxix), and which expands our consciousness of self and other on its ways to include wider contexts of life and of ourselves as a species on lands of the Earth.

How we relate to ourselves and the world around us contains the how's of what we feel, i.e. our human condition, the how's of what we think, i.e. our cognitive motivations, and the how's of what we do, which then builds relations and relationships with the world.

Embracing Polanyi's favourite reference to what he called 'tacit knowing' and that 'we can know more than we can tell' (Polanyi and Sen 2009: x), talking about relationality is then a very comprehensive way to talk about human nature, which adds inner sensing and perceiving as another dimension of life's interconnectivity. By adding our embodied ability to sense the environment as an ongoing activity of life and letting it have a more tangible influence on feeling, thinking and acting as the scope of human nature inquiry, we are also letting ourselves revisit the question about our human nature in healthier, more inclusive contexts.

4

Therapeutic and Philosophical Contexts of Wellbeing

Philosophical preoccupations over the subject of human nature can be very different: metaphysical, moral, ethical, liberating, concerned with human potential (eastern philosophy) or concentrating on how people simply are but they can also be related to its therapeutic aspects. For Plato for example, philosophy was a therapy for the soul, something that everybody should exercise in order to live well, and the concept of living through change-affirming open attitude has been known to pre-Socratic circles already, with Heraclitus's (Heraclitus and Kirk 1954; Kahn and Heraclitus 1979) work as its most acclaimed example.

Somatic movement education and therapy as a field of open inquiry into human condition resonates with a wide range of both philosophical and psychological paradigms. Deborah DuNann Winter points out that psychology, seen as a modern development of multiple philosophical traditions, 'has rarely been seen as an environmental science – as having something relevant to say about how we got into our mess and how we might get out of it' (1996: 4). In the realm of therapy though, the significance of the contemporary emergence of somatic psychology and body–mind therapy, as Barratt indicates, is an 'indicator of the profound change that is occurring in our most fundamental understanding of what it means to be human' (2010: 2).

Consequently, to perform any kind of counselling work within the current contexts of the twenty-first-century world-state, it has never been more important to rely on a proper ontological perspective from which every therapist practises and from which he/she views and supports their clients. What a therapist considers to be his private view on human nature and our relation to the wider life context will not remain without consequences and might be either implicit or explicit to their personal morale and the grounding philosophy for their counselling practice.

Another reason for staying very conscious of an ontological perspective is also a commonly seen tendency among therapists to integrate a number of working methods and to pursue an integrative approach. In his article 'Psychotherapy, ontology and therapist positioning: Why simplistic integrationist approaches don't work', Murphy (2014) advises that while staying open and flexible to all possible ways of working with clients is always helpful, a badly designed choice for the methods which do not integrate well on the ontological level might be quite hazardous to the services on offer and hinder possibilities for change and development.

The question of how we view the nature of being human and our worldly experiences and how we should go about fixing any imbalances in life must lie at the heart of every therapy. It creates a grounding bond between the therapist and the client, helping to shape potentially new openings in the mindset for those who seek therapeutic support.

The three most distinctive ontological stands among psychological traditions belong to different schools of modern psychology. It is important to mention here that modern psychology has its continental roots in pre-twentieth-century philosophical psychology represented mainly by post-Cartesian philosophers like Benedict Spinoza, Gottfried Wilhelm Leibniz, Thomas Hobbes, John Locke, David Hume, David Hartley, John Stuart Mill, Immanuel Kant, Arthur Schopenhauer or Friedrich Nietzsche, to name a few. They are ontologies of psychoanalytic and cognitive behaviourists as well as a later emergence of the humanistic tradition, which could be viewed as an earliest reaction to the predominant assumption about the body–mind alienation seen as a natural human condition, and a turn towards somatic psychology.

One of the most significant works on the borderline between philosophy and psychology, and the mentioned turn towards more embodied thinking, can be prescribed to Edmund Husserl and his thorough rethinking of the historical telos in western thought and its split caused by the dominant interpretations of René Descartes's *Cogito, ergo sum*.

Husserl's *Cartesian Meditations* is an important work that points any philosophical contemplation towards intuitive methodologies of self-knowledge and which, as Husserl wrote, is fundamental to all sciences. Pertinent to the work presented in this book, his phenomenology is guided by self-reflection and ontological intersubjectivity. And his methods of transcendental insightfulness and reflective intuiting as relevant to creative, movement-based processes of conceptualization are discussed by me in detail in 'Dynamic composing: On choreographic processes of conceptualization as a way to artistic knowing' (Dako 2010).

Joseph (2013) and Murphy (2014) present a contextual overview of the clinical approaches; however, any highly detailed description goes beyond the scope presented in this subsection. What is perhaps crucial to mention is that both the psychoanalytic and behaviourist traditions were driven by fixed pre-assumptions about human nature. The humanistic tradition was perhaps the most open to versatile opinion and individual study, the development of which created an entry point for somatic psychology to take shape.

Murphy (2014) describes that the psychoanalytic view on human nature is that people's behaviour is highly determined by unconscious motivations and drives, shaped during early years of childhood. It is through the moderating operations of the ego that the assumably uncontrolled and harmful instincts and innate drives can be harnessed.

A therapist is the only expert of their clients' unconscious. It is thanks to therapy and their objective therapeutic climate that the unconscious material of such drives and impulses is revealed to them. The contents of the unconscious cannot be made known to clients themselves without the therapist's external help and would otherwise remain undiscovered. It can be summed up that the psychoanalytic view presents people as inherently irrational and destructive and follows a clinical model of 'performing psychology' akin to that of medical psychiatry and working within the illness ideology. It is also where an assumed idea for a positive change in an individual is their rational effort in reordering the thought processes and strengthening the rational ego.

From the traditional behaviourist psychological view on human nature, we are born into this world as a 'blank slate' or 'tabula rasa', as it is sometimes known. Here, it is thought that a person's basic nature is neutral, neither personally nor socially constructive or destructive but remaining malleable to its shaping through life experience in people's immediate environments.

Over time, the therapeutic methods derived from this ontological standpoint have been developed to engage the client in therapeutic tasks which are to learn or unlearn certain behavioural patterns. The therapist is best thought of as someone that does not get personally or emotionally involved but who offers their clues in directing the clients to the tasks of the therapy to re-educate or 'repaint' the canvas, so to speak. An assumed idea for change in this tradition that sees an individual as a cultural being is necessarily dependent on others and cannot be separated from a change in the social group to which an individual belongs.

Finally, in humanistic psychology, which could be understood as an umbrella term for all experiential therapies, including somatic movement and expressive arts therapy, the therapy shapes and goes with the client's direction. Therapy itself is not seen as a treatment method to the 'sick' but as an open, educational process concerned with personal growth.

Humanistic-experiential therapists trust their clients' inner resourcefulness and so the therapy aims to promote clients' innate tendencies for growth and self-directed recovery and create the right conditions for such constructive or transformative experience. They do not assume to know what is best for their clients, or how their clients should think or feel, and neither do they believe that clients need to be controlled or regulated by external forces. The ontological stand within this tradition of counselling work is that human beings are naturally equipped with inner resources for self-discovery and an inbuilt propensity towards self-realization.

This positive change within the mainstream psychology was first introduced through the work of Rogers (1961, 1967, 1969) who questioned the underpinning assumptions of Freudian psychoanalysis. He proposed the view that human beings are naturally motivated towards developing to their full potential and driven by their actualizing tendency as long as they have conditions to continue to do so. Conceptualized by Rogers, the directionality of such inherent tendency and the natural motivation force within human beings is towards the development of autonomous determination, constructive growth of the individual and optimal positive psychological functioning.

The idea of self-actualization as a source for change and the therapist's trust in the client's ability to find their own way in life creates the founding ground for all person-centred and positive psychology practices. The term coined by the leader of positive psychology, Martin Seligman (1991), focused on facilitating resilience and wellbeing rather than treatment of distress or psychological disorder. It is also where intuition and felt-sense are the guiding sensations and where the therapist's role is to support the client in finding those inner resources and to reconnect with the inner voice. The successful result of such reconnection is meeting the client's expectation to become true to oneself along with regaining the sense of value, understanding and respect.

Rogers's conviction is that

> it is the client and not the therapist who knows best which direction to go in remains a powerful and revolutionary idea and still represents a stance which is in opposition to much of contemporary psychology, with its emphasis on expert diagnosis, formulation, treatment and interventions.
>
> (Joseph 2015: 23)

Facilitation of wellbeing as the purpose of therapy might be seen as a connecting bridge between positive psychology, person-centred therapy and the therapeutic practice within the somatic movement approach. It can also be seen as being in quite an opposition to the mainstream psychology based on the assumption that the drives within human nature are predominantly destructive if not fitting the mainstream ideology of a socio-political order in which the clinical therapy is taking place.

Having said that, seeing the client as an individual in the wider world contexts of the bodily unconscious as well as considering the deepened embodied experience as the essential starting point in the study of human psyche can be first recognized within the work of Carl Jung (1875–1961). Jung's work can be seen as one of the leading precursors to the number of contemporary somatic practices and body–mind therapy coming from the realm of clinical practice. The profound effect of Jung's work within the already visible paradigm shift will become visible later, not only within psychology as a discipline but also as a shift in the general worldview within western society and its grounding objectivistic epistemologies.

Throughout the twentieth century, guided primarily by Jungian (Jung 2002) work on the psyche, the Anima Mundi, the known to us external world of the studied natural 'other' based on the linear epistemology of *self* and *other* as well as *cause* and *effect* relationality has noticeably begun to collapse. Both the human being and Nature, 'assumed to be understandable to the human faculties of reason because it operates on an unchangeable lawfulness that is reflected in the logical and rhetorical functions of the analytico-referential masterdiscourse', as Barratt describes, slowly became a motif of the past era driven by 'dominating mastery of the other' (2010: 24).

Following this significant epistemic shift, it also became more evident that such an attitude towards Nature has been functioning as a philosophically constructed assumption and not a real phenomenon.

Indeed, speaking from the practitioner's point of view, the moment we attend to somatic experience, the world of complex dynamics and non-linear interdependence of experiences takes over, whilst the known world of subject–object, man–nature or mind over body dichotomies prove more and more illusory. Aizenstat too makes a clear statement that 'in the realm of the World Unconscious, all creatures and things of the world are understood as interrelated and interconnected' and that 'in this wider view the human experience exists in a field of psychic relationships, one among the many' (2003: 3–4) and sensed through empathy, inspiration and creativity.

Engaged in movement and submerged in somatic experience, by which I mean stepping into the natural environment of the self–world, it quickly becomes understandable why overly scientific approaches of studying motion are failing. Coming to realize that 'our spontaneous experience of the world, charged with subjective, emotional, and intuitive content, remains the vital and dark ground of all our objectivity' (Abram 1996: 34), as David Abram describes, movement cannot be studied as a separate phenomenon, any more than human beings cannot be studied as separate from Nature. One is naturally embedded and ontologically entwined within the other, or, as in his article 'Self-realization: An ecological approach to being in the world', Arne Naess describes: 'relationally constituted within' (Seed 1988: 19–29).

The biggest challenge in somatic psychology then becomes our language and its conceptual limitations in speaking *about* the experience. This is an issue I will address more closely in the chapter on 'Felt thinking and languaging experience'.

Seeing body as a relational process, as the grounding principle of somatic psychology, it is important to remember that as in all relationships,

> most of what we communicate to each other occurs non-verbally, beyond the reaches of conscious awareness, through our posture, unconscious movements and gestures, the tone of our voice, and other subtle bodily signals of which we are usually quite unaware.
>
> (Hartley 2004: 221)

This is also why in this work I include multiple attempts of referring to different, more experiential forms of writing as well, which expand our ability to share more about the movement experience and concentrate on movement in its embodied dimensions.

Experiential movement experience in felt thinking can definitely be seen as practising philosophy per se. The phenomenological developments known to us, in terms of the method's descriptive endeavour at grasping experiential phenomena, offer a great base for expanding on that. Thanks to the life work of philosophers like Franz Brentano, Edmund Husserl, Martin Heidegger, Jean-Paul Sartre and Maurice Merleau-Ponty, human experience has become the primary subject matter in the inquiry into the psyche and the nature of being human. On this phenomenological ground, the embodied experience has quickly shaped as the study of the present moment which is both absent and present (in Jungian terms) and which creates a new baseline for considerations about self–other dualism.

Phenomenological accounts, including those that consciousness and mental events, and so our bodily consciousness too, understood as *intentional*, are always directed towards something, have definitely built bridges between our alienation from the mechanistic body seen as an object (or as 'other') and seeing the body as the creative self.

Nevertheless, it is also important to mention that the increased interest in 'the body' and the subject of embodiment in general, as observable among other scholarly disciplines like sociology or medicine and which relate to the phenomenological traditions, is not necessarily congruent with the essence of somatic practices and more focused on the representational issues or social uses of the body only. For further reference, and a recommendation for the reader, the issue about applications of somatic theory is informatively discussed by Martha Eddy in *Access to Somatic Theory and Applications: Socio-Political Concerns* (2000).

Now, as a known quality of the universe in numerous ancient traditions of the world, our Earth-based reality thrives on interconnectedness. As a scientific fact, we now know too that all matter is inseparable, and that the objects of our knowledge undergo constant transformation, also in relation to the processes of knowing them. Consequently, having arrived at the twenty-first century, we, human beings, cannot continue to depict or relate to the world in materialistic or objectivistic ways only.

We are living through times of biggest shifts in epistemological terms, moving from conceiving of the world in terms of external objects to co-living with them as embedded in a larger cosmological context of life processes. Even though somatic practices which incorporate an active sense for 'the natural' can be seen as a continuation of the phenomenological endeavour in its philosophical sense, this continuation does not necessarily mean a blind adherence to the original method.

It is important to notice that even though in his chapter on the 'Worldhood of the world', Heidegger advises that Nature 'is not to be understood as that which is just present-at-hand, not as the *power of Nature*' (Heidegger 1967: 100, original emphasis), he simultaneously defines Nature as 'an entity which is encountered within the world' (92), thus pointing us back to his practice of phenomenological intentionality, the consciousness 'of' experience.

In my view, the Heideggerian ontology of being-in-the-world does not create a complete ground for in-depth somatic study. Rather, as Abram proposes, since Nature is the world, it is easier to picture it as 'an intertwined matrix of sensations and perceptions, a collective field of experience lived through from many different angles', 'the ever shifting fabric' (1996: 39) which can be experienced very differently as it is deeply influenced by the ways we engage with it. If the worlds experienced by humans are so diverse, as Abram continues, 'how much more diverse, still, must be the life-worlds of other animals-of wolves, or owls, or a community of bees!' (1996: 41).

In felt thinking then, with the focus on somatic experience per se, instead of looking at the external world in search for answers and new clues about the growing complexity within self–other dichotomous concept, one should focus on experiencing self as movement, or movement as self–other, which in itself is the life–world movement experienced internally and not separate from its external reality.

In her book *Primacy of Movement*, which resonates with Merleau-Ponty's *Primacy of Perception*, as an ongoing pre-verbal reciprocity and the very soil for language as the more conscious exchange, Maxine Sheets-Johnstone points out that from all the known work of phenomenological tradition, it has only been Husserl's work that embraces both the etymological value of movement per se, and the movement-based ontological unity of humans, non-humans, and all animate forms of life. And she then elaborates further, here alluding to Cartesian ways of reasoning, on the stages of development from 'I move' to 'I do' and 'I can' in getting to know the world.

Again, then, this is just to depict that picking up on different threads within phenomenological tradition, only proves the increasing need for an ecophenomenologically based somatic inquiry. And it needs to be understood as a form of practice-based stepping up continuation and not an adherence to the already known methods, which I hope this study provides.

The driving inquiry behind the work in felt thinking presented here is to look for Nature in human experience and to address the questions of:

How can our embodied focus on movement as the source of all experience redefine our comprehension of our creative Nature/Self and help us reorganize our place in the world and our relation to it? And:

What implications on Life in general does such pursuit for wisdom derived from movement itself, and from placing the movement at the forefront of any ontological and epistemological study, have for the future?

It is my belief then that by approaching the subject from the perspective of movement experience, we can learn a lot about ourselves and our individually different but shared innate connection to the wellbeing of the Earth as well, as our wellbeing. Our condition can indeed tell us a lot about our nature, and about how we choose to live.

Initially, it might be assumed that if we feel good we live according to our nature and fulfil our natural potentials in life, and if we are not well it might indicate that we live against it, and so against ourselves. Yet is it just a cause and effect relation?

To avoid any deterministic attitudes or simply asking the wrong questions, in this work in somatic experience I focus primarily on the emergent insights coming directly through the experienced nature of movement/self without any assumptions or predetermined questions asked. Instead, I concentrate on the ontological study of movement's qualities of interconnectedness, processes of change and living relations within open inquiry.

Unlike the traditional schools of philosophical thought, which are predominantly oriented at getting to the essence of things by arriving at categorical truths communicated by notions, concepts and categories, i.e. by definitions and valid generalizations, what somatic experience offers, by being closer to eastern philosophies in that sense, is keeping the experience always open. In movement, I am simply trying to get as close to the source of experience as possible, to embrace that experience by sensually and emotionally tuning into it, and by sharing it first-hand without presumptions or tightly closing conclusions.

The analytical part of the work presented here, organized according to the emerged Three Dimensions of Practice, will try to do just that while becoming a living narrative of interwoven, personal stories in movement experience. Yet, let us expand on the ecological context of felt thinking in movement experience first.

5

Ecological Contexts of Somatic Movement Experience

I would like to return now to the opening point of this introductory section that movement is the most primal experience of life which both connects and disconnects us from the living, moving environment and the wider living community of the world, and that it is through movement that we discover ourselves in the world. It is my deep belief here that movement as a lived experience of the self is also what we should return to in critical times like these. After all, as Maxine Sheets-Johnstone too describes, it is the 'generative source of our primal sense of aliveness and of our primal capacity for sense making' (2011: 146).

And, as Life on Earth happens through movement, we have to start thinking of and broadening our awareness to the ways we are both carried forward and filled with movement of Life itself every single day. As Abram says, 'at the most primordial level of sensuous, bodily experience, we find ourselves in an expressive, gesturing landscape, in a world that speaks' (1996: 81).

Movement is every thought we think, every feeling we find within and every decision we make. It is not a visually registered phenomenon open to aesthetic interpretations only but it is the essence of being alive, and the way Nature induced us into our Earthy life. 'We dance to feel good, to celebrate, to bind community, and for sociality', as Fraleigh (2015: 42) describes. Maxine Sheets-Johnstone also sums up that 'this primal animateness, this original kinetic spontaneity that infuses our being and defines our aliveness, is our point of departure for living in the world and making sense of it' (2011: 149).

The problem with talking and writing about movement is that it is highly misunderstood in our daily, practical life and too illusive, too ephemeral in any aesthetic encounter. In the first sense, we assume, as Emilie Conrad writes that 'movement is information, using the same muscles in a repetitive way and so we end up establishing a locked system in which no further information is received' (Johnson and California Institute of Integral Studies 1997: 69). In the aesthetic sense we end up realizing that no language, and definitely no reductive scientific method of studying human behaviour can hold it still enough to capture in the conceptual realm. That is why writing about movement from an observer's perspective only is a futile endeavour.

What somatic experience helps us notice is that being in/with movement and speaking from the experiential perspective brings us to the essence of how we are in the world in a much more authentic, thus natural way. The primary access to the psychic depths gained in somatic experience lives in movement as experienced from within itself. The 'external' knowledge of 'what' and 'why' and 'how' will always stay incomplete as it does not allow for the softer layers of implicit being of the 'knower' to emerge.

Knowing, or getting to know, movement is a relational experience and not a conceptual job of a disembodied mind, as once thought. When movement is conceived as a mechanical conveyance to get you from here to there, it is not experienced as alive, growing and changing. Only a deep engagement in movement experience can give us a more holistic sense of what the nature of being movement really is. We are, after all, movement, and what we conceive of 'the body' is a moving phenomenon as well, and so is our primal world, as I keep reminding us here.

Conrad ([2007] n.d.) calls the fluid body an interpenetrating wave motion that has stabilized within a particular electromagnetic field on Earth and which is responsive to what she calls bio-cosmic nourishment provided by resonance stream of fluid as a basic element of life. 'We are in perpetual resonance with all fluid systems everywhere in the universe, functioning as an undivided whole' (Conrad [2007] n.d.: n.pag.). She says that a human being is aquatic, terrestrial and celestial and that 'what we call "body" is not matter but movement' (Conrad [2007] n.d.: n.pag.). She then continues: 'Movement is the fundamental reality. In my view, the "body" is a profound orchestration of many qualities and textures of movement – interpenetrating tones of fertile play waiting to be incubated' (Conrad [2007] n.d.: n.pag.).

I couldn't agree more.

Emilie Conrad also writes about her early observation that 'on organismic level of pulsating life force, human beings were interacting among species and environments that our more conventional selves were unaware of' (Johnson and California Institute of Integral Studies 1997: 61). In her own life-long explorations into the biological origins of movement freed from cultural constrains and seeing human beings as biomorphic, i.e. including all life forms, she went on asking: what is it to feel movement as a cosmic play in which form becomes mutable? Additionally, she keeps reminding us that creativity is 'our own inherent potential' (Johnson and California Institute of Integral Studies 1997: 62) and that refraining from enforced movements allows for a more universal connection to life.

Her work with fluid movement, i.e. internal wave motion on the cellular level, stimulated by breath and sound, creates the basis for my understanding of the functional, physical movement organization in regular sense. Water is the basic element of life that shapes and sustains our organism. So too is the Earth, the air and all other elements of life, which also change individually as a response to changing environments and which facilitate 'some transactions and responses as well as restrict others' (Johnson and California Institute of Integral Studies 1997: 62).

In a somatic way of looking at movement, this constant patterning and repatterning of the organizing and interacting life systems within our living somas is a most visible analogy to validating movement in its smallest cellular dimension as its natural capacity for internal reorganization, self-remedy and healing. Conrad's life-long work with fluid waves, the undulating and pulsating movement techniques and the fluid flow has shown amazing natural capacities not only for strengthening the muscles in any compensating function but also for regeneration of nerve and muscle cells from scratch.

According to Conrad, both cosmic and primordial sense of *being fluid* or *being water*, as a unitary aspect of all live on Earth, precedes all cultural–social weight of shaping our being with the earthly environment. Attending to the frequencies and energies of these subtle movements restores thus the natural cellular balancing potential carried in unique auric energy fields we, as living beings, are all born with. It also reconnects our terrestrial *being* as part of an ongoing universal process. In Conrad's eyes, the undulating movements are like memories of our umbilical tie to the planet 'carried by the movement of water in which electrical impulses impregnate soft waves with the immanence of what can be possible' (2007: xxvii) and with its own purpose.

And to return to my earlier reflective perspective on the currently observed cultural tendencies, while immersed in principles of what the Director of Indigenous Tribal Studies at North Dakota State University and a citizen of the Three Affiliated Tribes of the Fort Berthold reservation in North Dakota, Michael Yellow Bird calls 'exploitation colonialism' (2014), the subtle attention to qualities of modern life seems to have become to have little value in general and often treated as a childish endeavour.

It is then only in the ancestral, tribal traditions of the Indigenous people, outside western societies, that such practices, based on a living relationship with the Earth, have been culturally sustained and considered as primal sources of wisdom. Driven by his motivation for recovery, from what Yellow Bird calls the 'trauma of colonialism' (2014), I do agree that it is important to see the value in knowledge as not something we strive for or constantly move towards but also as something we are all born with. And, what is currently needed is 'to go back to what we know' (Bird 2014) in search of a deeper connection with the living Earth.

I then propose that somatic experience, as a form of contemplative practice, can become a living act of such reconnection, as well as a way of dipping into our primal resources for restoration that comes from being one with Nature, as an enriching form of what Piaget called 'animistic thinking' (1929) in human development.

Additionally, to further refer to the existing scholarship within somatic work, Anna Halprin, as one of the pioneers of working with movement in reflective experience, also talks about her own work with the primal movement motifs. These are nowadays seen as part of ecological psychology practices as something that takes us directly to the core of things, and Halprin explains that 'when you work in the field of dance, when you work with movement, you are getting down to the roots of humanness, in a way that words can hide the truth but movement cannot hide the truth' (Halprin 2012a). She also states that there are 'all kinds of connections between what we experience within ourselves and what we experience in Nature and that connection creates a wholeness' (Halprin 2012b) in our life experience.

In psychological terms, it is exactly what Winter describes as 'the study of human experience as a function of the relationships in the complex network of other organisms and physical systems' (1996: 241) with her comment on the fact that, here, in my direct reference to the capacity of the medium of dance and movement experience per se, any form of artificial separation of simplification of the experienced phenomena is not going to provide us with any tangible or reliable observations.

It has been a problem of psychology all along, Winter continues, that it 'has paid more attention to goal behaviour than to the process of moving in the physical world' (1996: 241) as well as that it has ignored the most primal part of our psyche: our ecological unconscious, which contents are the 'living records of cosmic evolution, tracing back to distant initial conditions in the history of time' (Roszak 1992 cited in Winter 1996: 250).

Continuing on the problem of the western psychology viewpoint, Winter writes:

From this perspective, our difficulty stems from our limited experiences of the complexity, beauty, magic, and awesome power of the natural world. Our hearts and our spirits are closed down because our culture emphasizes separation and autonomy, convenience and efficiency. Housed in separate homes, often not even knowing our neighbours, much less the natural physical world that surrounds us, we maintain psychological separation from each other and from the ecosystem of which we are an integral part.

(1996: 265)

In a form of bridging humanistic and transpersonal psychology, in his interview with Teri Carter, and influenced by the work of Anna Halprin but also other somatic work pioneers like Bonnie Bainbridge Cohen and Emilie Conrad, Jamie McHugh relates to the basic multi-sensory experience of Nature, and calls it 'interfacing with the environment' (2016: n.pag.). He continues that it is a form of connection between the personal and the transpersonal experience, in Jungian sense, 'when the environment becomes the source of the preconscious experience' and where we can absorb 'the medicine of diversity' (McHugh 2016: n.pag.), i.e. the unique elemental synergy of a place.

The sensory contact with Nature creates a very rich somatic experience between our inner landscape and the outer landscape of the body of Nature in the most primal sense. It is where 'every movement quality is the expression of the particular body system and the unique state of mind' (McHugh 2016: n.pag.), as the mind of a rock is very different from the mind of the sea or air, etc.

And, in times of extreme urbanization, as McHugh says, faced with the loss of vitality, we are not only losing connection with the environment but we are also losing consciousness which would normally be permeated by Nature, as a 'strong anchor' in creating spiritual wholeness in its active form of both listening and embodied participation as well as our visceral affection for the planet.

As a summary then, and in final support of grounding this work in somatic experience as an integral part of the methodology of felt thinking, I would like to refer to yet one more quote which hopefully sets this way of self-discovery onto not only a promising but also the oldest quest of rediscovery of the self in a larger context. In Thomas Hanna's words:

> Somatic Education is not only something new and unexpected, it is something of momentous consequence: it entails a basic transformation in our understanding of the human species and of the capacities of the human individual. That which we have believed to be unchangeable in the human creature has been discovered to be not, after all, so unchangeable. Such a discovery amounts to a reassessment of the nature of ourselves and of humankind.

> (1999: 188)

As David Abram puts it, 'although we may be oblivious to the gestural, somatic dimension of language, having repressed it in favour of strict dictionary definitions and the abstract precision of specialized terminologies' (1996: 80), I would like to see and conceive the human–Nature relationship as that of ongoing co-creating in movement, and its meaning 'rooted in the sensory life of the body' (1996: 80). The movement that starts and lives within ourselves, and upon which we can re-create and continue strengthening the relational ontology that our world view should be created upon.

I would like to refer to such '*co-search*' based on movement contemplations and what I became to call felt thinking as a form of getting to know ourselves better, as well as a way of rediscovering new ways of relating to Nature.

To conclude, within somatic education paradigm and its emphasis on the wisdom of the body in motion drawn from many ancient philosophies and body-based practices, but most importantly, based on the primacy of movement experience per se, I believe I can now suggest re-phrasing the term 'human nature' with 'the nature of being', or rather with 'being nature'. And, to start feeling into such a change, I would like to offer an introductory description of what primal movement feels like when I move in felt thinking:

A gust of wind
a growth, expansion or an earthy push out
a sweep of the intangible
a cold wash off
a hot soup
a squashing press
a secretive pull
a give-in with no looking back
a shot of a cannon ball
a mush of a tail
an opening to the poise of the day
a flattening spread
a firing alarm
a nourishing warmth
a withering sound
an embracing, too short a hug
a stomping temper
a marching whistle
a gift to be unravelled
a rising breath
a friendly visit
a disoriented twitch
a play, open to unknown
a glitch, awaiting fixing
a forward storm
a slithering hunch
a scent arriving from the around
an enclosed, wasted chance
a firm wall

a melting freeze
a …
a …
a …
an Infinity itself …
(breathing)
Movement – World – Me
being like a …
and
… a like being
Making being,
or
Letting be
in all life-shaping relationships between active and receptive ways of being …
The open to changeable dynamics of motion, Ontological Creativity …
The life forming elements in ongoing exchange.
Elements are movement, different qualities of it, created by co-creating Time/Spaces …

(Moving Thoughts Journal, September 2017 [edited])

6

On Somatic Ontologies of Human Nature and Its Day-to-Day Dimension

To keep building on the life-changing realization that we, human beings, are currently living through the climax of self-constituted environmental crisis, but in personal care for the living world's wellbeing, it comes as an immediate reflection to me that our human practices and ways of being, guided primarily by western traditions of modern-day ethical and metaphysical assumptions, call for an urgent revision.

As Brown and Toadvine emphasize, these basic, life-governing 'assumptions about the relation between individual and society, human nature, the nature of nature, and the nature of the Good – underlie all our current behaviour, both individually and culturally' (2003: x). As I underline here, all those daily assumptions are further reflected in our own wellbeing condition too, tormented by many chronic diseases that spring from this alienated, as a species, life conditions that we have been securing for ourselves over millennia.

The prevailing objectification of Nature as a resource to humankind or leisure-time destination at its best only keeps reminding us that we think we own the Earth and sustain this ownership by our limited understanding of it, guided by 'disembodied scientification' (Merleau-Ponty and Edie 1964), organized and limited to a set of natural laws.

The importance of deepening the understanding of our relational interconnectedness with the living world and implementing it into our everyday life practices of *being human* understood as *living amongst many other earthly beings* cannot be overly emphasized. It is of major importance that our deepened understanding of where and how we belong in/with this world dwells in the daily performed, minute acts of conscious practices that shape our embodied comprehension.

With our cultural focus on material productivity, it is often forgotten to give enough validity to the processes preceding our actions, and that *the felt* feeds *the thought*, and that before we are able to feel, we have to be able to *listen*.

That conscious listening starts with simply *making time and space* for being mindful and respectful, and paying an open attention to life presenting itself through our embodied participation in it, as an ongoing creation. Starting with breath alone, our quieted attention to it can quickly reveal the endless complexities of its movement and an ongoing and responsive change that is taking place, and that the interdependency of life processes on Earth is nothing to control but to co-create with, mindfully, in active reflection.

Those complexities of moving through life do also shape the layered-ness of everyday experience and give us an opportunity to support ourselves from all the perspectives that we are open to live by.

As a mover, for example, I give in, and yield into movement as a natural chanter carrying its kinetic melodies through my embodied engagements, experienced differently every time. As an educator, I rely on movement as the most natural way of relating to self and others. As a practising therapist, my clients' movement takes me on a journey I choose to travel along, fully engaged with an open-ended dialogue shaped naturally by its in-depth developments that often show the need for internal, subtle guidance through embodied listening or relief in moments of awakened reassurance. As a writer, working through and with movement, I rely on its endless inspiration that flows along with my lightest attention to life processes carried on within, be it in the breath or in any other embodied sensation that channels messages about 'the felt' and 'the thought' and 'the acted upon', moment by moment.

Yet, as my most cherished connection to life around, I experience movement as a *living being* in everyday life, guided by ordinary dependence on senses, imagination, instinct and intuition. It is the somatic depth of being able to engage with movement as a daily practice, grounded in an embodied sense of self as the living body, the 'soma' and a life-affirming intelligence and connectivity within oneself and a bigger, than only human, living world, that makes me appreciate that inborn connection with the animate.

How come then, that a simple attention to movement-based life processes can reveal so much about ourselves and our relation to the immediate environment?

Somas, as Hanna describes, are individual syntheses of cosmic elements that shouldn't be understood in materialistic terms as objects, but as 'processes of patterned movements' (1986: 48). In his introduction to somatics as a field, he imaginatively compares soma to the natural phenomenon of a tornado, the emergence of which comes from a particular combination of atmospheric conditions. Also, writing that soma does not represent a break from the conditions that preceded it, but rather it is their very unique synthesis.

Thanks to such open comprehension of an embodied self, as an extension of the natural conditions that created it, both individually and as a species, alongside all other species on Earth, one can rely on somatic experience as the most natural method for self-knowledge and self-regulation.

Somatic movement experience is thus mainly understood as a sensation and awareness-guided free movement engagement, which, with a trained therapist's support, involves an opportunity to delve deeper into unconscious movement processes. These often offer crucial psychological support in their reliable 'ongoingness' or a way of restorative discharge by releasing the held-in emotional distress to various degrees.

At the same time, somatic experience can also be a very creative journey of meaningful expression built upon open dialogues brought into movement through *sensual sensitivity* and *embodied receptivity*, and practised as a way of ongoing self-discovery as well as a reminder of larger than ourselves, contexts of life.

Thus, the interdependence between the processes of letting go by co-creating as well as co-creating by letting go is a vital part of working with somatic ontologies of movement. Yet they also are, as this work will seek to explicate, an integral part of realization that it is the internal focus on our own experience that can further our natural connection to the natural world. This therefore offers a lived alternative to the predominantly external orientation towards studying Nature through observation and detachment.

It is important for me to state here, supported by my professional experience within both artistic and therapeutic relationships, that people who struggle to enjoy their ability to move freely are often those who also struggle in finding their psychosomatic balance in life. Those limits do not need to be occurring on purely physiological level but are rather a result of many limiting habits or mental restrictions that build up over the years. Additionally, those limiting habits are visible in many artificially imposed and carelessly performed bodily actions.

It is also why, in somatic felt thinking outdoors, I continuously commit myself to staying attentive to the recuperative depths of being with Nature and to restoring the virtually endless possibilities of movement, be it physically or simply imaginatively, which can then be externalized in one's creative freedom as well as psychosomatic wellbeing.

Somatic movement experience, as the grounding reality to the practice of somatic movement therapy, creates an aiding opportunity to dive into and engage with what it means to alternate from a purposeful activity. When in day-to-day reality we are all devoted to performing certain tasks and actions by 'using' our physical being as a mere vehicle to such performance, it is through engaging with somatic experience, as contemplative practice, that we can give ourselves time and space to, literally, *move* away from the necessity of pre-planned, cognitive and often superficial functionality.

The very purpose of somatic therapy is to facilitate such opening and widening of our sensorial capacities to engage with the world and connect that experience with our internal feelings, sensations, emotions and imaginings in a more meaningful way.

Methodologically speaking though, when guided by somatic comprehension of what it means to embody life in movement, to approach a reflection on creative movement-based experience by addressing the very nature of that experience, and focusing on describing it meaningfully and deeply, one cannot deny the individually varied subjectivity of such an experience. Indeed, as somatic ontology of movement suggests, we all are endlessly individual beings too.

Human experience, in somatic movement engagement as a form of contemplative self-study, cannot easily be captured as quantified or measured. Instead, it can be more easily approached descriptively and creatively within the first-hand experience, as embodied, and individually shaped *phenomena* that one is only able to access through ongoing reflection.

When reflecting on the nature of movement while moving and contemplating in free movement, guided by the multifaceted practice of felt thinking in relation to the natural environment, it is like making an inquiry within an inquiry. With the main aim to reconnect with the real 'human' nature by connecting to movement as it is shaped *by*, *through* and *with* somatic, i.e. the physical, the sensuous and the imaginative experience of the whole self, what is being addressed is the very nature, and so the essence of human experience.

Is human nature different from Nature itself, as experienced through movement in relation to the immediate landscape, and is it at all? Can attending to movement reconcile the human with Nature?

While attending to such questions, it is important to point out here that embarking on such an inquiry does not mean anchoring possible answers in any deterministic way, as the questions themselves refer to personal processes of relation. The shaping processes of *what does it mean to live my natural self(?)* and *how does it relate to my wellbeing(?)* are but a few examples of how intimately personal the journeys in felt thinking can only be.

Having said that, to embrace how somatic experience of movement, as a form of embodied listening and co-creating, can best be expressed within the practice of felt thinking, I propose to narrow the focus of movement experience by simply following what the movement itself is suggesting – as an ongoing, reflexive and narrative inquiry that can only come through in full engagement with movement as a messenger.

The versatility of experience, as relating simultaneously to the mover's past and present, comes from the individual differences in movers' ability to 'be moved' by sensations drawn from various landscapes or environments while following movement experience *'in situ'*, following the emergent, and staying open to co-creating with *life in movement*.

With such an emphasis on the role of somatic experience in contemplative comprehension of the self, I would like to propose that by attending to 'the felt' while thinking about the human condition, we can also deepen what ecophenomenological method has to offer. We can inquire about what it would mean to promote a more embodied ontology of 'being *in* the world' in a phenomenological sense by 'being *with* the world' in the somatic sense of embodied presence and co-creation.

Such work could then expand not only on the original thought behind phenomenological and ecophenomenological intentionality but also on educational importance of embodied experience of co-creating, and what Sondra Fraleigh calls 'lived metaphysic' (1987: 56), of the self, the other and the natural world as ontologically interconnected.

The reflexive practices of *voicing* movement which are included in the presented phases of felt thinking are embodied writing, drawing, painting, crafting, sounding and vocalization, and, most importantly, being in movement as it shapes itself kinaesthetically in somatic experience through ongoing body–mind contemplation upon itself and life. This very process of moving, living, creating, becoming and reflecting becomes the practice-based method of felt thinking itself.

As Kim Etherington writes, a skill in counselling practice, as a major feature of embodied consciousness, is naturally developed as 'an ability to notice our responses to the world around us, other people and events, and to use that knowledge to inform our actions, communications and understanding' (2004: 19). And as a methodological remark, following Freedman and Combs (2002) as well as John McLoad's (1994) work on *Doing Counselling Research*, Etherington sees reflexivity as a form of deconstructive listening oriented towards discovery rather than verification that often begins with a 'not-knowing' attitude and which can eventually lead to truly new knowledge formation where often marginalized and tentative voices can be heard 'alongside those of the dominant Western discourses that value certainty, action and decisiveness' (Etherington 2004: 21).

The method of felt thinking in movement, as described in this work, has developed spontaneously over time, without any external plan to movement sessions but simply by reflexive, intuitive and improvisational following of what felt right in movement.

To further support the somatic practice of felt thinking in movement experience as an ontological endeavour, it is important to view it, following Nelson's (2013: 51) suggestion, as a 'softer' methodology obtained through critical reflection and double articulation between theory and practice. As, despite its qualitative feel, somatic experience of ongoing reflexivity can offer something very substantial. Unlike many post-modern methods pointing the inquirer towards the fragmented, undecidable and relative realities of life and the voids of absolute possibility, it reintroduces the focus inside oneself, the inward search, and reveals the most relevant and personally grounded worlds of ontological relation, that go beyond the skin layers.

Nelson also writes:

> In response to the increasing recognition that human subjectivity is inevitably involved in the production of knowledge and that not everything about the universe – and the place of human beings within it – can be understood through measurement, a substantial shift away from the data-based, 'quantitative' methods of the natural sciences has indeed taken place over almost a century in the 'softer' social sciences, in educational research and in the arts and humanities.
>
> (2013: 52)

Indeed, somewhere between the reflective 'thinking about' and the reflexive tapping into a more 'immediate, continuing, dynamic, and subjective self-awareness' (Finlay 2002: 532–33), 'a shift in our understanding of data collection from some-thing objective that is accomplished through detached scrutiny of "what I know and how I know it" to recognizing how we actively construct our knowledge' (532), does take place.

When working immersed in felt thinking in movement, everything that meets one's attentive or intuitive levels of reaction can be called perception. Those percep-tions are incorporated and become part of the ongoing movement exploration. Yet sometimes, the meaning of such intuitive exploration can become quite elusive. That is why every movement contemplation session is rounded up by a lengthy period of reflection, in expressive writing, drawing or crafting, as such palpable results of the movement-based inquiry help navigate the self-inquiry process during the stages of making sense of such fleeting, left in a moment experiential processes in somatic practice.

Making our somas sensually aware and conscious is normally a life-learning process. It is part of somatic education to deepen one's ability to bring a lot of the bodily phenomena to consciousness as well as to widen the ability to pick up and perceive the world through the bodily sensorium more fully. Directed by experi-ence per se, the daily processes of reflection become a deep inquiry into the bigger 'self' as well, while the movement experience can speak for itself, and picks up its lively and ever-changing character.

As in Authentic Movement, as one of wider-known somatic practices, one can experience a feeling of 'being moved', in the intuition driven practice-led inquiry as this, the movement experience simply arrives by itself, often causing a lot of confusion and the feeling of uncertainty or bewilderment at first, but eventually shaping its way through and finding its paths or voices. This is also why embarking on practice of felt thinking calls for a lot of personal ability to 'let go' by following the process as it unfolds in movement, as well as a lot of acceptance in facing the unknown, which is an integral part of any creative process.

Free movement is a living conversation, a meeting ground between what is or what comes into being, at any given moment, be it a sensation, a sound, a memory, a site, a scent, an impulse, a feeling etc. It is never only one movement/thing at a time but a continuous dance of moving 'things/being(s)' that create the experience prior to our conceptualizing filters coming into play.

Such intuitive explorations into movement accompanied by vocalized expressions of the experience are possible, as Anderson again points out, because 'intuitions often feel palpable as distinct perceptions into the nature of things, even as these perceptions vanish into the background of awareness when the focused, rational mind kicks in, searching for meaning' (Anderson and Braud 2011: 19). As Anderson further refers to intuition, as described from a Jungian psychological perspective by Marie Louise von Franz (1971: 37), as 'a kind of sense perception via the unconscious or a subliminal sense perception' that expands upon what is ordinary sensed (Anderson and Braud 2011: 19–20).

Another way to look at it is what Moustakas proposes, the intuitive intention of something in its absence as 'it announces something that has the possibility of appearing or that exists within the intuitive' (1994: 77).

It is then in embarking on such self-inquiry of reconnecting with the nature of movement in movement that the poetics of such process 'attend to the work of knowing as a journey of return' and where, as Romanyshyn describes, 'one comes to know what one has already known without knowing it' (2007: 13). To me, it is also where the processes of *re*-searching and *in*-searching merge naturally with those of *with*-searching or searching *with-in*, and which address and reflect on what has been lost on the way of growing 'out of' Nature, as we have as a society, and where the work of creative reflection becomes 'what asks to be spoken' (Romanyshyn 2007: 15).

Movement as experience on its own does feel complete to the mover in the moment of experiencing it. Movement feels like the ontology of all beings. The metaphoric and symbolic dimensions of movement experience are picked up implicitly within the intuitive sensitivities.

Nevertheless, it is in the sharing and making movement fully conscious and explicit, as well as more applicable in our daily realities, that calls for additional ways of understanding it in multiformatted ways. My hopes are that it is in felt thinking, as a guiding methodology, that such constructive help can be found, for any individual mover's experience. Yet, before the phases are described in more detail, let us now address the difficulties of sharing and languaging the depths of somatic experience.

7

Felt Thinking and Languaging
the Experience

Before the descriptive part of the ecosomatic, practice-based work on felt thinking in movement is presented in more detail, it is important for me to mention that while working with movement-grounded experience, languaging that very experience has been a constant challenge. Creative expression, both in speech and writing, often eludes the logical functioning(s) of everyday prose, not to mention any systematic writing. It eludes it not only in style but also in terminology and syntax, and suggests a more poetic, improvisational or neologistic dimension.

With my deep trust in authenticity of movement messaging, the self-explicit value of the expressive sharings has then been considered by me to be a qualitative addition to the standardly processed language-in-use. They are proposed here as an opportunity to engage the reader with its felt, sonorous dimension alongside the logically discerned.

In his chapter on the 'Landscape of language', David Abram describes how, since antiquity, the participatory proclivity of the senses has been transferred from the depths of the surrounding world to the letters of the alphabet due to 'the synaesthetic magic of the senses' (1996: 138). He writes that our senses are now 'coupled, syneasthetically, to these printed shapes as profoundly as they were once wedded to cedar trees, ravens, and the moon' (Abram 1996: 138) and that the anthropocentric language-based mode of existence cuts us off from the voices of the rest of nature.

Hall also continues that words assume more importance than they should. 'Words, after all, are symbols, and while it is the symbols that are used to describe what the people do, somehow in this process the symbols and the story they tell take on the life on their own' (Hall 1983: 84). This creates a new reality that is quite different from the reality felt in direct experience.

So, even though the utmost attempt has been taken to share the experiential material in its contextual relevance throughout, as a practitioner, I still sense that the reality of the written text is somewhat incomplete, or at least, distinct from what the original depth of experience of felt thinking in movement provides for the mover. Also, the living contexts of the historicity and futurity of that experience will always be known and felt only in the very moment of being with that movement experience, never to be re-lived in the same way again.

To continue though, the somatically developed method of felt thinking in movement helps to attend to the most natural and unconscious flows of developing thoughts in search of their intrinsic meaning. Complementing thus our conscious thinking, which is normally targeted towards more analytical processes that predetermine the action, enhancing the logical, linear functions of the mind, and which can even convincingly change our feelings about it. Neuroscientific research (e.g. MacLean 1965; Rorty 1980; Damasio 1994, 2000, 2001) reveals that feelings are indeed rooted in one part of the central nervous system, while words and logic are a function of an entirely different part of the brain.

To bypass conscious thought in somatic inquiry then is to dissolve the ego and the consciousness of the self and to open up any dividing lines between the animate and inanimate, or tangible and intangible.

Borrowing from Herrigel (1989) and bringing in an example of Zen, Hall writes that truth in the West is specific, whereas to a Zen master, it is all-encompassing and, paradoxically, the very essence of the self.

> Every master who practices [*sic*] an art moulded by Zen is like a flash of lightning from the cloud of all-encompassing truth. This truth is present in the free movement of his spirit, and he meets it again […] as his own original and nameless essence.
>
> (Hall 1983: 98)

In the western traditions, we look for truth in one place, while a Zen master knows that enlightenment can be found everywhere.

As human beings, we are definitely in the habit of construing our own selves, in language, as a result of heavy reliance on conscious thinking processes and which are primarily a construct of our own linguistic concepts, often culturally claimed. The methodology of felt thinking in movement though attempts to provide a thorough opportunity for continuous reconnection and balancing of the thinking with feeling processes, the processes that often get suppressed on personal levels as the societal levels of functioning in language take over.

Irigaray calls this staying in a 'linguistic universe' a closed and isolating choice and argues that the lack of cultivation of our physical properties handicaps our relational life and gradually leads to 'an exhaustion of our vitality'. She also underlines the fact that we know practically nothing about our 'natural belonging' (Irigaray 2017: 11).

Additionally, feeding into a similar perspective, in her ongoing work within the recently established International Bateson Institute, and what she coined as *transcontextual research* or the ecology of the conversation, Nora Bateson asks: 'How can we improve our perception of the complexity we live within, so we may improve our interaction with the world?' (2018: n.pag.).

In her online elaborations on how we think about living things, she describes:

> We live in the world that is filled with thinking tools that push us to material and logical patterns, languages, research programmes, definitions, labels, categories, diagnosis [...] and how do we begin to think about communication and relationships and set ourselves free, or at least be aware [...] of what these lenses are that we see through [...] and that will give us some leverage, and some deeper access to our own subjectivity.
>
> (Bateson 2018: n.pag.)

Ansell-Pearson too adds that 'language imitates our spatial habits of representation: it compels us to establish sharp and precise distinctions or discontinuity between material things, which proves useful (only) for social science' (2018: 57).

One of the realizations of this movement-inspired work is that there are a lot of epistemological errors in questions we are trying to ask in the first place and that every question reveals ways and/or conceptual biases in which we have framed the issue. This is also why it has been my motivation all along to include the questions that are being asked alongside the practice, and to reflect on the process of asking and answering a question from more than one perspective.

What art and nature have in common is that they function on multiple levels simultaneously. It is an ongoing, improvisational conversation with countless relationships happening at the same time, and which can feed or enlighten one another. Nora Bateson gives an example of that in a vine climbing a tree, being dependent on the Sun, shade, type of tree, seasons, weather, activities taking place around the tree, etc., including an impossible number of stories ... 'Imagine', she continues, 'what is happening in the process of growing a jungle', and she describes it as a 'continuous process of evolving, co-evolving, compensating ... impossible to even understand for a human conscious mind' (Bateson 2018: n.pag.).

Now, the context in which we can approach our relationship with a jungle is always dependent on our present situation, something that contextualizes our stepping into the jungle for us, and makes meaning for us. That present context also confirms for us that the stories that the jungle can bring up for us, as dwellers or visitors are always changing, and that we are always in a different relationship with both the self and the jungle.

Relationships through time are always alive. Bateson concludes that art and nature offer us a 'paradoxical communication form that we cannot resolve'

(2018: n.pag.) and which we can relate to *only* with the feeling, yet keep failing to understand. And that both art and nature give us an opportunity to have our own opinion without reducing it, as revealed in differences in our own perceptions in the first place, with them being of the emotional, visual, sense organ-based or narrative type.

> No directions, no front, no back, no sides
> And up and down
> Itself not pushing, wanting, addressing
> Itself out of nothingness and everything
> Empty, full, solid, dark, wild and gentle, wide and
> Open, narrow, dark, dull, and wet and, and, and, and, and, and …
> Heartbeat of existence.
>
> (Martina Polleros, *Cove Park Journals*, April 2018)

I read those words, recorded in felt thinking, as an invitation to tuning into the rhythms of a heartbeat, settled into an open possibility for continuation and otherness.

Also, on many occasions in her pioneering work on experiential anatomy, that informs my practice, Cohen et al. (2012) remind us that movement is our first language and that dance is the poetry of that language. In order to be fluent, dancers need to move both with ease and flexibility but also strength and openness to expression as a sharing process.

Even though being a dancer might not apply to many, we are definitely all movers. Movement fills our life in all its most minute presence of becoming in breath, heartbeat, blinking, thinking and its performed extensions in wider, emotional and whole-bodied activities.

Bainbridge Cohen also argues that our psychophysical geography, sensed in experiential anatomy, and the historical traces of our embryological development help us to discover where we are in this 'earthy', as I understand it, body and how we got there, as we all live differently unique qualities of movement that guides us in life (Cohen et al. 2012). By focusing our attention inwardly, experiential anatomy, as opposed to the traditionally practised cognitive anatomy in medical education, proposes a way to refer to the uniquely lived experience of the body, and bodily organs, in connecting to the particular functioning of the felt sense. It also refers to the mover to the actuality that being alive is experientially accessible.

In a similar line of thought then, somatic felt thinking in movement experience offers an ongoing possibility of reconnection with both changing and sustained qualities of movement that define our individual selves, and our own unique yet shared nature. It is also a method of voicing that experience in its all-encompassing 'now-ness' of unfolding, where the conscious mind in languaging the experience meets the unconscious mind by simply following 'the felt' in sound as vibrational movement.

It is an experiential time-space when and where the *reflective thought* meets *reflexive feeling* and when and where the *insightful newness* takes shape as a creative offspring of such meeting, adding another dimension to the mentioned two, and connecting in a multiperspectival experience of the self through past, present and future co-creative multitudes.

If the free movement can be compared to writing in time-space, then felt thinking can also be compared to the creative 'stream of consciousness' writing, where there is no questioning of the unfolding content happening. Instead, there is an uncritical opening for what wants to emerge by connecting oneself to all there is and all that we are able to connect to, embodying all our own psychophysical limitations, while growing the felt self in widening, animating and deepening our own relation to/with the living world of which we are both an active and passive part.

It will be the focus of the following section to exemplify and describe the three-fold practice of connecting to the eco-somatic depths of the self. Finally, to contextualize it well within other practices and theory, the practice will be further summarized in the concluding chapters, including my further recommendations for regular time in felt thinking as a daily practice.

8

The Three Dimensions of Felt Thinking and their Embryological Correspondence with Time/Space Experience

As I discussed already, the historical recap on literature on human condition reveals a standardized tendency to approach the subject from a perspective of a human being in a human world context only and it addresses our predominant conception of human nature as unique, thus different from the nature of any other life on Earth. Yet, when feel thinking in movement, as a practice of ontological reconnection, I continuously choose to look at human nature as the nature of being in movement, and acknowledge both differences and commonalities within wider considerations for Life on Earth, i.e. life in earthy contexts of time and space shared reality that we, as a species, come to live and co-create in.

I also mentioned already, alluding to somatic experience as free movement improvisation, that the creatively voiced and expressed content will be addressed and presented here by me as a potentially new way, or new depth of thinking, away from habits of only mental, i.e. conscious processing, a way that offers connections to the larger contexts of life.

The task of making good progress in the direction of thinking out of habit though, if we think of ecophenomenological philosophy as an undertaking concerning sensual perception, is 'not to leave the human behind but rather to broaden the horizon of our experience of life' (Ansell-Pearson 2018: 5) as somatic praxis suggests, and to think beyond our customary images of matter, as Bergson et al. (2007) proposes.

The freedom in movement expression then corresponds to breaking with the habits and conventions that govern life of the social ego, the ego that Bergson calls our 'superficial self' (Bergson 1955). It is important to refer here to Bergson's contention that human thinking, at least in its logical form, is unable to appreciate the 'true nature of life' and that our failure to appreciate 'the ocean of life we are carried within' explains why we are so alienated from life and our full condition of existence.

I do then propose exploring the method of felt thinking in somatic experience as opening up to new possibilities of relation to ourselves as living beings. The emergent and explicated through praxis dimensions of that living relation will correspond to different psycho-somatic phases at work.

The practice of felt thinking as embodied and ongoingly shaped perception will then be further described and organized into three major qualitative dimensions or depths that take place in the experience of the self. They naturally ingrain and permeate one another, back and forth, even if they seem to succeed one another in the written format proposed here.

Since psycho-somatic wellbeing corresponds to how we feel and perceive the self in time, and corresponds to many qualitative changes at hand, reflecting on the nature of psycho-somatic states through praxis of contemplative movement creates the major foreground of understanding our nature of being in/with time/space here explored.

It is important to clarify too that the described dimensions of felt thinking emerged from the critical reflection upon the collected material in my personal 'practice as research' processes, collected in *Moving Thoughts Journal*. My initial reflection upon the material was that it is of a highly metaphysical nature. As the practice progressed over time, my ongoingly reinforced conviction, and realization, was that the performed movement engagements differed in their experiential depths.

Depending on the versatile psycho-physical conditions of the sessions performed, I could feel and distinguish three different types of connectivity to myself and the environment taking place.

Additionally, there has been no determinant identified in terms of whether the movement sessions have been happening outdoors or indoors, yet the quality of movement engagement has been noticeably affected by the feeling of safety, intimacy and freedom of expression. Working with sound, movement and art without disturbing or being disturbed, without causing any form of commotion or being actively watched, has thus been a felt priority for every session.

The three stages or the three dynamics of engagement at work here, and what I propose to call the experiential transitioning through embodied flux of related-ness, correlate with the depths of the experiential quality that I was able to awaken and embody in free movement.

But they also correlate with ways of overcoming the conceptual dichotomies about movement in general.

Further still, they also correspond to the somatically sensed cellular levels of agency as discussed in contemporary somatic literature, mainly informed by the pioneering work on experiential anatomy by Cohen et al. (2012) and Olsen (2002). In my practice, these somatically sensed cellular levels of agency found their immediate correlation to a subjective perception of the self as ongoing, both becoming and differentiation in time and space.

So, the anatomical aspects of the experience of the self will be understood here through the metaphorical lens of embryological development of germ layers: ectoderm, mesoderm, and endoderm and their dynamic activity patterns, but also through the corresponding questions that attending to those layers of experience seems to be addressing.

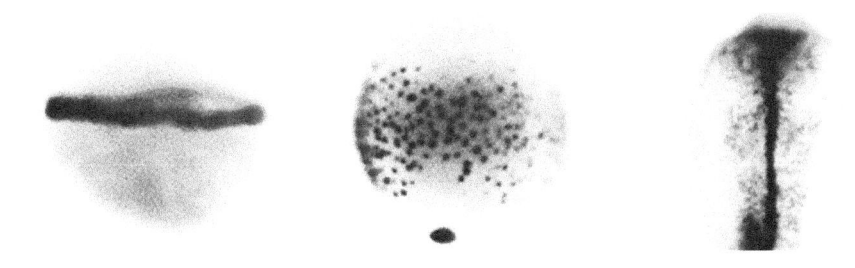

FIGURE 8.1: Dynamics of germ formation: (1) ectoderm, (2) mesoderm and (3) endoderm.

To explain in more detail, the germ layer is a group of cells in an embryo that interact with each other as the embryo develops and contributes to the later formation of all organs and tissues. The movement dynamics, as observed in both my own and other movers' explorations, show grounding similarities to the dynamics of germ formation observed in the images above, as the experience of free movement travels from the outer layers of skin and nervous system through the muscular and the bone-felt and onto the deepest, internal organs and cellular levels.

As brought up briefly already in the introductory chapter of this section:

1   During the first phase of movement engagement, there is a tendency for widespread, open arms and inquisitive encounter happening. The physical expression during this initial stage appears as mainly *horizontal*, following inclinations for sensual encounters through vision, touch, smell and willingness to meet.

2   During the second phase of movement engagement, a visible tendency for more dynamic encounters with the sensed dichotomies of experience takes place. The physical encounters deepen in psychological meaning creating a new dimension of relating through giving and receiving, i.e. experiential exchanging. *Multi-dimensional* expression of movement peaks at this stage too.

3   Finally, during the third phase of movement engagement, following the often exhausting exchange of phase two, a more *vertical* dynamic observable in movement takes over. Visible reaching up with hands or whole-body stretches happen which reveals strong connectivity between the grounded, the earthy and the more metaphysical, spiritual or soulful depths of experience to be taking place.

As an overview here, working with experiential levels of ectoderm, the outer germ layer of an embryo that gives rise to the skin, and the nervous system, the attended to questions are those of *Where* and *When*, creating a direct link to the *physical* time of experience.

Working with experiential levels of mesoderm, the layer that gives rise to all connective tissues, the attended to questions are those of *Who* and *What*, creating a direct link to the *psychological* time of experience.

Finally, working with experiential levels of endoderm layer, layer that gives rise to organs, digestive track and the respiratory system, the attended to questions are those of *Why* and *How*, creating a direct link to, what I call, primordial or *ontogenetic* time of experience.

And the emergent themes of experiential felt thinking in movement practice that create the three dimensions of relating to Nature/Self are:

1   Receptivity in the objective, physical time and its *ectodermic relatedness* as emergent from experiences of connecting to the living dynamic of spatial–temporal reality and guided by sensual presence, embodied listening and open attentiveness.
2   Responsiveness in the subjective, psychological time and its *mesodermic dynamism* as emergent from experiences of co-creating with the living dynamic of spatial-temporal reality and guided by experiential exchange, memory, emotion and imagination.
3   Responsibility in the primordial, ontogenetic time and its *endodermic intensity* as emergent from experiences of becoming the living dynamic of spatial–temporal reality and guided by insightful intuiting, gut-feeling, letting go, losing oneself and transforming.

It can be said then that the embodied connecting, co-creating and then becoming the spatial–temporal reality that the somatic experience in felt thinking guides the mover into, is then a form of re-living, in movement, the embryological stages of life that the body remembers.

The primal relationality of movement, emphasized by me, i.e. the towards and away from principle of movement, here too, becomes very present on the cellular level and its activity of both morphing and differentiation. But, let us look at the cellular development within embryogenesis a little bit more.

In her book *Bodystories*, Andrea Olsen writes that 'the human body develops from the union of two cells, the sperm and the ovum' (1998: 19). Beginning with fertilization then, the embryonic period is considered to be the period during which, the major structures of the embryo are formed. It is also when, by the end of week eight in embryonic development, that most of the organs and body systems are going to be established, by which time the initial two-cell stage of an embryo will transform into a million-of-cells foetus form.

According to most recent embryological literature (Webster 2016; Schoenwolf 2015), one of the most important phases in this developmental process of a foetus happens just into the third week, with what is called gastrulation or germ formation. It is when the trilaminar embryonic disc is formed to enable embryonic structures to be shaped by the three distinctive embryonic tissue layers of ectoderm, mesoderm and endoderm. Gastrulation is initiated by the process called the primitive streak – a visible depression on the trilaminar disc, and a crucial moment of cell formation.

The appearance of the primitive streak marks the point when it is possible to determine the physiological organization of an embryo, which side is left or right and where the main body parts will come to be. At this point in time, the cells of the embryo start migrating to different parts of the streak and begin on their path to specialization by forming the endodermal, the mesodermal and the ectodermal layers.

The ectoderm will form the external surface of the embryo: the epidermis of the skin and the nervous system and its sensory apparatus including the retina, as well as the touch, temperature and pain senses in the skin.

The mesoderm will form the connective tissues of the skeleton, the bones, the dermis of the skin, cartilage, skeletal and smooth muscles, and most of the cardiovascular, lymphatic and reproductive systems. Cells of the immune system formed in the bone marrow will also be derived from this layer.

Finally, endoderm will form the most internal systems of the lungs and respiratory tracks as well as the whole of the gastrointestinal track including all the organs associated with it, such as pancreas, liver, bladder, the tonsils, the thymus, the thyroid and the parathyroid glands.

Additionally, what remains important to point out here is that the three germ layers formation does not really follow the ectoderm, mesoderm and endoderm order. Rather, from the initial two layers of the embryo, the ectoderm and the endoderm of the bilaminar disc, the third – intraembryonic mesoderm – is formed. Thus the real order of the layer formation, despite its physiological appearance, is ectoderm, endoderm and then mesoderm. Mesoderm is then the last layer to be formed, as it appears in-between the original two and formed by the ectoderm side.

That interrelation and anti-chronological genesis reveal to me the complexity of body systems and that the divisive chronology of differentiation is as present at the embryological level as the synergetic, non-sequential generation.

Following this hopefully thorough introduction section, I would now like to turn us back onto the path of following movement experience itself. In what follows, I will introduce the practice of felt thinking in its experiential dimensions while moving with receptivity, responsiveness and responsibility, as the guiding phases of ecologically minded self-discovery in somatic movement experience.

SECTION TWO

THE PRACTICE OF
FELT THINKING
IN MOVEMENT

I

Moving with Receptivity
and Sensuous Co-presence in Physical Time
or
On *Where* and *When* of Being

FIGURE P1.1: *Moving Thoughts Journal – Towards Sensuous Presence (Embryological Curl)*, Cairngorms National Park, Highland. Photograph by Noemi Dako.

Being in movement, understood both as engagement in a most physical activity, like running for example, or an experience of a most subtle sensation or occurrence, like thinking a thought itself, cannot happen without its spatial–temporal relatedness, the where and the when. All movement happens through an engagement with/in time-space, and to me, the most extended version of such engagement in movement is in *sensual co-presence*.

It is when, and where, in felt thinking in movement, I become aware of the dimensionality of being, and when and where I sense that my own frame of spatio-temporal being co-exists in multitude of other. Following *When* and *Where* questions, that is questions about time and space of being in movement, opens ways for connecting to the living dynamic of being.

Nevertheless, having introduced the theme of this chapter a little already, the topic of time and space has a long history of posing a particular problem to philosophical reasoning.

Understood as seemingly easy, daily life reality, and so as the night-to-day interval pattern organized into past, present and future, on a closer look, it can seem quite illusive. With past and future being no realities, as the past does not exist anymore, and the future does not exist as yet, the only reference point seems to be the present, which is the model of reasoning about time derived ultimately from Aristotle's *Physics* (Aristotle et al. 1996). And yet, the present is always moving and can be reduced endlessly to an interval without duration, thus the only time existing is 'nothing but a point of time without any dimension; the point, we could say, at which past and future touch each other' (Zwart 1976: 3).

In philosophical tradition on the subject, there are three main conceptions of time: idealist, realist and relational. In his book *About Time: A Philosophical Inquiry Into the Origin and Nature of Time*, Zwart sums it up this way:

> According to the idealist view time is nothing but a concept and therefore dependent on (human) consciousness only. According to the realist view time is a self-sufficing entity, which is not dependent on anything else. According to the relational view, finally, time is also a concept, and therefore dependent on consciousness, but at the same time it is a function of the events happening in nature. In this view there would be no time without consciousness, but neither would there be time without events.
>
> (1976: 30)

It is thus important to consider our own relation to the subject of time and see if redirecting our attention from logical to more experiential data will open up any new possibilities for an ongoing referencing about our own being in time and space.

And if I do that, the following question emerges: Why has the relational theory not been agreed to and adopted into daily life as yet, on a wider societal scale? And why do we still depend on clocks as the most reliable, and so realist reference only? An attempt at providing possible answers to these questions, or making those questions even more rhetorical at least, will be attempted throughout the following chapters.

The main topic of Moving with Receptivity though, when guided by somatic movement experience, is to look closer at the processes of sensuous *connecting* to the living environment within and around oneself through attentive, embodied listening. And those processes encompass listening to all the movement-based sensations, the tactile, the visual, the aural and the intuitive. All the grasps and grips of co-presence-ing which happen through the experiential sharing of time and space, and of being 'here and now', whatever that might mean in personal experience.

The word *connecting* then has a very important function of underlining the conceptual dichotomies of being 'here and now' as opposed to being 'there and then', and the suggested framework of thematic sub-sections will indeed be meant as a way of building bridges towards a more fluent connectivity with the phenomenologically understood and somatically lived self in wider contexts of time on Earth.

The titles of the thematic sub-sections will then reveal a flowful journey from seemingly clear-cut discrepancies to more unifying perspectives, as felt in movement, as I believe that it is through one's practised attention to such primal abilities of relating to, and tuning into different realms of time-space that the differences and personal meanings about our own nature come through. And it is also where the initial dichotomies of thoughts become more permeable in felt experience, opening doors for shared connectivity.

Learning from the anthropological perspective, in his book *The Dance of Life*, Edward T. Hall deals with his culturally contextualized experiences of how 'people are tied together and yet isolated from each other by invisible threads of rhythm and hidden walls of time' (1983: 3) and how the shared organization of time became a primary organizer for all culturally specific activities, a way of prioritizing and categorizing experience, as well as a system revealing (or judging on) how people feel about each other, cross-culturally or whether they can get along, socially or personally.

In fact, he points out that nothing occurs without some kind of time frame (Hall 1983: 3) and that we all build our relationships to life thanks to and through personal, social and cultural frames of time. And those frames can also be related to as depths of experience, like in Bergson's words, when he says that there are diverse 'tones' of mental life and that 'our psychic life can be lived at different heights, now nearer to action, now further removed from it, according to the degree of our attention to life' (Bergson 1988: 8).

Hall also reminds that non-verbal, thus body-based communication constructs 90 per cent of total communication happening between people, with only 10 per cent based on verbal communication. And that the role of feelings, speaking from the Euro-American perspective, is generally ignored in socio-political governance.

While wondering about connectivity between the human and non-human worlds, it is then worth asking: how is it possible to maintain the wellbeing of our world-wide societies in the absence of feedback from the other 90 per cent of the body-based communication?

And I would here like to propose that in relating to movement, in a wider than behavioural study fashion that Hall proposes though, lies the link to wider than social, cultural or human communication, and indeed, a possibility of connecting to primarily relevant, ecological dimensions of our species as well.

It is the two-fold role of this section to reveal how somatic experience of movement and its constituent, sensual connectivity to the living environments, both internal and external, can help to self-discover and connect to one's personal dimensions of lived and embodied time-frames, as well as how to awaken, grow and expand our ability to flexibly move between different, often contradictory frames of time-space that fall within or outside our own, human life-time.

Consequently, as the narratives born in movement experience progress over time, the initially dichotomous phraseology of meeting the external world as described in this section on Moving with Receptivity will undergo multiple transformations by the time it reaches the section on Moving with Responsibility. And, the reader will be able to observe that the terminology changes overtime too, throughout the three dimensions of practice, into being more inclusive and more integrated, creating thus better grounds for eco-logically and eco-ethically inclusive comprehension of human–non-human being Nature/Self.

9

In and Out

The biggest contention in philosophy of time has always been that we keep confusing, or keep limiting time to space ... To me, the habit of spatialization of experience, as mentioned above already, reveals itself as simplification, the superficial perception we normally limit ourselves to and which excludes the full potential of our human sensual apparatus.

The proposed, here, *somatic receptivity* in movement experience refers to deeper layers of relatedness that corresponds to *feeling* time through pacing, frequencies and other qualities of co-existence as opposed to picking on spatial bearings from occupying space only.

To me, somatic receptivity conveys an implicit co-presence of time and space in the experiential dimension and includes patterns, rhythms, frequencies and shapes, both visible and invisible to the eye that our embodied attention brings forth into movement experience.

To start with, I propose looking at embodied receptivity as a form of connecting or wit(h)-nessing a bodily movement-led method of 'being with' or relating with whatever enters one's attention in the fullest way one can possibly experience, starting with the bipolar dynamics of the breath.

In my own notes on such experience in the *Moving Thoughts Journal*, I write:

> In my practice of opening to the Earth, to the skies and the wind around in movement, I often get rocked by giving in to the breathing patterns of being pulled up while I breath in and down into yielding onto the ground on the exhale. And whenever I enter that relational movement pattern I re-experience breathing as a primal relationship between the air and the Earth.
> I thus re-live my own belonging to the Earth as a place of rest and comfort.
>
> At the same time, it is the Earth that provides all the support for another lift up to come, and helps me rise up. Air in, air out, the Earth is breathing alongside with me, through me, and around me. And it carries a lot of playful quality in how it handles that relationship with the air.
>
> I then grow in my attention to full body breath that reminds me of the spatial directionality of the body, able to move in all the directions at the same time, even

if on different scales of engagement. Obviously, breathing with my back will be less prominent than with the chest but it is still moving receptively.

Free movement deprived of purposeful directionality by 'giving in to the body' and following the arising sensations helps to listen to otherwise silenced bodily messaging. For me, for example, it often reveals the deep need of shifting the 'upright' hierarchy of walking by releasing the feet into the air, as well as the heaviness in my head by bringing it to the ground for immediate support and comfort. The spontaneity of moving in relation to breathing whole-bodily wakes up all the possibilities of being in space.

And by entering such freedom feel-able and enabled by my unbreakable relation to the ground, as a lively and far from flat surface, it lets the directionality express itself in possible motion.

Its source reveals itself to me as that coming from the centre of the Earth, eliminating thus the simplified view of gravity as working downwards. Gravity is all-directional, radiating all over the globe in its all-embracing squeeze, and that is what comes through in my free movement as well. Different parts of my body have different needs for this open dynamic of Earth's breathing along, for being more or less resistant to either up or the down. A lively relationship.

And when I move like this following my breathing patterns the left and the right constantly feel like one and the same direction, contradicting itself yet complementing each other. No matter which direction I choose it always becomes just one. Up becomes down, left becomes right, all dilute to just forth and back, or the push and pull or yield and rise.

Just to make me realize this is exactly what breath does as well, moving towards and backwards, not necessarily in and out, as I normally perceive it, in its relational encounters.

I breathe in to meet the world with my chest movement directed towards the world as it reaches out and expands, and I breathe out back to land within myself.

At the same time, I can understand my breathing in as taking a bit of what I need from the Earth's air only to breathe out what I have to share. That way, 'in' becomes the 'out' for the world around me and 'out' the 'in'. And my common understanding of what is the 'in' and 'out' in breath exchange refreshes into a whole different dimension of relating in, to and with life, while noticing how limiting the linguistic concepts of spatial engagement are.

Like when we say 'movement', meaning something unitarily singular, while the way it is experienced through endless complexities of bodily sensations is an array of multidimensional activities of various spatial-temporalities happening at the same time within the living frame of what we simply call 'the body'.

Continue moving as I do, without actually doing much physically, I experience being functional on possibly infinite amount of frequencies, and this basic push and pull relationship of Earth and air so active in me creates a lively circularity, in, with and around me.

I feel this relationship as soft and gentle in its creative enterprise yet I know it is the same push and pull that can create most violent punch or furthest retreat in other movement contexts, and I feel its implicit potency for any change, and those felt possibilities are endless. Like moving in a straight line is possible only in a framed time/space context. Take away the frame and the movement starts to flow, chasing open possibilities of curves and winds.

And so when I enter the studio and release an obligation to perform within the uprightly correct world of human standards, I always land on my fours first to enrich my hands with the touch of the ground. And I often let my feet glide up in the air, while lying on my back, to compensate for the upright frame, but also to shake off the fears, as I yearn for the safety and support of the ground.

That very repositioning change alone creates a different set of conditions for being with the breath. And shifting to this more supported, almost resting position sparks a wonder in me, even though I feel stationary, I continue moving. Movement never stops, just like the breathing in life, it simply shifts frequency to a 'silent' mode.

And since movement of the breath can albeit change into something so subtle that we don't experience it per se, at least not consciously, practising openness to breath as movement helps me appreciate my embodied functionality to play with the multiple, the endless and the infinite within the temporal spans of such deeper attention.

And it is the infinite carried in the temporality of the breath as movement that unites me with the time-space of each moment and provides the grounding to the felt now, as both the temporal and the infinite dimensions make each other possible in every transition from breath in into breath out and into breath in into breath out into …

A shaping life relationship between active and receptive being and its ontological creativity of transitioning.

(September 2017 [edited version])

And I round up this introductory session on receptivity in felt thinking with this drawing (see Figure 9.1), entitled *Being,* where one can observe an initial, at this first stage of felt thinking, tendency for the 'stretched out' into a very open composition.

Some say, engaging in improvised movement like that is like moving in the dark, a daunting experience without a clear purpose in sight. After letting the breath be my guide in it though, it feels right to say that I experience the dark, or the unknown in movement pathways as being very conscious of the light and all its vision-based limitations.

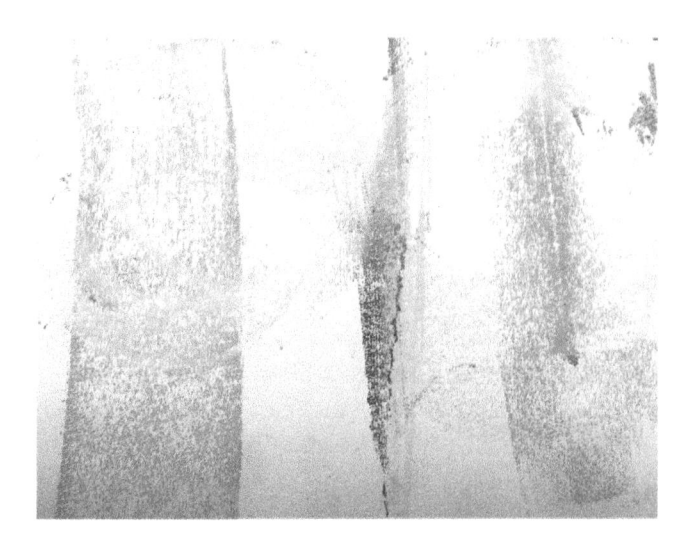

FIGURE 9.1: *Moving Thoughts Journal, Being.*

Moving with eyes closed makes me realize that the external world, guided by daylight, offers too many distractions. Learning to be conscious of my invisible, internal activity of breathing within the darkness of the experiential, is a gift that could be recommended, especially to those seeking to restore many aspects of functional integrity.

Movement supported by the dark, or the invisible paths of the breath within the bodily landscapes, gives a lot of release and gratitude for the life it sustains for us, in its ongoing, transitional exchange of 'in' and 'out' environments.

And to zoom out and look at the richness of this verbalized session, it can be stated here that breathing is often regarded as a basic sign or a guiding activity of life. Yet, in daily life, it often takes some physical distress to become more conscious, if not more appreciative, of this life-sustaining and seemingly silent motion. In somatic movement education, attending to breathing is an important aspect of slowing down which then creates an open possibility for attentive, embodied listening.

Breath, with all its different patterns, depths and rhythms, does communicate a lot about one's present psycho-somatic condition but it also reminds about the ongoing exchange between 'air taken' and 'air given' happening for us, the living beings, all the time.

And the fluidity between making the breathing conscious and its self-regulating, unconscious *carrying on* can astound many.

Ontologically speaking, 'being with' suggests right away a form of encounter-exchange, a relational co-presence with whatever is being witnessed, and so it relates to both, with-nessing and witness-ing at the same time, like in Authentic Movement practice when the mover is offered a non-judgemental attention of the observer. And even though I use the term wit(h)nessing exchangeably with 'being with' in somatic sense, its original meaning should be connected to Bracha Ettinger's concept of co-poesis as part of her wider work on affect in art making as a more-than-visual encounter that involves all the senses.

Ettinger (2006) reminds that each of us, living beings, is already in relationship before any assumption of an independent subjectivity is made and that life is ontologically relational, should we chose to attend to the compassion-driven feel thinking. Ettinger introduces or rather re-introduces compassion, along with hope, wonder, awe and reverential respect as primordial affects which, as she says, have been largely omitted in psychoanalytic work up-to date and oriented mainly towards the study of affects of anger, anxiety and abjection. She claims that art making processes that aspire to our sensual perception reveal that compassion is as much archaic and opposes the common belief that any revelation of compassion is reactive.

And in my somatic experiences, the felt thinking with breath seems to grow even more accommodating, merging the feeling not only with the thinking but also action, i.e. my physical movement, and most important of all, with my ability to listen.

In fact, the skill and quality of listening comprises and foregrounds the entire feeling-thinking-moving process and gives it its depth and responsive meaningfulness in ever changing contexts of attention.

And it is in the listening itself that I am being reminded that, '[i]f breath-in is a response of acceptance, the breath-out is a gift to the world; it is me returning a favour' (*Moving Thoughts Journal*, September 2017). And when I stay with the breath in my continuously expanding sensuous listening and connecting, I get to experience that internal darkness that every breath-in gets to travel on before transitioning onto its light-driven way out. And I get to feel think yet again that darkness is very conscious of the light. It can be experienced both as an empty space yearning towards light and as an escape from light too, a safe, rich and self-resourcing rescue place, depending on what draws and speaks to me more, from one moment to the next.

Endless creativity dwells in those possibilities of transitional relation, like every colour added to an emerging painting takes its choice in shading or lightening up the forthcoming shapes.

Is it then, I am asking myself, the light that brings up spatial realizations of the dark into the visible shapes, or is it the dark that provides the detectable contrasts as supporting backgrounds for a visual encounter to take space? And I am looking for answers to that question in the following streaming movement events, both in studio and in the open air:

I'm lying with my hands up tight
Pressed against my eyes
I create this darkness that
Gives an escape from the light
But it's very conscious of it ...
[...]
Taking my hands off my eyes
Into the light
And I see animal faces
They just come up
While the darkness meets the light.

> (*Moving Thoughts Journal, Felt Thinking in Movement*
> audio transcript, August 2017)

And later:
Cradled by stones and boulders
Of my local cairns
And blinded by the sunlight of this glorious
Cloudless day,
I feel like working with coal pencil
And draw and listen to the shadows ...

I just saw a baby deer ...
That disappeared in a blink ...

FIGURE 9.2: *Moving Thoughts Journal*, Kingswells, Aberdeen.

And listening to the baaaa-ing sheep …
While a lot of planes pass by … into the clear skies.
(drawing)

The sheep became quiet …
I don't hear them anymore …
And my little friend, deer, re-emerged
As (s)he was hiding in the dry, tall grass …
I'm thinking of belonging to the landscape … through time …

(Moving Thoughts Journal, Felt Thinking in Movement
audio transcript, May 2018)

FIGURE 9.3: *Moving Thoughts Journal, Boulder's Thought.*

And just like breath taking its shape and transitioning between the internal and external landscapes of light and darkness (see Figure 9.3), I feel that in movement is my chance to speak with space and that the sensual responsiveness to spatial conditioning gets translated into every sensed change, as in the following experience and the drawing that follows it (see Figure 9.4).

With my open palms, I'm letting the sun go through my skin …

And I know that all those trillions of cells that I live by are feeling it. And they are drawn into that open conversation.

They fluently adjust and open up to the invitation of the warmth.

And that warmth is like a gentle touch, travelling with air, spread by sudden gusts of wind.

The surface of my skin becomes much deeper, it widens internally and externally. It enlarges like a sponge filled with water, with texture and volume. It is letting the air meet the watery base of every cell, really. And that expansion and thickening of the skin layers has a soothing effect on the functional operations of my whole interior.

I feel more water-y, and I take shape of the rock underneath me through the softened skin and its cushioning effect. And that feel of belonging … so comforting …

If it was cold, I feel that the reaction would be the opposite. The skin layers would shrink or flatten up, tightening the density, becoming more of a protective container than a meeting ground.

(*Moving Thoughts Journal, Felt Thinking in Movement*
audio transcript, April 2018)

FIGURE 9.4: *Moving Thoughts Journal, The Butterfly's Reach.*

And on another occasion, an openness to a different form of exchanging with air, whole-bodily, through gentle touch, and following the 'in and out' pattern, reveals to me its most rewarding effects of being able to connect more and more to the spatio-temporal qualities of the ground. And the Earth feels not only present in my own experience of the self but also in the grounding me support. And felt thinking in movement continues guiding the way for such responsive and grounding companionship, as an experiential exchange between the elements of air and earth, as I reflect:

With all the soreness in my entire body, due to some heavier training earlier this week, I am trying to collect all the energy from the painful places and from the pain itself.

I feel like whooshing myself … and when I think of collecting energy, then all the whooshing happens from the peripheries, my toes and heels and fingers and elbows being directed towards the centre place, towards the heart and the solar plexus.

Maybe because it feels like this is the place where all the energy can be received back and transformed into something new, so after all the whooshing is done towards the heart and the solar plexus my breath goes directly there, to spend some time.

And then, an automatic second round of whooshing happens, but now, in the other direction, as if the air wanted to be pushed out of that centred spot from right at the bottom of the rib cage toward all the peripheries, toward the palms of my hands, toward the head and toward the back, staying on the waistline and toward my toes and the floor, front and back.

It's like giving myself a bit of propelling wind power to reach out to the world from the solar plexus central's spot. The movement is quite balanced and symmetrical and yet the roundness and dimensionality of the spine contributes to experiencing all those spatial connections around me as I twist and turn in all directions.

My elbows are catching a lot of windy, windmill-like kind of momentum together with stepping backwards and sideways.

I am feeling like I am filling up this whole space with that expansion, moving from the painful places, physically painful. My head is not heavy at all now, it wants to be taken places. It feels much lighter after discovering that feeling down or overwhelmed or overstressed depends mainly on my own attitude and it just takes that little bit to tweak it into a bit more of a playful mode, a bit of being exactly where I am in movement.

And I am letting all the thoughts travel downloads, into the body, into the ground where they get digested and looked at in a bit more real, comprehensive, down-to-earth way, instead of being chased up into my head, and into the future projections while making a lot of vicious circles as they charge forward too quick.

(Moving Thoughts Journal, Felt Thinking in Movement
audio transcript, May 2018)

And I follow this exploration with a soft pastel drawing on Voicing Air (see Figure 9.5) while feeling enriched, mentally and physically rebalanced.

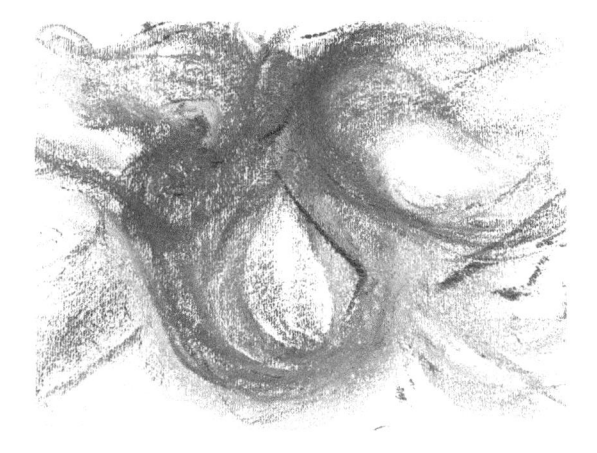

FIGURE 9.5: *Moving Thoughts Journal, Voicing Air.*

10

Now and Then

As described already, the sensed 'in here' and 'out there' in spatial transitioning of the breath feels like connecting all the functional activities of the living soma in practically unaccountable ways. And, as receptivity begins to reveal itself in emergent movement, I begin to notice that it relates to other spatio-temporal and often dichotomous experiences of the self.

In this sub-section, I am looking at movement as functioning in most non-linear ways and as a complex relationship between *Now* and *Then*, with *Now* being the focal point of attention, and *Then* relating to any time outside or further away from *Now* both in the past and future times, unlike our common understanding of time as linear.

In fact, in movement, I experience entering an open realm of experiential content that escapes any sort of linear categorization. Clock time shifts to being only a frame for ordering my daily activities, but not a real point of value or quality-related reference. From my practice, I already know that one minute of personally meaningful explorative time in movement experience can take me on endless trips to the imaginarily real time of reflection, anytime.

Thus, the Now is responsive to my attention, as portrayed in the pictures below (see Figure 10.1). The more I am sensually present the bigger the Now, that I mean and feel.

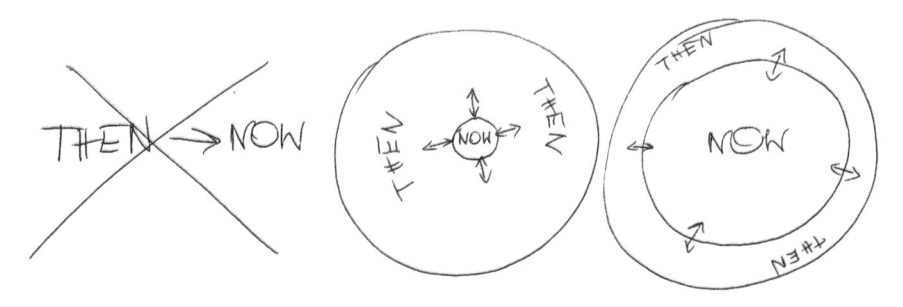

FIGURE 10.1: Shifting perception of 'Now and Then'.

And, by awakening the sensitivities of the skin receptors in the Now, doors open for me to imaginary travelling, and given an opportunity to find more support and rejuvenation in the *in-search* – a natural passage to the childhood realm is found. And it starts in simple bodily needs, as introduced already in the previous sub-section, for balancing the Ins and Outs, as the senses thrive on both air and water supplies. Like in yawning:

Yawning …
I can sense it performs air balancing for me
as it takes in and gets rid of access air at the same time
Opening different channels
Cleaning
Clearing up the eyes
As they become full of tears
Watery …
In and out
Stretching out into the world
Open mouth
Open ears
Watery eyes
Like all the connection
all the openings between the nose, eyes, ears and the throat
and the rest of the body, down to toes and fingers
want to open
and re-establish
rebalance
Yawning … when standing
My hands open, my chest opens
It pulls it out
Head goes up
My feet want to spread out
My toes part
My back wants to stretch
And I'm in a new relationship again …
I spread out, almost like with wings …
Not only the air gets rebalanced
But all the watery systems
And my connection to the ground
Its texture and its temperature
The air makes me light
And loose …

It activates directionality
In relation to all the space around me
Even my back feels like it's breathing better now
Very airy
I feel like my bones weigh nothing
And the sound can move me
It can lift myself like a feather
Scooping air and spreading it around
Scooping ground and spreading it about
My feet are so light
I feel like squatting for more opening to happen
I'm throwing myself around
And being thrown at the same time
Who is doing the moving?
I don't know
My toes are taking off
So my heels can hardly support the whole body
As it wants to fly
My hair is so delighted to fly
The longer it grows
The more fun it has
I need to sit down to give my feet more air
They don't want to be on the ground
They want to be where my hands are
In the air
They want to do their clowning and jumping in the air
So carefree
And childish
Exploring the air
No child can say no to that
And the way I move the feet
It makes me want to put my hands on the ground
Infantile ridiculousness
Of freedom and shifting hierarchies
Letting other parts have their closer relationship with the ground.

(Moving Thoughts Journal, Felt Thinking in Movement
audio transcript, August 2017)

Now, I'm asking myself again, how often in our daily life do we bring our hands to the ground? We generally teach our kids not to do that, while bringing both feet and hands onto the floor is such an enriching experience in movement. It awakens multiple instincts for natural connection to the Earth and our repressed, or dissociated rather, in upright postures – ecological unconscious. And perhaps still, a connection to our own, as a species, as David Abram (1996) describes, more-than-human nature.

It is no wonder that, in societal terms, children show the most developed connectivity to the world of both fauna and flora, as physically their bodily skills exceed those of a regular adult in flexibility and embodied curiosity for contact, the olfactory engagement and freedom in expressing the physiological needs, as the just exemplified, initiation of yawning.

Our sensuous development certainly does hold a primal role in establishing our relationship with the surroundings, and, following the spatial–temporal unity, it also reveals one's relationship with our temporary realizations.

Realizing that our senses work very differently in relation to the distances they can individually cover in establishing a basic form of contact is a thorough ground for such considerations.

And so, the reach of a human eyesight definitely makes human beings a primarily visual species, with our hearing capability falling second, then the sense of smell, touch and, finally, taste. While relying on skills of proprioception, the kinetic aspect of spatial arrangement between what we pick up sensually seems very obvious, providing us with direct and ongoingly updated information on distance and proximity.

Attending to the use of senses, as mentioned by Zwart (1976) too, can be definitely revealing in the way spatial–temporal interpretation is already implicit in our embodied perception. It is nevertheless not easy to agree with Zwart that correlation between senses comes down to our primitive ways of telling the linear, i.e. causal relation of before-and-after, as in the relation between seeing and hearing. And he does mention its paradoxical nature himself, that the complexity of time is far more sophisticated, and that any form of ordering should be rather seen as part of survival-related skill-set of locating self and other in space than as an attempt at the abstract conceptualization of time.

Zwart also argues that 'primitive man' has been much more conscious of the events happening around him than of what occurred inside him, and that it is unlikely that he would have been conscious of the succession of his ideas before he was conscious of the succession of external events (Zwart 1976).

Questionably, again, after closer examination of my own experiences of opening up to spatial–temporal connectivity, it is difficult to say what precedes or presupposes what. Similarly, I am not able to say whether it was the developing sense of infantility in me that made me touch the floor or the intention to touch the floor that made me feel like that. And so the exploration continues:

> The bouncing, down and up movement reminds me that I am travelling constantly with the Earth and as the Earth travels spinning around itself and the sun, and who

knows what else, because I am sure the sun is not stationary either, I just want to feel that movement in the air that lands on my skin as I open up to receive it with the whole surface of my skin front and back and sideways, with my eyes wide open, with my attentive ears, and my hair loose.

I've been asking myself that question, for a while now, why have I lost the fun in this, while it's such a glorious bliss,

To move,

To follow the movement,

To follow myself in it.

To play with that wind I create myself while charging through the space, through air …

And travelling on the rays of sun, caressing my own emotions in it,

Flying … gliding with the feeling of resting on the air and then receiving that bounce back from the ground …

(exhaling, sounding, singing, running around)

Just running, just running …

Enjoying the lightness of every fall and every bounce back, the freedom of manoeuvring and voicing on the inhale and the exhale (sounding …)

(moving, singing, drawing)

I do feel humbled by what I am receiving …

And I want to grow along with it

Appreciating every moment …

Soothing my own frustrations within that appreciation …

And moving with it,

Not necessarily forward …!

(*Moving Thoughts Journal, Felt Thinking in Movement*
audio transcript, May 2018)

The described 'practising openness' in receptivity to one's environment can be readily interpreted as a skill we are born with and which we are equipped with as children in the most playful and carefree stages of traditionally seen personal development. Yet, since a developmental journey is often seen as a path on which new skills are acquired, the skills that are to lay solid foundations for a successful adulthood, I would like to propose looking at it with a different lens, i.e. as mentioned already, *give* and *take* or *towards* and *away from* the process, where alongside the gain there is a continuous compromise happening, if not plainly a loss, of childhood skills.

Traditionally, we call it a process of 'growing out of', which suggests a safe leaving behind our behavioural drives and transitioning onto 'more serious' outlook on life. It also relates to many theories within the field of developmental psychology, the scope of which exceeds the focus of this study. In somatic therapy though, this mentioned 'growing out of' and 'leaving behind' often reveals an unnaturally suppressed relationship to our 'past self' which is not translated properly or incorporated in a healthy way into our 'ways of being' in contexts of adulthood. Why is that?

Well, in the western time system, it is commonly assumed that an agreed period of time, a day, for example, is an empty container, waiting to be filled with activities we agree to take upon ourselves. As a consequence of that mindset, failing to perform, cancelling any activity or experiencing a different result than initially expected will most often be seen as time-wasting. Judged by such standards, if we do manage to fill our diaries with all the planned and delivered deeds, we feel like we have lived a full and productive day.

Hall writes that in that way, western culture seems 'unusually self-centred because our time system keeps reminding us that we are the only ones who can fill those containers', and that, 'time itself is seen as neutral and its only value is that it is relentless and unfeeling; it waits for no man' (1983: 84). On our journey from childhood to adulthood, we often use this system to judge ourselves as well and consider our life achievements in the light of our own expectations, making them look like a success or a failure.

Abram connects such thinking to our basic comprehension of time, saying that 'if alphabetic writing was an important factor in the emergence of abstract, homogeneous space, it was no less central to the emergence of abstract, linear time' (1996: 185).

The levels of receptivity to the outside world and its different lived dynamic, as experienced in felt thinking, can be very helpful in integrating and adapting oneself to various, often novel life scenarios, as well as deciding not to mind certain things. Somatic experiencing points us in direction of an accepting attitude towards different dynamics directed elsewhere without creating any alienating attitudes within one's psychic orientation limited to self or other, and without the feeling of frustration. There is always something emerging in the ripples of *Now-ness*, even when lying down still.

And, in line with circular comprehension of time, in my experience of the malleable *Now*, Hall (1983) too mentions many Indigenous, polychronic cultures in the world, including that of Quiche, who live by comprehending time through multiple circles of relation. First circle being that of sacred time keeping itself, then one's ancestral lineage, then one's relatedness to the Earth and its nature spirits and finally to one's relationships to the larger community.

In dealing with so many experiential levels of relation, an important feature of Quiche's tradition and divination is 'the use of the body as a sender, receiver, and analyser of messages' (Hall 1983: 88), and where the blood circulation, pulse and muscular twitches can all tell the story and where their local healer does not interpret the felt dynamic diagnostically, but analyses it in search for their intrinsic meanings.

This new in western thought, yet old in other Indigenous cultures of the world, way of relating in/with time-space is definitely present in somatic experience of the felt self, and my further elaborations on the subject will become even more descriptive in the following sub-sections of practising receptivity.

11

The Shared and the Unique

In the light of movement-based theorizing, cultural differences can be understood as different movement patterns, bound to time and place/space of how people experience the world. The way I feel it, with time and culture being inseparable in many ways, it is possible to say that cultures live through time as much as time lives through cultures, i.e. that we create time by creating intervals, shapes, patterns in life – quite in opposition here with the Newtonian view of time as an absolute.

Hall supports this view of time, as being made, with the fact that there are multiple examples of cultures, with that of the American First Nations Hopi and the Sioux, that don't even have a word for time in their vocabulary. And that this 'hidden cultural grammar of our relation to time/space defines the way in which people view the world, determines their values, and establishes the basic tempo and rhythms of life' (Hall 1983: 6).

With the twenty-first-century world becoming increasingly intercultural, and in an ongoing attempt to account for interpersonal and intercultural differences, it is becoming more and more evident that our individual experience of time in its global contexts has been widely neglected and should be given closer attention.

Being unaware or else only peripherally aware of living primarily through socially or culturally imposed pace, as well as through digitized reference to clock-measured time, we are constantly positioning ourselves somewhere in the middle, without the full spectrum of internalized time of the soma or the externalized time of the living environment in its wider ecological contexts being addressed. Or, without being given a chance to speak through our behavioural choices on the implicit levels of embodied movement experience.

Even though I provisionally agree with Hall (1983) on the importance of bringing the differences between people and cultures forth as a fruitful way of conscientious development as a species, his outlook on the problem does prove typically anthropocentric, when he states that 'life for the human species is the ultimate value against which all else should be measured' (9).

Critically then, I would like to propose looking at creative experience of movement as a gateway to a much broader, and ecologically relevant way of self-study and personal growth. And I would further imply that eco-somatic movement practice can be a practical tool for balancing the inward-looking search for personal meaning grounded in the shared unconscious with externally, environmentally oriented growth in sensuous connectedness.

Realizing that time can be a very different experience to different people helps me understand that it is primarily a product of our minds, a mental environment, which corresponds, or not, to our relationship to the ecological time of the seasons, annual cycles, and other temporal and/or local aspects of Nature.

This is to say that one can often experience a discrepancy between the culturally or interpersonally imposed tempo of life and one's internal need to adjust, with either speeding up, if feeling held back, or on the contrary, to slow down, when one feels tailgated, and allowing more time and space for a particular activity to ripen or develop.

Paradoxically, as repeatably experienced in movement, velocity appears to slow down when the right rhythm is established. In fact, straining and working against the natural sense of self is the enemy of a balanced life rhythm and often comes across as the felt dissonance in psycho-somatic functioning.

When enough is done to re-establish the rhythmic synchrony of one's psycho-physical self, it can be further developed to improve a wide variety of disorders that go along with being out-of-sync, therapeutically, and regain the 'self within the world compatibility' and maintain the necessary stability in life.

There are also many psychological, physiological and neurological effects on the body taking place while attending to the natural tempos of bodily movements in somatic experience accompanying the fact that awareness of time ceases to exist in a deeper, meditational state. And more thorough exemplifications of such instances will become visible throughout the descriptions of practice to follow.

12

The Temporal and the Infinite

I mentioned already that having created too many devices as time measuring extensions to the experiential, embodied skills we naturally possess in telling the time, we have fallen into a trap of relying on the clock too much and have forgotten that looking out there for answers is not bringing balance in experiencing time in its periodicity and rhythm of events within our own internal processes nor in the living nature around.

It is definitely not coincidental that our original, analogue clocks comprise of a face and two hands. It can be described as a consequential development then that beginning with the movement of the sun and its shadowing made us associate time with movement per se and that this movement is always directional, from the east to the west. And even though it seems like a unanimous pattern experienced by all, a traveller's early realization of time zones reveals to us that this movement of time is always place-dependent.

Attending to experiential movement proves quite quickly that we are able to participate in an array of different dimensions or categories of time and give it a different frame of focus. The way we think about time does not often align with how the time is lived.

Einstein's scientific explanation of time's relativity as depending on the speed with which the clock is moving in relationship to the speed of light holds as much as the biological, body-in-built clock that gets out of rhythm when people travel by plane through geographical time zones. Personal time, biological time and clock time experiences, to name a few only, can thus be as distant as different universes and our internal timing mechanism of good or poor health reveals the synchronicity or out-of-balance states that respond to experience.

Over and over again, my attention to qualities of movement helps me realize that the estimated billions of years of Life on Earth have evolved within, and thanks to the rhythmic cycles of light and darkness, the celestial movement of our planet in relation to the Sun, to the Moon as well as farther universe contexts (Dako 2015b). What becomes obvious in my movement experience is that no form of life can evolve in a timeless or non-rhythmic world, and outside this physical time of the Earth, but only in response to the environmental patterns of change, from light to dark, from hot to cold and from wet to dry. And that, as life evolved, the external cycles became internalized and took on lives of their own following the self-established endosomatic timing for all internal metabolic processes.

Yet, what happens inside is continuously congruent with the outside world and can be observed in hormonal levels of the blood depending on times of the day, month or year cycles, and evolving in what is called 'exosomatic timing' (Goodridge 1999) for activities like sleeping, mating, eating, being born, hunting, etc., reflecting on the rhythms of the external environment.

On personal levels, as revealed in the following movement stories in more detail, time can also be experienced very differently, in various emotional, psychological or physical setting contexts, with the difference being felt primarily in the speed of the time passing. It is a subjective perception of time to be either crawling or flying by fast.

Somatic experience tends to slow down the experience of time to practically a standstill and translates it onto more primal rhythms of how the calm body functions when attended to in a contemplative state, with all the body systems slowing down and relaxing accordingly, yet continuously opening onto the external time frames more. Such experience helps us sense the physical timing of the Earth way more than in a rushed tempo of everyday life. Especially so, since the majority of our daily life happens indoors, in architectural separation from the outdoors's influence.

Metaphysical experiences of time/self, as described by Sondra Fraleigh (2004) for example, and sensed similarly in my movement experiences, are the ones most intimate and personal. Knowing that we are born with an individually incarnated sense of rhythm that yearns for forms of regularity as well as implicit ways for sustaining and creating new patterns of its own. And I become very sure of that when I am trying to feel into my own heartbeat on an audible exhale, as here:

I am working on my voiced breath out
I am muffling it with my hand
And can experience how
The wave of my voice that meets my hand
Is shaped by the beating of my heart
And when I keep my voice stable
On the sustained tone
It goes into a wave pattern
And I can feel through my voice
My heart beating pattern …

(*Moving Thoughts Journal, Felt Thinking in Movement*
audio transcript, August 2017)

It is my suggestion then, supported by the practice of felt thinking in movement and having one's individual wellbeing at heart, to rather move in direction of understanding time as a subjectively felt, lived dynamic, and not as a linear, measurable entity.

The internal clock that human beings shape and develop already in the womb, like other mammals, remains the living part of the maturing life-sustaining systems, the circulatory, the respirational, the metabolic, the lymphatic, etc., throughout. This internal clock is also securing and enabling the organism's ability to adapt to all kinds of periodically occurring changes in the natural surroundings.

And in my experience, this connection to the bodily processes, which consists of a continually reoccurring events, like the pulsing of the heart and expansion of the lungs in search for air, definitely develops my sense of regularity and continuity that can safely adopt and pick up different dynamic only to safely return to their own.

And with that feeling of return to 'normal' comes my sense of attunement to the continuous Now, as I feel think:

I know it is Monday
But my movement sees everyday as Now
Anyway.

(*Moving Thoughts Journal, Felt Thinking in Movement*, August 2017)

Also, as another example about the conceptual and the embodied differences in telling time, in his philosophically deductive, in my opinion, chapter 'Measuring time', Zwart (1976: 50–64) moves very quickly from connecting to the internally sensed rhythms as the basis for counting time as counting events, to abstract counting. He describes the shift from relating to events observed and experienced to counting in numbers as the most primitive way method for measuring as counting one, two, three corresponds to the number of times said.

Speaking from movement-based perspective though, I believe that counting is a more complex multi-sensory experience that connects the visual, the aural and the tactile experiences of children adapting to the material representations of life, and using their fingers in this activity, of which we have ten, is no small coincidence for further development of decimal systems in maths.

The other aspect of maths, i.e. of it being a highly imaginative endeavour, also confirms to me that abstract thinking, being so helpful in teaching us how to stretch or shrink the Now into different frames of time, is grounded in our physical capabilities to feel through every cell of the body, be it the skin, the gut or the bones, and which again grounds this capability in the stable functions of repeatable and recognizable patterns of breath, heartbeat or the shape of our skin.

And in my breath-enhanced movement experience, the natural permeability between the temporary and the infinite time frames becomes more and more feel-able, while I voice that:

> Staying with the breath for a while can have an illuminating effect on how this seamless activity connects the temporal contexts of life with its infinite dimension. Each inhale urging for its upcoming release, and each exhale carrying a continually intensifying invitation for the next breath in.
>
> When I feel my breath moving while I move with the breath, the divine presence of the infinite in each breath reveals to me its relation to the temporal, and translates itself into a movement form.
>
> It can remain within the breath alone, with calmness in the body overall or it takes a wider shape creating a gesture or a reactive move, opening up the dance floor to other responsive and conditioning factors like the temperature, the sounds, the smells, the thoughts and sensations but also physical limitations enlarged by anything imagined.
>
> After all, my chest can be sensed as both, a claustrophobic container or an endless wave, depending on the scale of the manifold engagements experienced.
>
> (*Moving Thoughts Journal, Felt Thinking in Movement,*
> September 2017 [edited])

Historically speaking, to position ourselves in human time-telling contexts between the temporal and the infinite, it is no coincidence that the motion of the Sun was preferred as it presented the most reliable, in its continuity and uniformity, process. It thus became the most convenient and simplest method of contextualizing, on Earth. The method of telling the time has then nothing to do really with the real nature of time, yet more reflects our own nature, i.e. that in preference for convenience, stability, convention and external reference.

And Zwart (1976: 58–64) describes in further detail man's preferences in methods for time measurement, with Galileo's law of inertia and movement at a constant velocity, like that of a pendulum, taking its precedence over discovery that the motion of the Sun was not completely uniform. The fact that resulted in temporal replacement of the Sun clock with sidereal clock and leading towards establishing the clock of physics as fundamental and standard clock, which hypothetically, according to the laws of nature, proceeds absolutely uniformly.

Other physical methods of measuring time as the flow of water or sand through a narrow aperture in water clocks or clepsydras, or chemical processes of timed combustion, have not been exploited extensively, yet there is a real probability that they did help in discovering the fact that the days, based on the rising and the setting of the Sun, are not equally long. In any case, the dominant thought, based on observing the Sun, that existence equals measurable occurrence remained dominant, even though the flowing nature of time, as it continues to do so today as well, kept escaping the logic, including the logic of languaging it.

And to give it a final experiential example here, when I move my hand through the air, as a playful experience of the co-creation between the temporal and the infinite, with my hand conceived of as a temporal entity and the air as the infinite, I notice experiencing the cold. But when I bring my hands together, palm to palm, without touching them, as the play between two temporal entities, as I feel they are, I experience the sense of warmth.

And I feel think then that both the temporal and the infinite are making one another possible in such a dichotomous difference-awaking relationship, but their interdependency is better felt than measured. It is when attending to personal levels of experiences alike that we realize that cultural generalizations are both helpful and limiting at the same time. Like movement itself developing towards and away from, multi-dimensionally, at every moment in time, means that we always move towards something while moving away from something else, at the same time. We just customarily choose to focus on one movement at a time, and hardly ever on its other, simultaneous activities.

And while the movement of life is never exclusive, it is our conscious choice to open our receptivity to wider frames of its multidimensional presence.

13

Reflective Synopsis:
Moving towards Sensual Co-presence

My ongoing explorations on receptivity in movement keep reminding me that being on Earth, as we all come here to live, means coming into something specific, something temporal and conditional and which comes from and goes back to being in an open sense, the omni-being. Similar to what happens when we make art or when we move with no real plan, things take shape through becoming a living part of the temporal with all its shaping capacities, resources, limitations and the individual connections to the limitless. The *Now* feels alive, welcoming and responsive.

I then begin to feel think that our conscious mind comes from an attachment to the temporal, as a survival tool. But the real skill in living a meaningful life, as it shapes itself in my experience, is to stay close to the relationship between the temporal, i.e. conscious and the infinite, i.e. unconscious realms and in keeping that 'back and forth' or the 'towards and away from' movement exchange open and permeable. We all participate in and are part of that dancing dynamic of creating and being created at the same time. One cannot be one thing without potentially being its opposite other, just like our skin is both a breathing home but also a restriction and a physical limitation.

Summing up my own explorations of the often dualistic reality, movement teaches me that being is not a singular, but interdependent process of agreement between the temporal and the eternal. And that I live through time as much as time lives through me, just like my movement is not separate from me, and yet I give it its form, which I can look back at in reflection. Reflecting on my connection to myself in time, as my movement unfolds, proves to me that on the plane of eternity, time, as a concept, does not exist, it comes into existence only through its temporal occasions.

When I feel into the somatic experience of movement I sink into its fluid nature and slowness, leading towards rest and active stillness. If the subtlety of movement resembles and thus reconnects me to the eternal realm, its fluid nature makes me think of coming into life temporal as a spillage that sooner or later goes back to the eternal flow of time/space.

We say 'currents of life' meaning life as a creative opening in an eternal flow of (s)pace, but we keep forgetting how relational that opening or closing is. And that relationality is ontologically implicit in movement as an ongoingly living and variating pattern of forth and back, the *towards* and *away from* transitioning, an ever-present and creative exchange of seizing and beginning.

In her book *Relationscapes*, Erin Manning sums it up in Bergsonian terms too saying:

> For Henri Bergson, as for theorists of 'embodied cognition', the relation between perception in all its modes is one of reciprocal reach-and-return. This cross-genesis of action and perception opens onto thought. Every perception is already a thinking in action. Every act is a thought in germ.
>
> (2009: 2)

Importantly though, the method of connecting sensually to the subtleties of co-presence(-ing) with all life around in movement-based experience is not suggested here in replacement of our culturally standard ways of measuring time by clock, as indeed, it is a useful tool in daily organization. My intention here is rather that perhaps a bigger amount of attention to our bodily 'feeling the time' could be adjusted and introduced to the daily agendas, not as a derivative but a complementary clock of guidance towards our own wellbeing.

And I am not talking about participating in one yoga class per week, as it has become a cultural standard already, and the duration of such class is exactly one-hour clock time anyway, but about practising experiencing time without numbering the units passed and developing a feeling for accommodating the self in open relation to time lived as varied and responsive dynamic.

It is that dynamic, which originates in the interrelation between the nervous, respiratory and circulatory systems experienced internally, that eludes our capabilities for logical explanations and which appears to me, in movement, to be able to expand towards various accelerations or shrink towards a standstill, cease or pick up, and which forms or deforms endlessly on its creative paths onto its experiential realizations in the materialized, i.e. physical realm.

The activity of philosophical wondering in somatic *receptivity in co-presence* provides me with moments of slowing down which offer new windows for relation to Life to develop, and slowing down helps the energetic power stored be redirected in ways that benefit my health, i.e. towards places, or wounds, that need attention. The ongoing connectivity between the lived opposites, as in breath-in and breath-out, keeps escaping the attention; it is not easy to grasp and hold onto. But the implicit need for realization is there as I hear myself say that:

> The warmth of the breath out
> Meets the air in the light
> As if it was about to waste
> If there was 'no difference'
> Was it to come back to or stay in the dark.
> It is yearning to be useful
> To be given a chance to be part of
> Other things.
> [...]
> Speed is about making statements
> And drawing attention
> Always accompanied by slowness
> To complete the movement pattern.
>
> (*Moving Thoughts Journal, Felt Thinking in Movement*
> audio transcript, August 2017)

And with those words in mind, it is becoming apparent to me that moving forward in life too fast becomes depleting by having no connection to the past, and slowing down helps me achieve that. Moving too slow, or unambitiously, on the other hand, is not productive enough in a way that it wastes a capacity for creating new things in contexts of specific time-space momentums.

Relying deeper and deeper on felt thinking awakened in movement, I keep reminding myself that the grounding agreement in the ongoing debate on time, and especially between the two most contrasting world views: the scientific and the philosophical, or the Einsteinian and the Bergsonian (Canales 2015) to be exact exemplifying, is that there is no time without movement. And so, if the universe were to slow down to speed zero, there would be no time.

The resonance in that thought does stir a question though about why we keep choosing to define time in life as moving forward only, while body's memory is an unused, or underused, to say the least, reservoir of past experiences we keep revisiting. At the same time, as intuition points me to conclude, we also store a lot of hunches towards future engagements as we live projecting ourselves onwards, often beyond the immediate future.

To further engage with the processes of re-connection with the natural world in multi-dimensional movement, I will now provide a further scope of reflections on the theme of receptivity coming from a wider circle of movers and their experiences in felt thinking outdoors, and which naturally merge with the many continuations of my own movement explorations.

In the following chapter, I will then offer a selection of shared stories awaken in receptive movement experience while meeting the land with open senses. And hopefully, bring to light even more personal depths of experiencing sensuous presence in felt thinking, collected with a group of fellow movers during a spring time, on-site residency within the Loch Lomond and the Trossachs National Park, Scotland.

14

Connecting with the Land:
Stories in Sensuous Receptivity

FIGURE 14.1: *In Sensuous Receptivity*, Drumdollo, Aberdeenshire. Photograph by Anna Dako.

What a Place!
My head aches with excitement.
How to settle?
[...]
To reside
To re-side with the land
To move across the boundary
And face backwards at the place
You once were
And to see that other past self
And its former situation.
Here now on the side of this place
I am another me.

(*Cove Park Journals*, April 2018)

FIGURE 14.2: Cove Park, Loch Lomond and The Trossachs National Park.

To feel into the land's presence, to 'be with' the place, to fully arrive. These are the opening steps to feel and think about our own belonging in full receptivity. After all, residing *in* Nature means something else than re-siding *with* Nature.

The cared-for *with*-ness while moving outdoors helps to open the attentiveness to the living agency of the place, and the agency of living Nature itself, within our moving/thinking/being processes of experiencing our own human nature in somatic movement experience, as movers. It also creates an opportunity for an opening shift in the mover's mindset to happen. That is, the shift from questioning 'How can I experience my own nature in Nature?' to 'How can this living environment help me experience my inner Nature/Self while I am offering my own presence too?'

The already described analogy between felt thinking processes and the embryological processes of germ formation, i.e. the primal dynamics of movement, helps also to facilitate the possibility for deepening the experience, from outer layers of the mover's sensual peripheries to the deepest, gut-based relation to the natural world around, in an open and exploratory manner of circular re-searching while heading 'inwards', as an *in-search* within oneself.

At the same time, the *deepening inwards* in self-inquiry in felt thinking is accompanied by a revealing tendency inscribed within the open questions that facilitate the discovery in both directions at the same time, both inwards and outwards.

And so, as a group of movement practitioners, while meeting the place in open receptivity we begin our explorations of sensual encounters in the vast landscapes of Scottish Highlands by awakening and widening the breadths of our *sensual presence* through embodied listening and open attentiveness. And such explorations devoted to the outer, ectodermic layers of skin and sensual sensitivity, mean bringing everybody's attention to the underused capacities of our senses first.

The sense of smell, hearing, taste and sight, they all operate within the parameters of our head mainly but expanded onto touch, which resides in vast territories of the skin, they can create a vibrant and inclusive system of experiential resonance with the surroundings.

We set off hoping to renew our individual relation to time and space in an inclusive attention grounded in the *where* and *when* questions. 'Where/When does Nature *out there* end and Nature *in here* begin?' With the spotlight cast on borderline territories between eyes closed and eyes open, between movement and stillness, breath-in and breath-out, or touching and being touched, the explorations begin to take shape.

> Me reaching out
> Me wanting to connect
> Me opening into my senses
> Hearing, listening, smelling, touching, and
> tasting to the you, the other, the outside
> It is my voluntary action
> A willingness to meet, first
> and then when this happens when the
> gateway is open – I am with – the earth
> becomes body, erotic, warm, a dance
> evolves, creates itself, is, loves, feels, becoming
> familiar, close, not yet merging.

(*Cove Park Journals*, April 2018)

FIGURE 14.3: *Opening to Receptivity*, Cove Park, April 2018.

Then the first sensations of somatic re-adjusting become felt. The yawning comes along. And so, after those initial connections of 'being with' other life in the landscape have been established, in such an amazing example of compassionate co-presencing, a form of bodily re-balancing of water and air happens automatically. And the overwhelming amount of little sensations all over the body, awakening in this encounter, allows the mover to ponder over what's around, available to the senses. She then continues:

> Here I am sitting on a bench of moss.
> Sun on my face, my naked skin of feet and legs
> little insects buzzing around
> birds in the background
> [...]
> soothing, calming, giving me the feeling of
> endless existence.
>
> (*Cove Park Journals*, April 2018)

It is fascinating to notice how quickly those first encounters with the outdoor scenery turn into relational stories in reflection.

Soon enough another mover describes the force of nature that comes strong in her first visual encounter with the landscape, and a strong feeling of a 'come back', as if belonging to one, or more, elements of nature. There is no thinking process involved, she indicates, just an automatic, natural claiming of herself to nature ... as she realizes a powerful pull towards sitting by a tree, and

> being nothing more
> or nothing less
> than what the tree is.

(*Cove Park Journals*, April 2018 [translated version])

This first encounter with the place reveals to her another bipolar sensation of beauty that stirs an emotional meltdown in adoration while realizing the awakening sensation of power that is collecting internally within herself as a response to such an overwhelming beauty.

How do I feel with my dual nature? She is asking herself while exploring walking outdoors when blindfolded and supported by another mover's guidance in a dyadic work of movement-based exploration (see Figure 14.4). And in her journal, she shares a story about her childhood, when her mother used to put her barefoot on the grass, and she would scream. She didn't want to be put on the grass as she was scared to step on ants and accidentally kill them. Even when walking on paved paths, she writes, she would not walk in a straight line, trying to carefully bypass any crawling ant.

And now, walking blindfolded reminds her of walking barefoot, as she experiences that the ground under her feet is exactly how she finds herself to be too, delicate and careful, but also, in a way, brutal and dirty. And that this walking recap helps her to free herself from that tightening memory of the childhood days, which she has been carrying within herself for many years, without being able to embrace its full meaning. It also balances for her, as she describes, her two longings, one for life and one for death, in most harmonious proportions.

She then continues that harmony confirms for her, that there are no felt borders between the self and nature, as everything permeates everything. And that constructive and powerful sensation she receives from nature makes her feel not scared at all of the assisting it also cruelty. She feels she is cruel as well. And just like deep water, she can be calm and peaceful, but carry the potential for lethal action under her skin all the time. And that, thanks to that very moment of realizing it on the walk, safeguarded by the presence of another mover, and tossed between the calmness of the sunshine and the cold blasts of wind, she feels, she can finally stop fighting it within herself, as nature is both gentle and dangerous at the same time.

The experiential interactions between self and other then, similarly to my own movement explorations, seem to be shaping into overlapping intervals of *towards* and *away from* movement. The movers share a feeling of being drawn and pulled

FIGURE 14.4: *Dyadic Walking*, Cove Park, April 2018.

outwards, reaching out towards life around, yet constantly redefining their own need for 'life unfolding backwards' and for returning to the inwardly guarded sensations.

It is also where further explorations into movement backwards follow:

Backwards
Into
Into what is
Back
Wards
Backwards – forwards – wanting to walk
Insecurity, much more scared walking backwards
Insecurity of my feet, silence
I have touched the land even if I was only on my feet
I feel it on my skin
On the surface on my body through the body of other
Through the land's body, I am.

(Cove Park Journals, April 2018)

And so the complementary forces in reaching out in two opposite directions at the same time, both harmonious yet contradictory, become very present to the senses

FIGURE 14.5: *Cove Park Journals, Acorn, Yoni, Female, Spider, Mystery*, Cove Park, April 2018.

during the first encounters of being outdoors in Nature, and reappear in different forms for other movers as well. As in this drawing above, entitled *Acorn, Yoni, Female, Spider, Mystery.*

The way I see it, the drawing further reflects on the felt symmetrical, both open and enclosed workings of the picked-up dynamics when encountering the place. Its title-based reference to the feminine energy of Yoni, which in Sanskrit is interpreted as 'the womb', 'the origin' or the 'source of everything', and conceptualized as Nature's gateway brings its immediate relevance to the very place of our residence, Cove Park, with specific emphasis on the word 'cove' as a coastal inlet or a bay.

Thus the presence of water, and its activity within the living landscape, as in the welcoming it bay, i.e. a cove, which itself is being shaped by the water too, seems impossible to ignore. A cove, the sheltered, precipitously walled place with its rounded opening as if a valley extending into a hillside. It embraces many local, Celtic stories, including those based on the omni-presence of water as the sacred power of the feminine.

A particular landscape indeed, creating a double reason for feeling as if 'falling into' the feminine, as if the Nature's motherly embrace reawakens all the 'belonging' instincts, and the internally succumbed need for continuous guidance, that helps one feel safe to open up. Thus the following words emerge:

Placing my Pearl into your Oyster
This rubbish
This man rubbish
Has ruined this world
Bring back the woman's secrets
Let the Goddess lead us.

(*Cove Park Journals*, April 2018)

And in the following up movement stories, there is also a strong reference found to the relationship between the Moon and the feminine, and the sudden change of life context, as if arriving out of a structural organization of ordinary, civic, life and into the flowful circularity of the outdoors. The loss of connectivity to the circular patterns of life within her own body rhythms, as experienced by another mover, corresponds for her to the loss of safety as well and the coming with it feeling of averseness or indisposition. She says,

[…] body wants to go forward, body wants to go back, back to the time when things were regular, regular as the way the Earth moves in relationship to the Moon, in relationship with the moon, without our looking through glass walls at the moon, there is no 'Moon thing', there is no moon, it's a rock looking back at us, with no us there, there is no Earth. No Earth, no Moon. […] I arrive from places where I have to be, structures that make me be a certain way, and here untethered my womb goes round and round like a planet, except something in the relationships has gone asunder, I want to move back into the regular solar system but my womb is off course, off circuit. […] This is what happens when I arrive – immediacy plus intimacy of outer space.

(*Cove Park Journals*, April 2018)

And while her gratefulness for finding herself within this rich landscape of a cove, and out of the city, builds up from the internally experienced place of entropy, her reflections over 'the watery' in her own implicit nature switch focus onto the

FIGURE 14.6: *Cove Park Journals*, no title, Cove Park, April 2018.

loch and its awe-inspiring luminosity and the sky with its depths of the dark blue colour that she calls the 'exotic sensual velvet blue that radiates luminous darkness' (*Cove Park Journals*, April 2018).

And as her drawings are never on a separate piece of paper she continuous over it:

> What I would like to share is deep blue – a colour that belongs only in nature – that is to say it should never be reproduced or flat, it must always, as the guardian illusion of the sky stay luminous – luminous darkness is my nature maybe, fluid.
>
> (*Cove Park Journals*, April 2018)

As shared above then, these first attractions to the presence of the feminine energies of the place and the self in it, bring up the feelings of overwhelming helplessness as an individual, and an immediate sorrow felt for the lost. The strong influence of the element of water, which makes one participant say that 'it is so much easier to be a part of everything when alone' (*Cove Park Journals*, April 2018) is picked up by another mover who, in longing for companionship too, asks:

> The Truth for Me is that I am never alone
> with my thoughts
> The Gods are always there
> The Goddess always present, beneath and all around me
> It's my human body I become alone with
> This Earth Goddess does not always have arms like a human companion.
> (*Cove Park Journals*, April 2018)

And as the theme of the watery feminine continues throughout the movement reflections on sensuous receptivity, I find more and more co-related contemplations upon how the landscape itself creates stories, that we personify to connect to the individual past, and how one can show their respect for the landscape or a place simply by listening to those stories and their '*silent voices through the hills and lakes*' (*Cove Park Journals*, April 2018, emphasis added).

And as the movers continue their sharings, the interconnecting themes of openness and closeness, beauty and death, cruelty and playfulness and the internal need for guidance take shape in yet another story, constantly weaving in the intimate narratives captured moment by moment (see Figure 14.7). She writes:

> Travel wind, travel
> Travel to those places and those days
> Travel through past and present
> And future when I'll be old
> And the story will come
> To an end and it will be fine
> And I will witness and listen to another story
> Teardrop falling down
> As the drew
> As the drew drop in the morning in the grass
> [...]
> As the drew drop in the morning passing

From the grass to the tip to my finger
I listen to the story
Of a gate closed
Of a gate open
While you hold the pearl and you stop and pause and breathe
And the breath follows the wind
And the wind follows the breath
And then you stop
And then your voice resonates
I listen to the story and the story
Talks about what I see
And the story talks about the landscape
Sailing.
How to sail?
Be led
Be led
Be led
The eyes and the lake.
Sunshine resting on the face, surprising
In the laughter?
The laughter, the laughter.
The voice more than the words,
The playfulness.
Stop – open the eyes. Try not to be god and be led and
then you cry and listen to your story.
[…]
As breath becomes dance
Crying, crying, crying …

(Cove Park Journals, April 2018)

FIGURE 14.7: *Cove Park Journals, Movement Session Stills*, Cove Park, April 2018.

And while on a similar outdoor exploration, connecting to the themes of time and space, another mover mentions her deep need for continuous walking and continuous exploring, discovering and finding. And so she does find, as she describes herself, that it is through her old interest and liking for bones in her own body-work-based praxis, that she got drawn to a hidden in the grass and well-preserved sheep skull.

A beautifully kept treasure, as it seemed to us all, when she brought the skull intact onto the shared terrace space, overlooking the lake.

FIGURE 14.8: *Cove Park Journals, Shapeshifter*, Cove Park, April 2018. Photograph by Jack Wylie.

The felt penetration of the themes of life and death, as well as the now and the past, is then very much present for all. And I find another example of such dual reality experience in that of two movers who were having their first encounter with the local sheep herds, but they experience it from two different perspectives.

One mover describes it as having an amazing exchange with the sheep that respond to her low voice by running towards her to re-gather as a herd. She then decides to continue that exploration by singing to them, only to later see them casually return to their less attentive and widely scattered grazing.

Surprisingly though, another mover, while on her own 'wandering in Nature' session happens to be at the same time and the same place as the mover interacting with the sheep, only to tell her own story as a witness to the same encounter. And she shares it in her own words while wondering:

Where does the wind come from?
Trying to figure out, the orientation

It's easy for me,
having no spatial sense to lose myself, so …
Where is the west, where is the east, where is the north and where is the south?
This morning I tried to remember where I saw the colours of the sunset … behind the hills
So, wind might blow from the south, from where I come from …
Is it where I come from, or is there a place where I come before I come from?
Nature, what is nature? Is this place natural?
[…]
What is this word?
What are we referring to? Historically, philosophically?
When does the issue of nature come from?
Romantic poetry, philosophers, age of modernity …?
The sheep! All running down the hill!
The sheep are all down!
Ah! Let's go and catch them!
(running)
Ha!
I see a shape, somebody, I don't know … if it's a person or a pole …
It's someone! Someone who is talking to them, someone who is provoking them!
And they run down the hills!
And there is here, this landscape …
What nature are we talking about?
Has this gorse always been here? Or someone has brought it?
Was it the wind, was it the land, was it a person?
Somebody is singing!
Somebody is singing to the sheep and they respond!
They are all there!
Responding!
And I would like to meet them
I would like to meet the singer.
That's amazing!
(laughing)
And daffodils are also there, like an audience!
Have you seen them standing with their heads curious? They are so curious!
Daffodils are yellow and … curious!
And their curiosity makes them … innocent?, maybe, maybe?
Hey!
They start to respond!
And it's not only sheep, and it's not only rain, and it's not only my voice!

And oh … can my voice travel to a place behind that hill?
(screaming)
(baaa-ing)
(laughing)
Oh can you hear the sheep responding???
(shouting)
(laughing)

(*Cove Park Journals*, audio transcript, Cove Park, April 2018)

Such reflections, interlaced at the same location, reveal how the same moment varies and differs in individual experience, depending on how your own story meets the time/place. Time as both container for experience as much as the experience of time itself finds its way into words. And so, as if an ongoing discovery of the unknown that shapes our individually unfolding and overlapping stories of encounter, the wondering about Nature continues:

Does the sky think?
And if it does, does it think like you and I?
Or does it have a different thinking way?

(*Cove Park Journals*, April 2018)

Or,

Does the water in the bath know the water in the loch? Do they resonate, do they have a deep connection, do they hear each other or sense a presence or just do the relationship bit, without the sensing, which is kind of how I like it?

(*Cove Park Journals*, April 2018)

And then I hear another mover continuing the wonder:

A river …
Is this a river?
Water running …
[…]
This is not a river
it's something much smaller
[…]
This is not the way I'm used to hearing water
I'm used to hearing waves

but there is something that I know about the river
even if …
(shouting out loud)
even if I don't know rivers well
There is something I know about you!
I know about you
I know you
I know you
It's the images
It's the sounds of other stories
Other stories make me know other places
as if I have visited there
Other stories
Other people
I was in their books
I was in their times
I was
I was
I will be
I will be
In other stories with my stories
I will be in other places with my places
Like that time
Like that time
Like that time
I didn't stop while the tree was falling
Like that time
Like that time … I felt
Like that time …
Like that time … I woke up
Like that time I woke up and I didn't know who I was
But I felt
I felt it so true …
[…]
Something that is as it had to be
as it was always …
This place is historical
We cannot say this is nature
This is a mingling of choices
A mingling of choices, of shaping and adapting …

[...]
Let's walk and feel the time ...

And she continues the story ... as she keeps finding and picking up more and more wool from the ground, and keeps walking and screaming running across the water:

> Awwww ...
> Why are our faces so ugly?
> People should look up at the sky
> And smell
> And smell
> And smell
> Fresh air
> Fresh air
> And listen to the water flowing.
>
> (*Cove Park Journals*, audio transcript, Cove Park, April 2018)

And so, a reflective look at the stories gathered here brings up a few important findings.

Opening this chapter with an image of an embryological curl (see Figure 14.9) on a stone, it became quite suggestive in multiple movement explorations that any 'forward in time' or unfolding movement in receptivity happens *through* or *with* inclusion of moving backwards.

The embryo too, while opening up to the world in its uncurling movement upwards, wherever the upwards is, does move backwards in relation to its spinal organisation. Additionally, that same movement backwards in forward development, as it came up in further explorations, brings up the vibrational opening in the respiratory system which comes as a humming sound on an inhale.

Conrad writes:

> All movement becomes elaborated by the breadth of breath. Wave motion is fundamental healer in which all aspects of our existence can move with greater communication. Increasing wave motion permits greater possibility for biological life to communicate with itself.
>
> (2007: 143)

And that this fluid movement of the breath enhances health and wellbeing beyond our capacity to name.

The experienced fluidity within such transitioning, carried on waves of voice and sounds of the living landscape, does hit many hard surfaces on its ways though, or physical limitations, or mechanical malfunctions as well. And yet, they do become part of an ongoing and collectively felt process, seamlessly turning into occasions for spatial–temporal redirection.

The audible presence of sheep voices around has also impacted our movement explorations in letting us feel we reside in the Scottish land flocked by livestock. Even though it is supposed to be the most wildly kept land of the National Park, human dependency on other animals becomes very apparent and such dependency-shaped and often one-sided relationship to other life feels part of the landscape.

Yet, moving in open receptivity creates also a strong connection to our child-like nature, which is best cultivated through the sense of open curiosity and just being 'out there'. A form of longing to be with Nature, outdoors, definitely awakens. The true sense of being with, as shared by the movers, comes into place when walking on the grass barefoot, instead of sitting comfortably overlooking the landscape from an indoor perspective. It provides a form of liberation and satisfies the deeply hidden longings for tangible contact and playful connectivity, thus the omni-present gestures of opening arms to meet the world around.

One of the movers also mentions it being impossible for her to concentrate inwardly on herself in the presence of such 'calling' Nature, as she has to give in to being pulled outdoors constantly in search of reconnecting with that longing for being truly *with* Nature, and letting the disturbing sense of questioning the self, disappear.

And yet re-connecting with Nature, in going back movement, comes with a lot of grief, and much of the grief comes from the left behind and re-membered childhood perspectives. But it also comes with feeling grateful for such re-connection, and I cannot sum it here any better but to quote:

> I feel very grateful. Gratefulness permeates the water in my cells and the over-full womb, water is my everywhere and everyone carrying information and releasing me in tears, I could drink myself, I'm so grateful. Thank you for bringing me here.
>
> (*Cove Park Journals*, April 2018)

Thus, the sensual presencing in receptivity, both inwards and outwards, becomes really tangible when the experiential connectedness between many dichotomous realities of Nature is addressed as *felt* and not limited to conscious thought only.

The growing openness to change in voicing the experience, reaching out, or 'coming into touch with' presents itself as lived in individually contextualized time, or timelessness, and its personally shaped relevance. Things relate to the mover as long as they attract their attention and yet the scope for attention seems always open for more, or for 'the different' to join and take place, again in the opposite, and playful, movement of distraction.

This soft yet changeable dynamic of the feminine Earth does seem to permeate the explorations in the overall sense and serves as a welcoming ground for the shaped stories of the *Where* and the *When* and the accompanying imagery of opening, unfolding, reaching out, meeting and embracing.

And in my first open movement encounter with the local sheep, I experience the similar happening. My arms open wide to sense the associated softness and gentleness that fills the air when sitting by and being with the herd of sheep for a while. Their silence feels precious, as I know they feel comfortable about my presence, perhaps just cutely curious. And my bare feet feel eager to meet their piece of grazing land, rich in sheep scents and wind-caressed bundles of sheep wool.

FIGURE 14.9: *Moving in Receptivity and Sensuous Presence*, Kingswells, Aberdeen. Photographs by Ronald Dako.

I play with the wool for a little while and feel into its qualities. I stay low, at sheep height and my movement becomes wool-like too. It spreads softly and stretchingly. My fingers become my new sensuous openings, curious and attentive just like the sheep themselves, without causing much commotion either. My alertness grows around me as well, and the arms are often tempted to check what's behind, while I am beginning to move my whole body in circular sway-like movements, staying low, and swirling backwards towards the observing me sheep.

Being amongst them brings so much bliss and openness to my breath's forms. And I feel they know what it means to be present for themselves and others, at the same time, much better than we humans do.

Ingold (2011) too adds a word about our capacities for a wider comprehension of the living world around, saying that once we recognize the primacy of movement in the animic cosmos, the wind in its blowing, or thunder in its clapping, becomes just as other organisms and persons living in the ways peculiar to themselves.

And speaking from her personal practice perspective, Sondra Fraleigh too confirms that 'we can listen with our somas when we give up grasping aggressiveness. We can hear others – the paces at rest, the disturbances, where and how the next movement is forming – that we might follow and be present without judgement' (2004: 126).

Moving in somatic receptivity embraces just that, for me, and for other movers. I am out there with the land and the sheep but I am also here and now, and movement makes that connection easy and natural. It is also *where* and *when* that I feel – I am more than my physical self.

Breathing out - Reaching out - Forward / Backward - Time / Timelessness - Space / Light / Spaciousness - Darkness - Attraction / Distraction / Breathing in / Breathing in - Distraction - (Cruelty) - The Feminine - Water / Land - Balancing - Dual / Bi-polar - Folding / Unfolding / Unfolding / Darkness - Spaciousness - Attraction - Beauty / Danger - Stillness - Past / To Guide - Life / Death - Open / Closed - Change / Now - Listening - Resonating / Stillness - Stories Unfolding - To Be Led - Now

121

II

Moving with Responsiveness and Experiential Exchange in Psychological Time, or On *Who* and *What* of Being

FIGURE P2.1: *Moving Thoughts Journal – Towards Experiential Exchange*, Cairngorms National Park, Highland. Photograph by Noemi Dako.

Silence is a doorway to the undisturbed openness
Silencing with things and beings around is a connection in itself
Silence is not the lack of sound
It is the sea of unborn sound
It is the sea of the extinguished or the spread out sound too
It is the void of transition.

(*Moving Thoughts Journal*, September 2017)

Reflecting back on this stage in my practice, the attention to the awakened sensations (as described in the 'Moving with receptivity' chapter) transitions slowly from the peripheries of tactile, aural or visual backgrounds to the forefronts of the experiential engagement. And this transitioning from, but also *with* sensuous listening helps me move through and with changing states which I feel are due coming.

The initiation of change, in movement qualities, comes in spontaneously, and in its own time, as the vibration-stirring oxygenation and the fluids pick up tempos in my cellular functioning. I experience some spread out tingling and other motivational thrills in my body. The felt thinking processes that sprouted from attentive listening begin to grow into new relationships with the vibrant silence as I keep moving and keep following the movement into its more spread out and more dynamic outbursts.

It continues its workings on levels that exceed the peripheral nervous system and exceed me making sense of my perceptions and engages the deeper layers of the muscular and vascular systems, tipping into the emotional relevance of every movement initiation.

And, as an important side note here, it is interesting to consider that tapping into the vascular, circulatory system, which genetically evolved over millennia, reminds me of the fact that every human being develops the length of veins that goes three times around the Earth's diameter. How can such a fact be excluded from our conception of human nature or our natural, heart-felt bonding when growing up?

Andrea Olsen helps out here saying:

Although we often consider emotions irrational, neurobiologists tell us that they are intricately interwoven with the circuitry for rational thought. Emotions are relational, essential to humans as social creatures. Because emotions involve the speed and thoroughness of the endocrine system, we often describe them in the language of water, as fluid states: a flood of feeling, a wash of emotions, a flow of warmth, a surge of tears, a wave of happiness; or as a process: bubbling with laughter, drowning in grief, frozen in fear, or swimming in excitement.

(2002: 194)

Moving forward from the watery stories described in the previous chapter, it is the emotionally interactive co-creation of voicing and silencing, or moving and not moving that opens the reflective analysis of the experiential material gathered in this chapter, and in this second dimension of a movement process. Again then, with the focus on bringing the intrinsic meaning of movement-based experiences to the fore, the attempted here continuation of an explanatory look at movement material will go alongside its thorough contextualization and thematic verification with what it means to move with responsiveness in the psychological dimension of experience.

Ansell-Pearson writes that 'as we move onto ontological appreciation of the past, psychological consciousness is born and emerges only when it has found its proper ontological conditions' (2018a: 84–85). Connecting then again to Bergson's philosophy on time and space, as he develops the thought while grounding it in his own interest in biological sciences in *Memory and Matter*, Bergson concludes that 'the greater the power of action of a body, symbolized by a higher degree of complexity in the nervous system, the wider is the field that the perception embraces' and that 'there is no perception which is not prolonged into movement' (1988: 56–57).

And indeed, reflecting back on the contemplative content of the gathered material, it can be easily noticed that the increasing intensity of psycho-somatic engagement in movement is inseparable from a qualitative progression in what I already described as the relational *towards* and *away from* movement, and which Bergson similarly depicts as forces of attraction and repulsion, as a living framework for the mover's perception.

And while attending to this widened activity allowing for random voicing of movement to take place offers release with every sound passing through the throat, it also comes with a lot of contraction in the diaphragm. Again then, I experience this basic movement pattern – tightening for action and release for relaxation. Let us look into more detail within movement experiences at this stage.

15

Voicing and Silencing

What a busy space
It is windy
And apart from the clock ticking
All those voices and noises happen on the outside of the space
And yet, they fill the space
Feels like the walls can stop the wind
From being felt on the skin
But when I hear it outside
I am with it
It is with me
So the sound on my skin picks up the sound on the outside, easily
All the random noises around
As I am embracing the regular …
Ticking …
Tick tock tick tock …
And my movement goes into syncopation
Into the playfulness
In between the stable paths.

(*Moving Thoughts Journal*, August 2017)

As I did before, I am keeping my voice stable on a prolonged exhale, with my hand held gently on the chest. It takes a few moments of being with that sound-y exhale to discover that the wave pattern of my voice is shaped by the beating of my heart. Again then, I can feel through my voice – my heart beating … I can tune into its rhythm too. And as I do, it changes its pattern simply by me being aware of it.

I feel I can now start interacting with myself as if, which I feel I am, with (an)other. And the movement I engage with begins to feel more and more interactive itself, and full of capacity for change, as if I am sensing into its innate potential for reciprocity and interchange. I also become aware of how much of my ordinary ways of being (in) movement can be shared in the dynamics of voicing it. As I feel think that:

> Movement comes with sounds, like the wind.
> I wish we could hear the Earth move through space.
> But the breeze is already a good sign of it.
> Like a layer that hugs the Earth as an expression of the spatial relationship
> between the cosmos and the permeable surfaces of the Earth.
> The relationship that shapes the Earth every day, every sound, every breath.
>
> (*Moving Thoughts Journal*, September 2017)

Our soft tissues embrace the silence in its slow, functional movement, seamless conditioning of its water, air, earth and fire resources ... always feel-able with touch or the penetrating attention. This natural balance in constant motion is self-sustaining but not independent of conscious thought or any other external input, i.e. my daily experientials.

And as my explorations continue, I feel more and more capable of expanding on what I was once taught in traditionally held lessons of physics simply by continuing my felt thinking in movement and involving sounding against different proximities in the enclosed space. I move about and come into different relationships with floor, windows, room furniture and walls. I sense that sound bounces off and becomes sharper on hard surfaces. The soft surfaces muffle and quiet the sound. And my yearning for something soft in comforting myself can thus be seen not only as a physical aid but also as a longed-for passage to engage with the quiet, restful silence and a doorway to the soothing infinite that I feel resides within me.

Interacting with sounds in space is full of meaningful responsiveness that helps me discover what the body needs.

Perhaps there is even a sound of thoughts, that we don't know of, as our hearing does not work very inwardly, does it? If thoughts can be heavy or light, moving fast or slow, they must have different sounds and frequencies as well. And my explorations continue outdoors too, on another occasion, while experiencing the mentioned heaviness of thoughts, that accumulated in an earlier, mentally exhausting process of verbal exchange, causing me a lot of psychological heaviness. I then voice that:

> From stiffness from overload
> And intellectual turmoil ...
> A need of silence arises,
> Followed by a search for it ...
> The magic of a hidden corner

Found as formed … by chance really …
Composition of shrubs …
Growing towards the sun on one side,
Only to become a shaded hide-out for seekers like me today,
To find asylum, in their unwanted side.

(Moving Thoughts Journal, April 2018)

And so the shaded side, just like the longing for soothing darkness or sleep, becomes the door of connection for the deeper, often hidden frequencies of functioning to take over. Closing eyes is an awaited already step in bringing the past 'self', or selves, closer to the felt present, and so is my place of sitting, hidden in the side of a bush on a wet mossy ground. I then continue:

It is through the open kinship that I feel I am able to reconnect with the animal voice
(bird singing)
inspired by my morning bird-watching
(bird singing even louder)
I can hear you!
I've been so appreciative of those tiny birds waking me up in the morning …
One of the robins was following me for a while.
(Baaa … Baaaaa … sheep voices)
(sitting in silence for a long time …)
I need to find my friends, sheep.

(Moving Thoughts Journal, April 2018)

A precious time in active re-connection with myself, while being attentive to the busy lives of the animals around me, and their time spent eagerly on minding me.

Bergson argues that time involves a co-existence of past and present and not simply a continuity of succession and that, owing to its character as a continuous multiplicity, the duration cannot be made the subject of a logical treatment. Different degrees of what Bergson calls 'mental state', and which I would rather call 'psycho-somatic transitioning', correspond to how we feel and perceive time and to its qualitative changes, and not just to any simple measure or a number. In movement, I feel that states of consciousness can permeate and melt into one another without any precise outlines or affiliations to a defined quantity, and where past and present states enter an interactive dialogue.

Reflectively speaking then, the creation of movement cannot be divided into its separate parts as it is an act of certain quality in progress, but the complexity of the experience makes human beings think of a time in frames, which we call states, thus making the conscious thinking of time easier to comprehend.

Bergson also argues that time/space relationship is like that of intensity and extensity, and that it is through the quality of quantity that we form an idea of quantity without quality (and our habits of representation), not the other way round. Thus, he suggests that time is primarily of qualitative nature.

And, as I continue hearing my voice shaped by the beating of my heart, I do feel that if living a life is 'becoming time' in Bergsonian terms then my own nature is similarly, primarily qualitative. And that to allow the universal character of any scientific quest, the quest for certainty and lawful obedience of movement is to make an assumption that movement is subject solely to forces of attraction and repulsion that arise from the defined points of reference, without any regard to the energies encountered between the defined points.

This is the vision of some singular and exclusive arrangement, like in an experiment of controlled conditioning, grounded in deterministic thinking. Just as affection, as Keith Ansell-Pearson writes, is not a simple movement from an inner intensive state to an outer extensity, simply because 'it is intimately bound up with the modifications that inform the movement of one body with other bodies' (Ansell-Pearson 2018: 26), vibrational movement carries on the multitude of playful dissonances.

And this innate dynamism of movement and its constantly relational folding and unfolding resonates its truths in my carefully observed transitioning between voicing and silencing. It also translates well into what Ingold describes as a 'reanimating thought' when he writes about the attitude of openness, saying that 'those who are truly open to the world, though perpetually astonished, are never surprised. If this attitude of unsurprised astonishment leaves them vulnerable, it is also a source of strength, resilience and wisdom' (Ingold 2011: 75).

Playfulness in responsiveness allows for just that. And I carry on familiarizing myself with my own voice, when I just freed it from singing in words, as one would normally do, and let it be 'whatever comes' in sounds. Then afterwards, I write:

There is space for the voice
to fall back on and rest into ...
My voice is not lonely or alone,
it carries on the rays of sun,
even though it might feel too shy,
or overwhelmingly dizzy,
as it spins into its own well ...
I'll be most patient ...
It nourishes in hope and soulful being
and feels invited by the buzzing sounds
of the visiting bees and flies ...

and the birds chirping along …
And the fresh air from between
the mountains and the sea.
There is so much light in the sounds of my voice …
Light, Space, Sound, Voice …
No wonder that birds, the airborne beings
thriving on sounds and the singing melodies and colours.
They simply live their element!

(Moving Thoughts Journal, June 2018)

It feels indescribably uplifting to discover such an immanent connection between light and sound in movement. While Emilie Conrad too adds that breath lights us from inside while 'sound emerges as audible breath, suggesting new forms, dissolving density, refining movement and perception'(2007: 141–42). And that:

> The body can be seen as a resonating chamber in which the play of breath becomes a kind of music. The versatility of breath invites ranges of new sensations, responses – new awarenesses develop, new relationships are formed. […] Breath enlivens our internal functioning, allowing more to exist.

(Conrad 2007: 141)

And in this movement exploration, I keep coming back to an image of a bird with two wings but four legs. Voicing the light in me definitely lets me think of wings, but my grounding habits keep adding legs to the imagined bird.

I am then beginning to be more playful with how the air that passes through my throat, and the vocal cords in the larynx, behaves not only on its 'normal' way out but also on its way in, while on an inhale. I visualize being able to sweep the internally, mentally drawn image of the bird off its four feet on an inhale and imaginatively helping it fly out on an exhale.

And the undiscovered capacities for sounding on an inhale amaze me so much that I continue blending the sounding both on inhale and exhale throughout the remainder of this movement improvisation. Experiencing all these qualities of air that passes through me in a playful exchange of sounding, opens up new ways of relating to air as element; the element that permeates every inch of my body in cellular breath through membranes that respond to its frequencies and which transform them from closed up to open in curious exposure.

My relationship with gravity changes. Sharing the space through, in and with sound is elevating.

16

Moving and Not Moving

Life is way too complex to be captured in a written text in its magical connectivity between anything and everything, between something and nothing.

Light is a guide, but the silent darkness embraces life as a whole and gives it a never-ending chance for coming back, anew, strengthened by not being, or being it all at the same time.

(*Moving Thoughts Journal*, September 2017)

One of the strongest realizations of my ongoing work as a practitioner and a mover is that even when I stop my body from moving, lying on the floor with my eyes closed in stillness, non-movement is not obtainable. It exists only artificially, as a physical reference to a different dynamic taking place, but movement itself never ceases.

All the internal activity of ongoingly functioning and life sustaining bodily systems becomes vibrant in my quieted attention, away from external distractions of outwardly shaped senses.

And so, if non-movement is still movement, just timed differently, the conception of myself in time also reshapes as a living passage. But what does that mean if I already experienced that movement in its purest sense is one direction in its omnidirectionality.

I am then feel thinking that every moment in time is an ongoing movement too, which makes any present moment a past moment in the future and its future in the past. And that, in turn, makes every moment past, present and future as much as none of them at the same time.

Aligning with movement, the unison, the stillness, the passage …

The layers of depth don't matter in a line

At the back of my neck, the shifts grow as arms, reaching out of the muscle tissues, searching for inspiration … counteracting the visual take … of the Moon … sipping onto the movement of the clouds …

(*Moving Thoughts Journal*, March 2018)

I start initiating some back-and-forth movement and realize how much of a conscious choice it is for me to stay swaying in a straight line, as it takes the slightest redirecting, or distraction of movement either upwards or downwards, in relation to the ground for example, for a curve to emerge. And the curve initiates change into the exiting bounce right away. This little opening in the closed circularity of back-and-forth movement is all it takes for the movement to enter a new relationship, and another one, and another one still, as it unfolds continuously into another shape if not locked, consciously, in a flat space or an agreed choreography to be performed. It keeps on going, potentially everywhere, until I make a choice to stop.

And with this movement–stillness relationship, another one, the one of dwelling or being on a journey can be associated. David Seamon writes that movement is generally associated with 'newness, unfamiliarity, exploration and courage' (Seamon and Mugerauer 1989: 227). It is linked with carrying the person away from what is stable and towards confrontation with place, experience or ideas. Rest, for a change, relates to spatial order and familiarity, while maintaining experiential and historical continuity.

He then defines dwelling and lifestyle involving regularity, repetition and cyclicity grounded in care and personal concern for the place, things and people, thus the most self-conscious way of living within co-dependent environment. And such 'living within' could be related to Ingold's elaboration on the primacy of movement, when he says that 'in the animic ontology, beings do not simply occupy the world, they inhabit it, and in so doing – in threading their own paths through the meshwork – they contribute to its ever-evolving weave' (Ingold 2011: 71–72), and that the animic world is in perpetual flux.

Considered in a temporal sense, the dwelling–journey relationship, like that between balancing needs for movement and rest, signifies 'a process which occurs over time: the experience of leaving one place and going to another' (Seamon and Mugerauer 1989: 228). In this dialectical relationship between the old and the new, as Seamon describes further, one has to, on the one hand, become free of the old world yet use it as a ground stone for creating a new place of dwelling, and, on the other hand, let the new world speak and determine itself.

The relationality of any decision in life, and its authentic reconciliations, always works both ways, even though we feel the initiation of movement directionally, and what is new at first becomes the known constant over time and provides us with psychological security.

The presence of thematic permeability of movement resonates strongly with the, present in all the chapters, element of water. The element that perhaps is the most binding to all other as it is to the human experience of self as Nature. I can here refer to Buttimer's words that

> all over the world one finds in art and poetry, in science as well as fiction, water as symbol for home and reach, security and adventure. For so many writers and artists, the very presence of water – lake or ocean – was an indispensable condition for creative work.
>
> (Seamon and Mugerauer 1989: 275)

And when re-imagining movement of time, water is definitely the easiest to refer to, and the one with most changeable dynamics. Most mutable and complex too (Johnson 2001). It can flow, or it can stand still. Yet still just on the surface, perhaps, as the depths of many waters on Earth hold many mysteries, just like the one I experience when lying down in stillness, while realizing the watery activity in me. 'Water's capacity for multidimensional expression likens it to the human capacity for revealing our changing inner landscape through emotion', Rae Johnson (2000: n.pag.) continues. It runs hot or cold, just like our relationship with staying put or being on the go.

17

Fast and Slow

A similar observation is made when I pay attention to what happens in-between movement and stillness while speeding up or slowing down, and so while relating through pacing.

What becomes apparent is that speed is about making statements and drawing attention and it is always accompanied by slowness at some point in time to create a full movement pattern.

Slowness, or stillness, becomes then a point of reference to the realization that a 'different' movement has occurred. And so I think about it in comparison, realizing that we can only see clearly as long as whatever moves, moves along with the same or similar speed as we do!

And I can here compare it to two instances. One, of looking at a painting, for example, while standing still as we (the painting and I) both move alongside the same speed of the Earth turning. And, two, of looking at a rain drop while it's falling down in a pouring rain, or a chosen object in sight while spinning. In the latter case, it is impossible to connect fully, visually, kinaesthetically, but we register an impression of the activity, performed as if in another time/space.

Movement thus, as a quality of being appears to me as created by coexistence of different time/space(s). Just like me taking only five to ten minutes of physical clock time to experience many lengthy adventures in psychological time of an experience. Or, as in my private practice, working with many clients who keep prolonging the session guided by a feeling of time being brief, while it has been more than one and a half hours on the clock!

Hall writes that perception of time is deeply embedded in specific contexts of situational experience and that 'it is extraordinary and paradoxical that the very activities that are most rewarding and satisfying are those in which time is experienced as passing with extreme rapidity or in which the sense of time has been lost completely' (Hall 1983: 148). And experiencing movement somatically is full of such impressions, indeed.

Yet, time being relative can have multiple meanings. The relativity of time in its modern physics usage means that time is in some respects dependent on the observer. Other times, time's relativity can appeal to the fact that every individual has his own sense of it and that 'this psychological or subjective time can simultaneously fly for the one and crawl for the other' (Zwart 1976: 30). And so, following Zwart's suggestion, it should seem more appropriate to use the term 'relational time' instead of 'relative' time, although such usage is not yet very common.

And my realization to this point is that elements, which I have built up relationships with through coming into contact with different objects both indoors and outdoors, are expressions of different qualities of movement as if created by an exchange between different time/spaces as well. And that the sensed creative input that translates into my movement comes from the fact that creativity is ontologically embedded in movement (or motion, in more general terms) and that it thrives on openness to the changeable dynamics of possibility.

It is also at this stage of movement engagement, following its initial stages of relating with receptivity in embodied listening and sensual awareness, that the movement picks up in expression following either up-tempo movement or slowing down in relation to the forthcoming psychological awakenings and the bodily needs in the present moment.

It is when all the awakened content of my own relation to the sensed wants to be shared in expressive co-creation. And, with me, it comes in different formats on different occasions, through up-tempo movement, through voicing and singing, through tears or shouting breaking out or through more tactile ex-change and interaction with objects in the space or landscape around. Most common change though comes through up-tempo, very dynamic movement engagements which are executed in most random and interactive ways and which open my movement up to all directions at the same time, complex syncopation with sounding and testing my own limits of any physical relationship that I find myself with.

As in the selection of these sequences, I have captured the stills as in Figure 17.1.

FIGURES 17.1: *Moving Thoughts Journal.* Video stills by Anna Dako.

This portrayed in its specific dynamic stage of practice reveals its characteristic intensity of movement. The internally sensed change comes about through vigorous and energetic exchange between the internal and external stimuli, and includes an intensive spatial engagement, a lot of rubbing, swishing, pushing against, pulling, twisting and spinning. What felt as vibrant and active in its potentiality before now meets the space and fills its extreme points of high and low, left and right, etc., and its omnipresent belonging. It feels like the created through attentive listening connections and awakenings seek their embodied realization in numerous meeting points and that all the physical limitations of the attempted movements are included in this inter-relational action taking its time and place. I keep bumping, falling, hitting and yet the fluidity of movement in general carries on, as if all-inclusive.

My voice also joins and creates its own ways into and out of movement. It is very shy at first, then builds up some lower tones through more stimulant movement postures and finally, becomes part of the sharing and giving itself to the exchange, as it translates its sprouting melodies into words too, and then phrases, as in this one: 'Dizzy voice, come and walk with me, come and dance with me, come and sing with me' (*Moving Thoughts Journal*, audio transcript, June 2018). It also becomes visual (see Figure 17.2) in the after-movement reflection.

FIGURE 17.2: *Moving Thoughts Journal, Dizzy Voice Sprout*, June 2018.

And on another occasion too, the woken up sensitivity of hands and feet start spreading out its curiosity about all the newly possible spatial relationships (Figure 17.3).

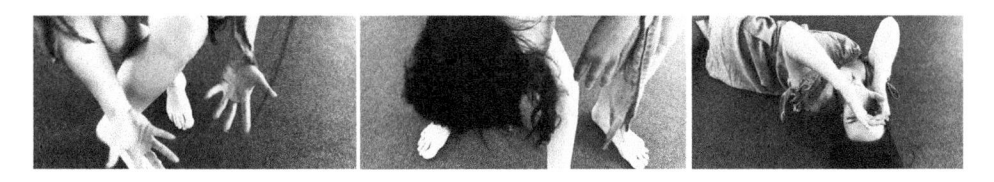

FIGURE 17.3: *Moving Thoughts Journal.* Video stills by Anna Dako.

And my voice becomes more and more the integral part of my movement experience. And it keeps becoming very visual too, as in the collected works (Figure 17.4).

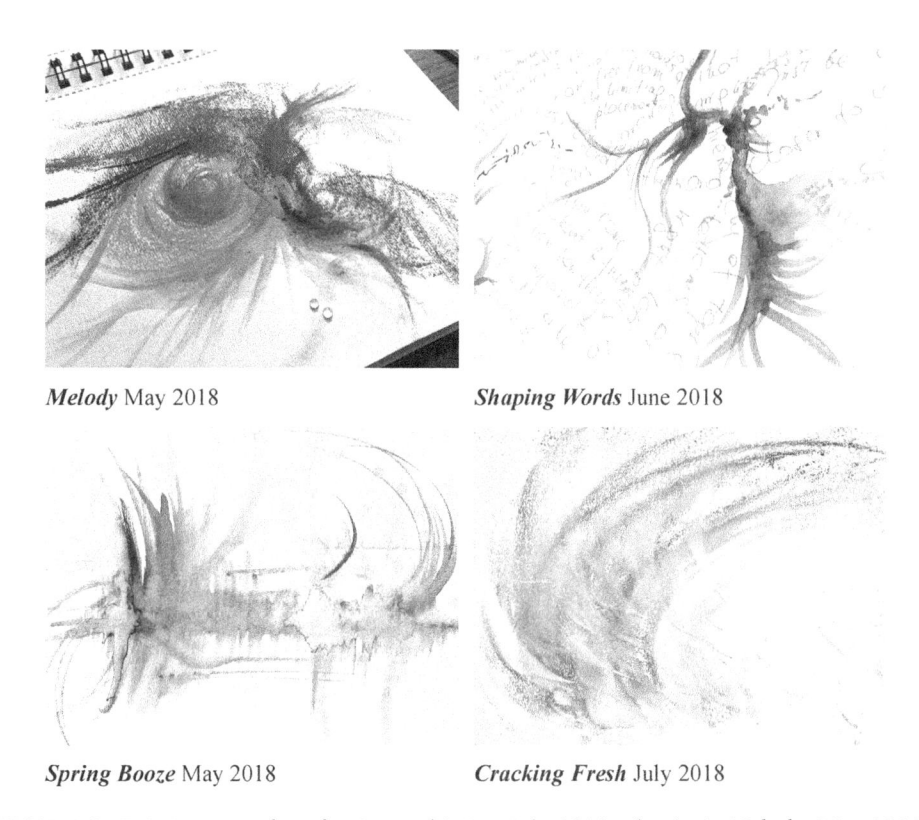

Melody May 2018

Shaping Words June 2018

Spring Booze May 2018

Cracking Fresh July 2018

FIGURES 17.4: *Moving Thoughts Journal* (May–July 2018 selection), *Melody*, May 2018; *Shaping Words*, June 2018; *Spring Booze*, May 2018; *Cracking Fresh*, July 2018.

And this open dimensionality of expressiveness finds its ways out in both sharply outward and softer, circular motion, while I keep experimenting with co-creation (see Figure 17.5), as in the work here, drawn together with an animal friend.

FIGURE 17.5: *Moving Thoughts Journal, Co-creation*. Photographs by Anna Dako.

The prolonged and slower in expression curves mingle continuously with the fast-paced, both outward and inward swishes of paint. Noticeably too, it is when I also decide to start combining media, and so movement merges with voiced expression alongside changing the tempos, as much as water paints start creating combinations with dry pastels, and pencil work on paper.

Lines co-create with written words, and the white background moves forward, becoming a visible part of the work's breathing space. I also begin to sense that the transitional spinning winds in eventually, either up or down, as my movement explorations tend to smoothen up any sharp shape as if it was not part of the subconscious willingness, or the natural way of psycho-somatic unloading. And during another felt thinking session, this emerges in a very confident voice while lying down on the floor within a triangular shape made of cushions:

Lines, ropes, threats,
walking paths
canoeing on the river
(singing, humming a tune)
rowing, rowing with a stream
following the stream (singing the words)
stretching one way
forgetting
forgetting about the rest ... the rest of the world
being selfish
moving forward
is being, being selfish
especially, if you walk up the river stream
why wouldn't you agree to follow it?

while practising the withnessing
the withnessing the river
so withnessing, is a choice
choice of being open to whatever comes
and yet with time it will eventually switch to doing nothing
or giving up, like sitting still
and at any given moment it can switch back
to being with
it's always that
while being something else
becoming more of the living Earth's journey
while sitting still
following the river stream
it's an agreement to be taken on the journey
to become that journey
but diverting through awareness
gives that journey an opportunity
to have a beginning
and an end
and a beginning again
through those transitioning stages
withnessing cannot be without those transitioning periods
nothing can
as everything belongs to
some sort of a process
in one or multiple realms
day and night
also have a different relationship
in different places on the Earth
day becoming a night can be a slow fluent process
or it can happen abruptly within minutes
and perhaps hours
like anything else that lives
can also be as abrupt as seconds
and so the transitioning
may have different dynamic
of being fluent and flow-like
within the circular shape
or a bit bumpy and fast, switching directions
and moving in a rectangle, or diamond shape

movement can also transition
into something completely new
with only traces of recognition
to the old process it transitioned from
like in an open shape, any open shape
and so any thorough transition
does have a recognisable
repeatable pattern
that keeps looping
that keeps coming back while moving forward
more spontaneous change
continues more abstractly
with endless possibility
of coming back and looping
or continuing on its own never-ending path
and I guess it's the same to say that
endless possibility of something
does not exclude the endless possibilities of something else
and I think this is exactly why
we have two hands, two feet
two eyes, two ears, two nostrils
up and down sides of the lips
the singularity inherently contains the possibility for its dual nature
like the duality creates perfect harmony of oneness
in embrace
being one and two at the same time
is the playground of multiplicity
of creation
of desire
and rejection
of choice
and uniqueness
and my embodied-self embraces possibilities of it all
even when I'm doing 'nothing'
(exhaling)
aren't we a glorious space with openings
the openings create a possibility of random movement
without being bumped too sharp
without being redirected too quickly.

(*Moving Thoughts Journal*, June 2018)

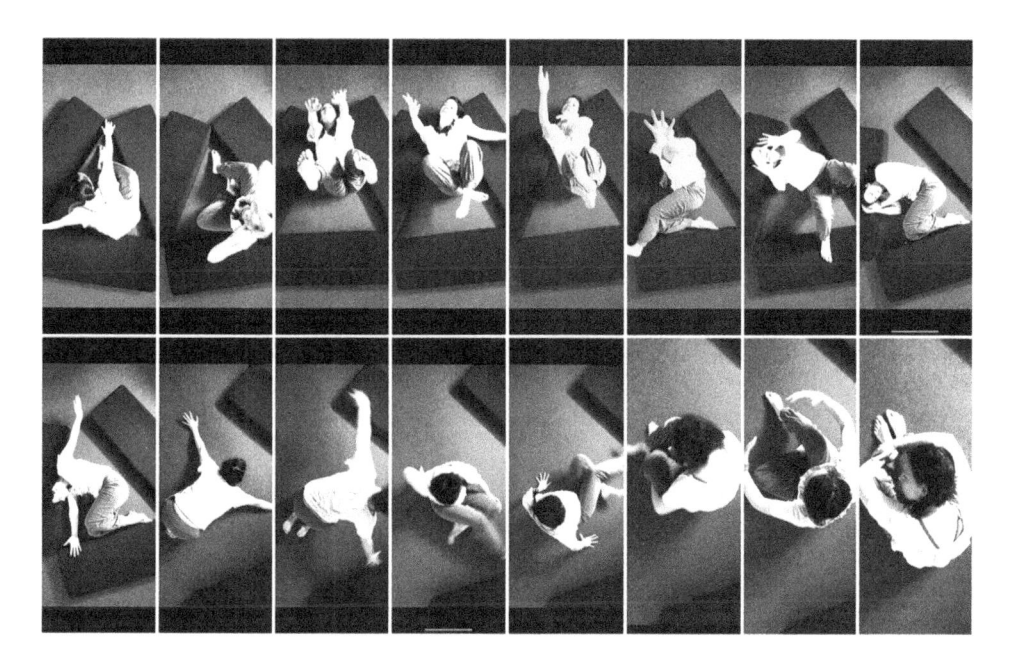

FIGURE 17.6: *Moving Thoughts Journal*. Video stills by Anna Dako.

And as depicted in Figure 17.6, the tendency for further development of this felt thinking is opened up by the need for more air and more space as well as for more connective movement again. I start moving the cushions wider apart creating in-between spaces first and then continuing to spinning and turning on the ground ending up in an embrace with myself surrounded by open space.

An image of whirl-like, infinitely small point of selfhood emerges surrounded by endlessness of 'otherness' and which is my own creation at the same time. My reflection on geometrical, permanently closed shapes and straight lines makes me conclude on their limited feasibility in the natural environment as constantly re-shaped by permeating forces of nature and elements. There are no straight lines, unless we are able to keep two points connecting the line's beginning and an end out of motion, which is, ultimately, impossible.

In the natural world, to keep a straight line of a ship, for example, one has to always account for a corrective action, as the ship will slowly wander off course. This corrective action then, defines movement's purpose, but it can also help us realize that fast movement can only be followed by reflection, a possible look back in adjustment, whilst slow movement makes time for reflexivity while it emerges and shapes its own course of meaningfulness.

18

Purpose and Willingness

Had I been seeing the world perfectly with my eyes ... I might have never become a mover whose creation thrives on the magical mysteries of the unseen.

(*Moving Thoughts Journal*, September 2017)

At this stage of thinking through the gathered, in responsive movement, material, it is interesting for me to ponder over the physiological facts of responsiveness and that within over six hundred individual muscles that construct the muscular system in our body, there are three major types of them: cardiac, visceral/smooth and striated muscle.

Striated muscles are voluntary muscles, like those found in legs and arms, and they can be easily and consciously controlled. Smooth muscles are involuntary, like those in the lungs, heart and digestive system, and require no effort to move or function, as they function automatically, under the control of the subconscious regions of the brain. Following on from the awakened sensations in the nervous system, the muscular system receives its ability to move in response. The muscle tissues are both excitable or irritable, capable of receiving and responding to stimulation from the nerves. They are also contractible or extensible, as well as elastic and adaptive, which means the muscular system can be changed in response to how it is used without losing its capability to be able to return to its original, resting shape and length.

Again then, the deeply felt innate nature of movement being relational in the way as it keeps creating innumerate possibilities between its ongoing tendency of back and forth pattern seems to make itself visible in the properties of the muscular system.

It is also noticeable when we consider the functional, ongoing bounce between muscular hypertrophy, i.e. muscle's enlargement with increased work and atrophy i.e. its muscular degradation, if deprived of work, or the workings of a muscle tissue itself, as stretched between abduction and adduction, or extension and flexion with rotational movement connecting and adding all the creative dimensionality to our physical capabilities.

Having considered that, I begin to think, that perhaps I should inspect my own relationship with the visual world, as my poor vision might be revealing to me the way I have been trying to see too hard, and developing a myopia, instead of concentrating on relaxed, through natural connectivity, receiving and responding.

The strenuous effort of meeting the world out there with clear(er) vision, which might also be interpreted as clear(er) understanding, definitely shows me how I use my eyes and how tired they get by the end of the day, as I put continuous stress on the ocular muscles at work through squinting. I get reminded that straining is the enemy of any form of synchrony in rhythms or seamless connectivity.

Vision too is a form of active connection of meeting to receive, followed by a muscular response. The more in sync we are with the image in front of us, the more details of what is taking place before our eyes can be perceived. Phenomenologically put, Merleau-Ponty too reminds us of such inclusive reality of embodied vision, saying that we belong to the visible and can be seen, while at the same time we are also our own sources of vision (Merleau-Ponty and Lefort 1968).

And, as I am trying to use more mindful ways of relaxed seeing, I begin to feel think that I have been blaming my eyes for malfunction in providing that clarity of vision instead of helping myself in using the eyes properly. The field between the proper and improper functionality of any systemic organization is vast, and I am now beginning to understand my ability to see more as the meeting ground between the seen and the unseen, the felt and the not felt, and that it can be of many faces, and not simply as an *on* or *off* functionality.

At this stage of movement engagement, I realize that our relationship to ourselves can change daily, even though we definitely have some ongoing characteristics that become part of our personality. And that the cultural primacy of vision, similarly addressed by Luce Irigaray (2017), Maxine Sheets-Johnstone (1999) or Elizabeth Grosz (1995), does not need to indicate mastery, but as co-creating personal imagery of the world in a unique way. For soma, as Fraleigh reminds again, 'is not rendered visually, but through proprioception, kinaesthetic knowledge of one's spatial and temporal condition at any moment' (2004: 128).

And yet, sometimes, embracing the intimacy of self in an open and informed way is as difficult as saying hello to a stranger on the street in the middle of the night. Developing one's capacity to trust the innate creativity of movement enough to carry on diving into its ways that unfold for the mover is definitely an underdeveloped skill, not only in artistic or dance education but in life in general. Yet, this is what informed improvisation is all about, and it is also what we learn when we refrain from too much enforced or purposeful activity and develop a sense of trust and safety in things that simply come our way as they do.

It is also when, for me, this animated stage picks up its own dynamic that shapes its own developments on such continuous and most lively exchange between what is given and what is being received as meaningful stimuli. And every smallest change to a quality of received sound, light, temperature, texture, sensation, breath, etc., can have a potentially most abrupt response from the awakened interconnection between the nervous and muscular systems.

And the felt *Now* in such an ongoing exchange, stretches and shrinks infinitely easy as I become, like a Japanese musician, an 'open score' with the music, like time itself, coming from within myself.

19

Being and Letting Be

A healthy life relationship between active and receptive forms of being, i.e. 'being with' means not over-producing, but being in balance with productive and receptive modes of being. Moving away from self and towards the outside is productive. Moving towards self is passive and relaxing.

Yet, life as co-presence is often violated by claiming the presence over the presence of other. It is an act of judgement, of prioritizing the self and taking advantage of contextual reality. And the other side of imbalance in co-presencing is living in a state of withdrawal and denial, without touching one's potential.

When I am *with* movement, sharing presence is an open dialogue, and it means both giving and taking, accepting and offering and finding ever new ways of engagement with life as it creates itself in the moment. And yet there are boundaries, and the boundaries are manifestations of the presence of other, as different, including the difference sensed within myself. I am being on my own and yet I always belong.

Thus, being *in* movement is very different from being *with* movement. The former is mainly productive, the latter, relational. Giving in, yielding onto the ground, is like admitting that you are the part of the Earth. And yet through being able to create different movements on top of it gives me possibility to distinguish myself from others in embracing it all oneness.

Creation is never separate from its source and becoming happens through both losing and gaining. And on many occasions of working outdoors and feeling how anything I do belongs to the living environment and its ongoing movement, I sense that I can see thanks to the Sun, but I can feel thanks to the Moon (Dako 2015b), as this most basic cosmic scene created for all life on Earth resides in me deeply. And with my earthy subconscious awakening, I write:

> I feel that my body remembers all life experiences, subconsciously. And all the collected life experiences become me, the living reservoir. And they can further

become whatever they want, and whatever they become, they are the seeds, for greater things, or they can be detrimental as unwanted context, as mistakes, or collected overload, the energetic collective …

I just found some sheep wool, again …

(*Moving Thoughts Journal*, March 2018)

20

Reflexive Synopsis:
Moving Towards Experiential Openness

Entering the experiential openness at this dimension of somatic practice can be a very challenging undertaking that connects to the psychological relevance of every movement underway. What remains critically important is to follow the authentically emerging clues for action and/or rest in their endlessly dialogic rhythms and following the sense of 'what feels the right thing to do' without second-guessing or judging our decisions against any cognitive standards.

With little prior experience of letting myself feel comfortable listening to my own voice shape its tones alongside being engaged in movement or art-making, for example, the depth of its connection to the emotional overwhelms at first. In time though, it presents itself as a natural extension to any movement performed and the most accessible aid at releasing, letting go off control, and letting myself be.

And this opening, an all-encompassing awareness brings about something more fundamental within me that I normally just sense, but hardly come into contact with on every day basis. And I immediately sense that that hidden voice is always there, hopefully for everybody, not to control but to add to a meaningful fabric of personal life that connects all to all in unique ways, and in which the authentic personality reveals itself through 'silent openness' (Seamon and Mugerauer 1989: 247–56) and 'sense of reciprocity' (Abram 1996: 137).

Hall reminds that in western thought, religion is one thing and social control is another. Yet, for many older cultures, with his specific example of Zuni Pueblo tribes, songs perform multiple functions, religious, ceremonial, social as much as they are also the reflection of 'the different currents in the sea of rhythm in which people are immersed' (Hall 1983: 171). 'The songs, therefore, perform an emergent, formulative function because they come from that unconscious, previously unverbalized layer representing group sentiments and beliefs' (Hall 1983: 157), yet the common misconception about rhythm is that it originates in the music, not in the individual.

It is then important to realize that vocalization and improvised singing or sound producing is a vital part of expressing one's identity which should not be separable from life itself. Practised in intimate settings that provide comfort and safety of expression, it is a complementary way of keeping in touch with oneself on the emotional level. Trying to open the vocalizing experience to the sounds of the environment helps to create new relational experiences of the self and shows how synchrony, as a natural way of 'being with' in sound, is our innate ability.

This easily achievable multilevel synchrony and rhythm, and what Hall calls *entrainment*, following the term coined by William Condon (1978) between two, or more, nervous systems, 'is so much a part of everybody's life that it occurs without notice' (178). With a more clinical reference to the cases of dis-rhythmia, i.e. problems with entrainment, as present in patients suffering from schizophrenia, autism and dyslexia, Hall says that if you can't entrain with yourself, it is impossible to entrain with other, and if you can't entrain, you can't relate. And then, sumps us that:

> There has always been great coherence in nature and it would be valuable to know more about the rhythmic interrelationships. Human beings are just beginning to recognize that there may be an underlying unity. It is necessary for us to understand that 'rhythm is nature's way', and it is up to our species to learn as much as possible about how these remarkable processes affect our lives.
>
> (Condon 1978: 179)

And that, with one-second-frequency delta wave being the basic rhythm of human behaviour, 'all human rhythms begin in the centre of the self, that is with self-synchrony' (Condon 1978: 181).

And while synchrony has been present throughout the first phase of my practice, the felt transitioning described in this phase is happening within my improvising abilities to syncopate as well. This is where the real playfulness and time-based exchange happens within the openness of creative movement exploration, and where I can express my own relation to time and space. Both positive and negative emotions feel intrinsic to the ongoing negotiation about my own, time imbued, identity. The character of rhythms performed and felt reflects body's energy levels as well as its internal needs for closer relation, either with higher tempos and frequencies or lower. This reflective action will also tell bigger stories of rhythms we live by culturally, or even generationally, yet we are not conscious of it, on every day basis.

And those many forms of felt entrainment happening between ourselves and the environment can be compared to Carl Jung's concept of synchronicity (Jung 1973), as experiences happening simultaneously by different people in different places yet sharing identical qualities, sensations or emotions, not to mention their implicit connection in meaningfulness.

Bringing Earth's collective unconscious as a shared ground to such experiences, Jung says that 'our concepts of space and time have only approximate validity, and there is therefore a wide field for minor and major deviations' (Jung 1963: 331). Visibly then, sharing informal patterns of relation is intimately related to the study of time as a cultural process, but it can also be a metaphor for larger, ontological contexts of Life.

My reflexive feel thinking here is that by following the tangibility of things only, even in naming phenomena, we create false divisions and contradictions. Our constant effort to rationalize experience takes away from the depths of the informal layers in natural connectivity with the natural world, the connectivity that we do develop if we follow the felt cues that life's creative processes store available to us. While naming and sharing about the experience is helpful in processing and accommodating it within our conscious mind, responding in movement, physically, mentally or emotionally is already an acknowledgement itself, of inner shifts and reactive change.

21

Co-creating with the Land:
Stories in Experiential Responsiveness

FIGURE 21.1: *In Experiential Responsiveness*, Drumdollo, Aberdeenshire. Photograph by Anna Dako.

Morning sun – an unbelievable blessing in this place – as if a veil had been lifted from the world – Scotland is the world's most beautiful woman who has to be hidden behind a veil.

The water refuses to just be a view – it moves.

(*Cove Park Journals*, April 2018)

Another day of shared movement explorations at Cove Park. Our shared time here brings a lot of new reflections carried over from day one and opens up space to more co-creative felt thinking. With my reflective wondering about how we can celebrate, participate in and embrace life fuller, to include our fears, grief and sorrows, the wondering that became very vivid to me after all the activities of moving in receptivity phase, I open the floor to hear other movers' stories. How can we get involved, be *with* and continue offering ourselves to other life of this land?

We start with much appreciated holding hands in silence. Just as we are sitting, in a circle, on the studio floor, overlooking the vast landscape of the resided in/with cove and its lake and the embracing it all – hills and mountains. Sitting, holding hands, and breathing together, sinking into each other's presence.

I experience those moments of silence as a very active time of new inclinations emerging.

Some movers feel like being more outdoor, some want to take it slow re-finding themselves in more secured settings for their movement practice. Yet, we all share the guiding thought of working through the limiting distinctions of what is outdoor and what is indoor by offering one another a mindful form of 'withnessing' awareness. And the proposed 'withnessing', or *being with* in shared awareness, shapes as wilful participation in the group's dynamic which is tuned by the senses and which does not necessarily mean 'witnessing' in the visual sense, i.e. staying within sight, or doing the same thing all together.

Rather, other sensual capabilities, like the audible one of hearing each other through vast open space, or simply sensing through shared presence come into picture and so are the individually sensed differences in qualitative dynamics which we are all trying to respect and bring forth for one another. And it might be, again, the mentioned already childish curiosity awakening and the longing for the difference that eventually takes over the group's decision, as we all decide to carry on the shared morning in formats of contact improvisation.

With today's guiding questions of *What* and *Who*, I am asking everybody to start our explorations wondering about: *What is the nature of Nature?*, without any further clarifications of what I mean by the question myself. And I hear the first response from one of the movers right away, saying:

I feel that for me, my mind does not understand the question, so I will have to find it with my body. I cannot really relate to it brain-wise, in a cognitive way, so my body really wants to move with it.

(*Cove Park Journals*, April 2018)

And so we move.

FIGURE 21.2: Video stills, Cove Park, April 2018.

The contact improvisation session depicted in the pictures above portrays its dynamic versatility. It starts indoor, in the studio, and then carries on through the open glass door onto the wooden deck and the grassy outdoors around the Cove Park facility. The material reveals an intense co-creation of movement extremes happening. The physical exchanges stretch in all directions: upwards, sideways, diagonally and downwards throughout both indoor and outdoor exchanges yet there is a continuous progression onto slower tempos and wider space engagements happening, primarily during the outdoor part of the exploration.

The way the group picks up the movement exchange in the studio comes again through sounding. At first very heavy, sighing and gasping happens alongside the wide-stretched and more individualized positioning of the movers throughout the studio floor. Hardly anybody begins the session off the floor. We are all pulled and caressed by the ground and its supporting push at first, lying down and waiting for growing impulses of movement to emerge. We then start creating different patterns on the floor through tumbling, resting against one another, sliding, crawling, dragging, twisting and worming into collective mounts.

Different meet ups, either in pairs or groups of three or four begin to permeate the session and create different exchanges that either pull the group back together or separate it into divergent, more local 'happenings'. Open curiosity with personalized levels of movement motivation, which comes from different bodily needs discussed earlier, comes through, naturally. And the process sustains its ongoingness as a whole, embraced by the walls of the studio space and with visible influences from sunlight cast throughout the space and the lively gusts of wind coming through the open glass doors.

Then, the active partnering picks up on re-emerging occasions for co-creative playfulness in sounding and vocalizing the felt and in motivational exchange in movement. There is a lot impacting others through movement taking place, as more and more energy accumulates.

There are lifts, supporting partnering, pushes, pulls and pull ups, twists, raises and sudden alterations in directionality happening at different corners of the room and all at the same time. And the sounding exchanges transform onto shared, and contagious within the group, bursts of laughter. It feels like a long awaited release to exchange in contact improvisation like this, as if the group needed that tangible companionship. But there is even more awaiting, as one after another the group 'leaks' out onto the deck and experiences the deeply felt difference in the quality of space, and time, we now come in touch with. Something that felt like calling when in the studio embraces us now with full exposure to the sun and wind, the bare wood under the feet and the living landscape around.

Delighted, with a few deep breaths delivered by the wind, the need for further stretching and opening the chest up wide takes over. And the group spreads out into further crawling explorations on the grass or giving in to a more mindful appreciation of how our bodies long for such spring time meet up while lying down on the grass or moving with 'what is being received' in a slow, contemplative way.

Everybody follows their own calling, and I discover mine in creating a better 'home', or nest rather, for the witnessing the group sheep skull, the 'Shapeshifter'. And while I begin gathering sticks and soft grass for the spot, the activity connects me to other movers, as we continue our exploration in extended 'withnessing', and I get joined on the task. Soon, the Shapeshifter finds itself not only on a softer, grassy bedding but also decorated with flowers and stones.

And the exploration carries on with more colours on the deck, while my movement grows in size and wants to be expressed visually with chalk drawings co-created on the deck's wooden surface.

FIGURE 21.3: Cove Park, April 2018.

FIGURE 21.4: Cove Park, April 2018.

The experiential relevance of time and today's wondering upon What and Who questions sinks in by now. Yesterday's strong calling outwards into the landscape grows its other end, as the notions of connecting to our inner landscape starts being visible in movement.

In one of the movers' writings I read about '*life unfolding backwards*', '*backwards into the future*' (*Cove Park Journals*, April 2018, orginal emphasis), as she herself feels like she is sinking into the background of the living world around. And that sinking in, in walking backwards, comes along with her feeling connected and being with Nature, as she says: 'Here I am with I am in everything' (*Cove Park Journals*, April 2018). With the toes being placed first on the floor before the heal, as she describes, it is like '*tasting the ground first, carefully, before inhabiting it*' (*Cove Park Journals*, April 2018, orginal emphasis). And then she continues onto this mindful reflection:

A sacrifice
A sacrifice of me-ness
Presence of lake, lakeness
Presence of sky, skyness
Presence of rolling hills, hillness
A sacrifice – I sacrifice me-ness
Becoming
Lightness
Cloudness
Grassness
Treeness
Sacrificing me-ness
Walking backwards
With all-ness inside of me
I see a woman –
Walking in front of me – backwards
Come – come, waving with one arm towards me
Come – come
Inviting me – calling me – breathing me in
Through her mouth – in – in – in – moving
Through her till I am released again – a circle,
Backwards – being swallowed, breathed in
Shaped and moved through her movement
Released – out – me – till I am swallowed, shaped
again. Backwards – circling – me-ness.

(Martina Polleros, Cove Park, April 2018)

In the meantime, it is interesting to point out that this reflection about the backwards movement towards the self has been happening within the practised on the day *witnessing in awareness*. The described sharing of the breath and re-becoming while sacrificing the self in releasing another yet the same self in circular motion backwards has been thus also physically witnessed by a few of other movers.

And suddenly, in an amazingly smooth and continuously gentle movement engagement, and, without her realizing this at any point of her reflective movement practice with eyes closed, she gets joined by another mover. And, together, they form a seamless duo in 'blindly' guided and wilfully followed movement exchange. And this slow ongoingness of movement unfolding seems to have built up in sense of comfort and peacefulness and in what I would call, movement's implicit potential for co-creation.

FIGURE 21.5: *Moving in Sync*, Cove Park, April 2018.

Knowing her own normally very talkative and communicative nature though, as I read the journal by the mover who was the follower in the described above contemplative duet, she is wondering about her inner ability to create a relatable contact with other movers simply by sharing presence and letting the primacy of language-based communication go. Her subtle 'double dance' then comes from her curiosity about letting her normal self, that guides, leads, pushes onwards and infects others with her own energy go, and about expanding on her silent presence in following, listening and responding.

And she is also describing a huge shift happening for her since arrival at Cove Park. From her normal interest in the darker side of her own personality, she is now experiencing a powerful presence of Nature she participates in inwardly, as if she was looking at herself from the inside, as she describes (*Cove Park Journals*, April 2018). She then adds that the way she explores the living landscape around grows out of her internal needs, which helps her understand her own nature better. And that transitioning between silencing and voicing in movement makes her feel participating in an open dialogue.

Then she writes:

My internal need for braking into pieces, conflict and crashing has disappeared.
Why – I don't know!
But it is nice to know that it is not obsessive in me,

And that it is not always ready to destroy.

[…]

I like my dark side, and I think I can brighten it up.

Conquer, lighten it up.

Oh gosh, I am drawing flowers, Help! Why? ☺

(*Cove Park Journals* [translated], April 2018)

Her transitioning onto today's explorations, coming from the following entry in the journal, happens with her strongly felt influence of the lake's waters. She discovers an immediate need to move with it, as well as to breathe-in the water, the air and the soil. And soon she discovers that it is movement itself that helps her work through the darkness she is experiencing internally as part of her own nature, as if it is movement itself that provides light for her to keep discovering the 'shades of the dark'.

And in her captivating interpretation of the opening question, she then writes that the nature of her own nature is to

hear, look, feel, receive, being in touch, impact, being open to influence of everything, everybody, no matter what, for joy, for life.

(*Cove Park Journals* [translated], April 2018)

She thus creates a unitary image of herself as Nature with this drawing to follow, as in Figure 21.6.

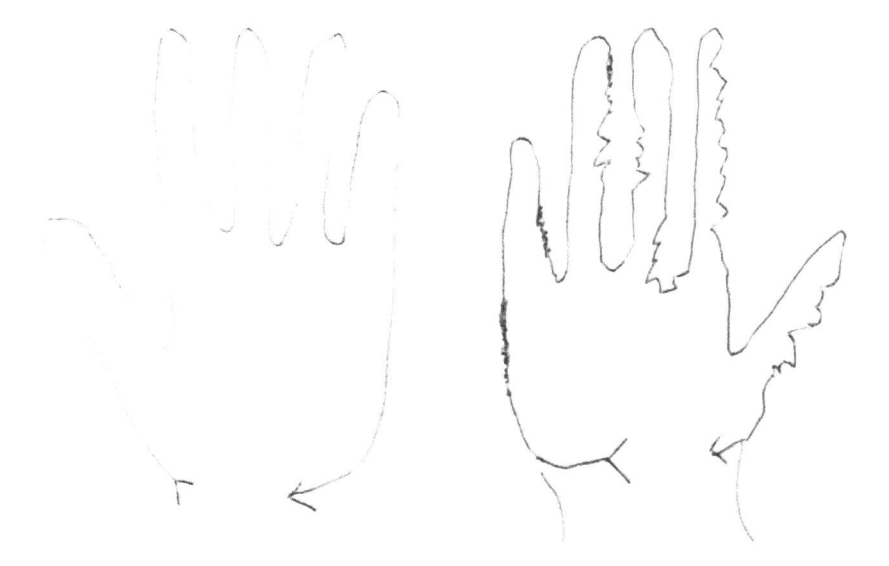

FIGURE 21.6: *Cove Park Journals*, no title, Cove Park, April 2018.

And with movement as the essence of Nature becoming stronger and stronger, another mover provides her own definition of it as well, as she delightfully writes that:

> Nature is the juice – the force that makes things go.
>
> (*Cove Park Journals*, April 2018)

And that:

> The natural is what moves by itself, unmanipulated – that in us which moves and is moved – which is to say – everything.
>
> (*Cove Park Journals*, April 2018)

And after experiencing feeling one with the natural world already on the first day, human nature as a theme in journals' reflections appears more and more, yet seems quite problematic in more conscious evolvement of the participants' thoughts. For some, human nature presents itself as very different from that of Nature itself or the nature of the self as defined above, because 'people are not so open' or 'they are the difficult nature that calls for patience and study' (*Cove Park Journals*, April 2018).

And the motivation behind saying this, as the mover describes further, is that nature lasts, and the feeling of its continuation and permanence calms her down despite the awareness of her own temporality. She thus has a sense of 'being in relation', or constant relationship, despite death, or embracing death rather, and thus being able to continue sharing the space with the natural world in this form of another. She would like to be able to contact, or be in touch with other people in the same way, yet, as she further describes, human imagination and human thoughts are different from being the way Nature is, here and now, as they need transformations that are withdrawn from the present moment (*Cove Park Journals*, April 2018).

And those findings about human nature, imagination and thoughts as she puts together into one reflection come to her after she had spent over three hours by the lake side. The lake that called her in the morning and which appeared closest to her own nature as well.

And yet, as she continues, the more she was thinking of getting and experiencing the closeness of the water through her own conception of it the more put off she felt in actual contact with it, as if put off by fear of it. 'My entry point to connect with nature, she describes, is through being an animal, I need to reduce myself to a simple form. The moment I join my thoughts of it, the contact with nature ceases, and I feel bad' (*Cove Park Journals*, April 2018). She explains further then that she wasn't able to 'get out of her head', and being in her head made her feel separate from the water.

Being with Nature as this mover experienced already physically makes her feel stronger, with a solid base, and confident that she belongs to a bigger picture of things. 'I have always been functioning on a "margin" of society', she says, 'here there are no borders, no margins, only multiplicity' (*Cove Park Journals*, April 2018). And she now realizes how much of the energy of the trees she actually needs, and how much of a most sensual experience it is for her to stay in an embrace with its branches.

Due to feeling rejected by the water through thinking of it, instead of experiencing it in/with her body, she concludes that it is as if Nature tolerated only being and not thinking. And then, she keeps going back to reminiscing her own death as being one with nature, and wonders why it does not scare her. It must be, she writes, because when I am open and in the receptive mode, as I am here with Nature, I feel complete, permanent and ongoing. I feel I belong with it in listening and touch, and when I open my eyes and think, my connection disappears.

And she follows up with these words and images (see Figure 21.7), full of flowful compositions of complimentary shapes.

> Tree, bark, moss, skin, liver, blood, water, stone, bone, head, voice, sheep, eye, soil, warmth, wind, air, omnipresent motion, change, breath.
>
> (*Cove Park Journals*, April 2018)

FIGURE 21.7: *Cove Park Journals*, no title, Cove Park, April 2018.

That there is something animalistic about being with Nature, about being in an all embracing relationship with it without a word or a thought has already been mentioned. And another mover too develops her own pondering over the mutually disruptive processes of *being with* and *thinking* while reflecting upon her own time with a tree. She writes:

My Tree friend
The familiar one
Wears clothes like me
Its dress is divine
Nature made this
So like me – armless, body spread
Rooted in the earth it
Supports me on my journey,
Shapes my movement,
Holding my window of weightlessness
Offering a view of the world above
I trust this tree,
Its skin beaten by the wind.
There is no room for thought when nature speaks
Like a key in a key hole.
What is it to connect with nature?
To be still, to flow, to be guided, to move with.
To arrive at a place.

(Cove Park Journals, April 2018)

And she gets joined in her timeless embraces with a tree by other movers, while she further reveals that

> human noise is the most disturbing, distressing thing. Noise/sound without soul or heart is [...] irritating. In nature there feels peace around sound.
> *(Cove Park Journals*, April 2018)

And the collected moments of meditative co-presence with the branches, the roughness of the bark in touch and movement with and against it without conscious thinking of it all takes over, as *being with* trees become a collective discovery of something we have apparently all missed.

FIGURE 21.8: Video stills, Cove Park, April 2018.

And yet, thoughts also move ..., as pointed by another mover, while she says:

I love being surprised by my own ideas, as they circle around and hit me again.

(*Cove Park Journals*, April 2018)

And then she ponders over Nature as animating force in forms:

Nature is what moves
The animating force
What can't be made up
What moves itself
What moves in us
What moves in water
Fire
Earth
Air
And all organic beings
And causes to be
Nature's what you can't make up
Can't control
Can't create
But can destroy – the forms –
Can't destroy the life force.

(*Cove Park Journals*, April 2018)

And she follows it up with these tree like, dynamic drawings as in Figure 21.9.

FIGURE 21.9: *Cove Park Journals*, no title, April 2018.

And by now, the felt, ongoingly moving and evolving relationships between languaging, words, silence, listening, being in contact with, touching and releasing begin to permeate one another, like water itself. And then the tree like imagery, and its dimensionality enters the language as well.

> Puddle stream shine stone wet
> Walk words
> Words walk
> One two
> Two one
> Legs walk
> Legs are form
> No two no one
> Stay on the path if you only have two legs
> When I was touching you
> I wanted to grow another arm
> I wanted to grow more hands.
>
> (*Cove Park Journals*, April 2018)

And pondering over the ongoingly moving nature of nature and its potential for change engulfs us all, while one of the movers creates this current-like and circular pattern in words:

> Change
> From pain to joy
> From illness to health to illness
> From fear to tranquillity
> From light to wind
> From tension to love from closeness to distance
> Impermanence
> Change.
>
> (*Cove Park Journals*, April 2018)

And then, she transitions onto wondering about the feminine, about being a woman and asking a question as a woman. 'What does it mean to be a woman?', she asks herself (*Cove Park Journals*, April 2018). And a striking contrast between her longing for both the intimate femininity and the sudden changes in life as 'the wild' surprises her. The strong images of the feminine and the masculine energies as co-creating at this phase in movement developments begin to spread.

Skin –
Today my skin
Sunshine
Sunshine on my skin
Breast
Breast
Opening the chest
Naked breast
What does it feel to be a woman
And take the clothes off
Skin
My skin is so pale
Sunshine where are you?
I want to walk naked
With the sun
Naked and safe
Safe and naked
Wild
I get dirty
[...]
Today I met bulls and I felt fear
I thought of my ancestors and these encounters in the fields, forests
With wild animals and fierce creatures
Fears
Threats.

(*Cove Park Journals*, April 2018)

And visibly, the themes of touch, embodied sexuality and ecstasis begin to show in the work with clay and other artworks as well. The felt ecstasis though, in my interpretation, is not a literal representation of a romantic rapture, but a 'heightened sense of awareness', as Fraleigh (2004:133) describes, and 'becoming one' with the movers' intentions in action.

In a chapter titled 'A dance of time beings', Fraleigh further says that dancing, with its constant relationship between containment and overflow, and, as a metaphysical artefact, springs from our embodied states and our embodied sexuality within the 'metaphysics of discovery' and helps engaging with 'anything for the pleasure of the doing itself and not for future rewards' (Fraleigh 2004: 119–23). She also says that 'opening present time, being alive to it through matching rather than mastering, is a possibility in all our work and play' (Fraleigh 2004: 123).

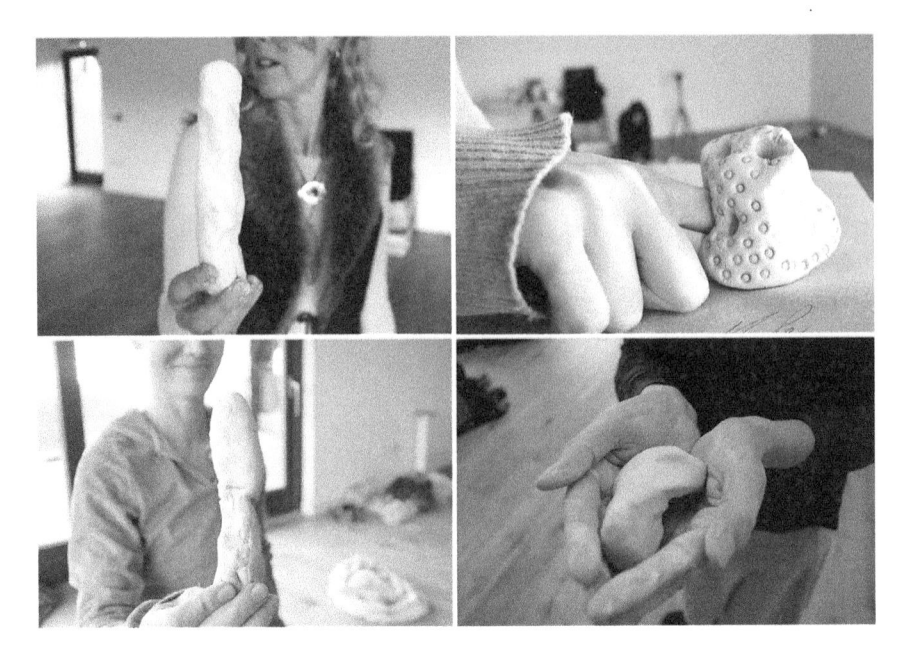

FIGURE 21.10: *Clay Work,* Cove Park, April 2018.

Taking on our sexuate belonging, as Irigaray too writes, with sexuation meaning the process of active individuation in embodied relationships with the living world around, brings us energy. It also provides structure to our relationships with other beings and compensates for absence of roots by compelling us to unite with 'the other' (Irigaray 2017). This does not occur through a mere sexual drive, but requires us to cultivate love with respect for mutual differences. And, with touch being a primary source of contact in somatic dance improvisation, embedded in proprioceptive space–time awareness, it definitely permeates the explorations on responsiveness in full engagement of our open and interactive selves.

It also creates connections to follow-up contemplation about the feared, life and death transitioning, being a natural process anyhow, and embraced within present-centered attention which provides strength and more gravity in handling the struggle, as described in another journal:

> I can feel gut bacteria and things inside the digestive track and the womb, working away, composting, being absolutely nature, incomprehensible, not measurable, not controllable, and constantly making or doing life and death.
>
> (*Cove Park Journals*, April 2018)

As the world both changes and remains the same, Irigaray continues, 'coming into this world amounts to exposing oneself to dying for living' (Irigaray 2017: 7). Thus, living entails the risk of death. Living, as she writes, involves perpetual becoming, and if we are not becoming, we are declining, we are constantly torn between omnipotence and helplessness. And yet, having experienced it in the shared practice already, I wouldn't necessarily agree here with Irigaray, as in my understanding, living to our fullest involves processes of letting go, which is a form of giving in. Thus, to me, there is helplessness embedded in omnipotence and the other way round too, as it is in the breath.

And so, the felt relation to the breath comes back again, as a soothing middle ground resonating somewhere in-between life's cruelty and its beauty, somewhere between being and not being, a sigh and an awe, and some(w)here where those striking differences belong together, no matter what. Or as Heraclitus famously reminds that 'just as the river where I step is not the same, and is, so I am as I am not' (Heraclitus and Haxton 2001: 51) And the cited above mover continues merging her reflections in between words and air-light paintbrush strokes, writing flow-fully that:

the breath moving through is always
beautiful thing, always power, life and joy
in itself
even the last one
crunchy feet stone words
toes rummaging in stones
rummaging in the heart
to find shapes to match
the matching disease
leads nowhere
but resonance is where it's at
the shine
the glisten on the stone
and in the heart
the tears in the eye and in the sea
it stinks here, it glitters

FIGURE 21.11: *Cove Park Journals*, April 2018.

Following other the stories unfolding in the journals, she too finds herself following the water calling today. And again, the same place by the lake and within each other's sight, as I find out retrospectively from the journals, creates two divergently different experiences for two movers. The described earlier rejection felt by the mover standing by the water and thinking about it in her conscious thoughts gets contrasted here by another mover's story of belonging to water, despite feeling unwell. The lake communicates with her and sets her off to carry on living, as being one, with water. And she describes her experience as the water telling her:

Go
Never mind the forms you are like water
You flow
I spiral in you
Move with me
Everything takes you
Go.

(Cove Park Journals, April 2018)

And to me, this caught in words water exploration goes along with this following one as well (see Figure 21.12), even though this one was caught in stills, no words, creating a very expressive language on its own. It tells another story too about being open to whatever the stream brings and about moving within its waters both up and down the flow, and simply, being with it in wonderous contemplation.

FIGURE 21.12: Cove Park, April 2018.

A path of discovering oneself relates again to the forth and back movement of striving towards discovering the self yet with the otherness of others.

Irigaray writes:

We search for a possible mediation in a common world already existing, and yet it is the one which prevents us from discovering our own 'to be' and a path towards a possible conjunction with the other as other. Rather we must listen to the desire of the other which attracts us beyond a horizon defined by sameness and the already common, a desire which remembers the ec-stasis from which we exist and calls us back to the questions of our human being.

(2017: vii)

And then I realize again and again, how revealing such wondering can be, as I continue listening to the recorded felt thinking over the nature of Nature by the mover continuing her lengthy walks and *being with* the open landscape:

I am here in and with and my heartbeat …
More and more …
Synchronizes more and more and more and more and more …
When I feel safe and sheltered.

(*Journal no. 5*, Cove Park, April 2018)

The mover describes getting lost or simply feeling lonely in the vast, open and empty landscape, walking for hours. And experiences a big relief when she finally rediscovered the bitten, human path. The open empty landscape may appear powerful, overwhelming and a little frightening as well, and the bitten path provides back more support for her hours spent on the wet, mossy, soft but rough to walk on grounds.

This is where, in the open Highlands landscape, walking barefoot again, she loses directions, loses herself and yet she feels this is how it should be, giving up on her front and back and diving into the landscape and 'being in 360 degrees', as she describes. And, as she continues, she feels more and more at home under the infinite sky, in the openness, where backwards means forwards in landscape's omnidirectionality. And when I listen to her recordings, I do hear her heartbeat in her walking … intertwined with the sounds of the wind …

And while walking she keeps wondering: What if all those shapes, forms, textures and qualities of the landscape could live within me? What does it mean to fully take it all in and engage? Then she feels being stuck in soaked shoes, a limiting her restriction. What does it mean not to want anything? And she feels nourished in silencing with the movement around her. 'Does the tree feel the same as I do when I'm touching it?', she wonders (*Cove Park Journals*, April 2018). Skin to skin, surface to surface. And in her continuous exploration in backward walking, she discovers that human beings moving forward all the time seem to be losing their real nature, the nature that is not separable from Nature around.

Then, by the end of the day, she shares in her reflective writing:

I am yearning for silence to hear the rain.

[...]

This place calls for time, a lot of time, or no time at all. Thoughts wonder, thoughts about my journey back. Transitioning again, different, me carrying a special landscape, wild, rough, beautiful with me, in me. I want more of this diving into, losing time, losing concepts.

Familiarity, pause ... no words come to mind ...

I feel the warmth in my fingers, warm blood ... my skin, especially my feet still sense and carry the barefoot walking on the land, in, with the land, they feel so much more alive.

I am grateful.

Connecting to the 'many sides' of nature, or the 'no sides of nature', every form every movement.

Beauty, no restrictions, no lines, no borders, no fences, no this and that, and that is this.

Free movement, possibility all over.

Being called into every form -

Shaping, moving, until we dissolve.

(*Cove Park Journals*, April 2018)

And I now connect it to Conrad's words, when she says: 'Every time there is dissolve, a new life can be formed' (2007: 94).

Then another mover too writes, after her intimately rich time of felt thinking about Life barefoot (as captured in stills in Figure 21.13):

FIGURE 21.13: Cove Park, April 2018.

I suppose there's no such thing as a dead thing ...
Life unfolding
Heart surrenders; hurts
Unknown all is
The Earth has my heart
I am married to the Earth

She holds me
A million years ago I began
My evolutionary journey
Ancestors plus ancestry
Are the starts and the rocks
So sad now …
Arising tears
Death and Life in each moment
What is 'this'?
I surrender and open my heart.

(*Cove Park Journals*, April 2018)

And I see this contemplation inspired by the found earlier that day heart-shaped fungi, growing within the bushes over the brook … on which she finger-wrote: HEART, and then held it in her hand and looked at it while sitting within the brook's moving waters, for a meaningful while …

FIGURE 21.14: Video still, Cove Park, April 2018.

Then, her song comes in as well, and the song goes like this:

When I Was Young
When I was young
I was the sun
Shone through the trees
Down to the ground

When I was young
I was the mountain
Knew all the birds
Had my own vision
When I was young
I was the river
Flowed through the mountain
Into the sea
When I was old
I was the ocean
Held all my friends
Throughout the end
I am I am
I am I am
I am I am
I am I am
We are
We are
We are
We are …

'Being with is nothing but being is nothing but IS', and to sum up our explorations on experiential responsiveness, I feel that this is exactly where we have been today, ongoingly – in the 'is-ness' of things, 'and, and, and, and, and, …' where we managed to sense 'the glimpses of the non-dualistic nature of life […] in wordless wonder' (*Cove Park Journals*, April 2018) and in full responsiveness on what and who we are, as part of the natural world around.

And my own experiences of finding that living and moving us agency within Cove Park's lands, as this second dimension into felt thinking takes over, provide me with another opportunity to follow the callings of the sheep, right after collecting my felt thoughts sitting hidden, in a shade of a bush, as described in previous section.

I walk driven by the sunshine, following the voices, and indeed, I soon encounter a big herd of sheep. I also see something we were supposed to mind as a visiting group, i.e. the Scottish farmland rule to keep all gates closed at all times – I see an open gate. I quickly check on the stirred with my approaching presence herd, seeing that a few sheep are indeed outside of their fenced territory, and I keep approaching slowly. The sheep freeze to observe all tendencies in my movement and they are accepting my pace, for a while, until I come too close. Then, in an instant, they flee and chase back through the open gate.

One sheep stays, though (see Figure 21.15).

FIGURE 21.15: *The Meeting*, Cove Park, April 2018.

(S)he is looking at me carefully, observing my every move and I slow down even more and start talking to him/her, as if I met a friend on a path, and together we slowly establish a 'safe distance'. The sheep releases from his/her stiff posture, as (s)he sense I stopped targeting her/him in the walk but simply start moving around him/her while talking. I sense her/him being brave, as the only one that stayed with me on 'the other side of the fence'. (S)he also allows me to take close up pictures of her/himself and continues grazing while keeping his/her eyes on me …

I continue moving around for a while and then open the gate even wider so (s)he knows (s)he can always go back, and I cross it myself and join the whole herd in my improvised movement amongst them, scattered all over the hill (see Figure 21.16).

The herd reacts as a group, or a 'super-organism' (Conrad 2007), they keep silent to watch me, then sound one another if they feel I approach them too close. They also rush away in packs to rearrange if I move too rapidly. And after a while of this improvised exchange in movement and sound, I encounter a spot with bare sheep bones, all exposed. I sit in contemplation, admiring the structure of the full length of spinal cord bones, and part of me, following my amazement in how airy the bone structure of the cord is, wants to blow some air through it, just like I used to play flute when I was a child. And similarly to a flute, playing different sounds with different keys, I discover each bone having an extraordinarily unique shape while joining them, on the inside, the airy hole is smooth and consistent in its tunnel-y, sleek shape, all the way through.

FIGURE 21.16: *Moving Thoughts Journal, Dancing with Sheep* (video stills), April 2018.

Again then, the experience adds up to today's wonderings about the interpenetrating opposites, the form and the flow or the structure and the living force relationships and makes it very tangible to relate, both physically and emotionally. I leave the site as I found it, including the open gate. I also finally feel, I have now arrived, connected and tangibly exchanged not only with this place but also with my animalistic self.

I sense the mesodermic dynamism awakening in my own bones too, and I feel ready for whatever comes next.

Moving Towards Experiential Responsiveness
in Psychological Time – Key Terms

Opening | Openness - Time / Timelessness - Forward while Backwards - Surrender - Releasing - Unfolding Backwards - Permeating | Penetrating - Feminine / Masculine - Ongoing Change and Changing - Co-creating - Cruelty - Abrupt Change / With-nessing | Danger - Noise / Resonating - Breathing in/with - Peacefulness - Living on in Dying - Beauty next to Cruelty - Moving with and Animating - Sipping into - Sounding into - Omni-directionality - Being in 'No Thinking' - Growing out - Never-ending - Animal Voice - Transitioning - Voicing movement - Open space / Endless possibility - Open shapes - Dynamic complexity - Complexity - Something and Nothing - Something in Multiplicity - Freedom in Multiplicity

III

Moving with Responsibility and Insightful Intuiting in Primordial Time, or On *Why* and *How* of Being

FIGURE P3.1: *Moving Thoughts Journal – Towards Insightful Intuiting*, Cairngorms National Park, Highland. Photograph by Noemi Dako.

I'm sitting on a big pile of rocks again,
　And 'on' the sound of underground water rushing underneath it all ...
　What a force ...! Built on all its grace ...
　It just has to travel ...
　I feel mainly water too ...
　Water ..., it its true relation to the earth ...
　Springing out of it, like a new born baby and then expanding and growing, and travelling the world, merging with other water species, shaping the land, curving the continents, and hugging it all constantly on the go, constantly changing, filled with air, then evaporating, to travel even farther, through the air.
　It almost feels like the creative life force is all about the ability to connect, permeate, and transform ...
　A will and unspoilt curiosity about delving into another element ...
　While sharing its own way of being ...
(Moving Thoughts Journal, April 2018 [edited])

My first thoughts upon the cited above, and awakened in movement, relation to the natural elements – pull me towards a quick refreshment of how we, as human beings, like myself, are able to physically, through the engagement of all the body systems, open up to the environment. Our complex nervous system, with its functional ability to coordinate all the activities of the body, is what we call consciousness or what Susan Aposhyan (1999) calls the 'natural intelligence', i.e. the intelligence that arises out of our bodily resources, and it is also where our human ability to know ourselves resides.

The complexity of the nervous system in human beings is definitely something that distinguishes and sets the human beings apart from the rest of creation, at the same time though, it is where we should find our deepest connection to the living environment too – for the mentioned coordination, happening within the nervous system, is an ongoing process and an embodied ability to both respond and adapt to the changes inside and outside of the body.

We live through and thanks to an ongoing dialogue happening between oneself and the environment around. And all life on Earth shares that quality of adaptive change, yet the sensitivity of human kind, which translates itself onto the physically achievable complexity of movement we are capable of, is definitely unique.

It seems that at this stage of my movement practice, I am entering the deeper layers of what simply feels right, and why and how the movement comes about. I am entering the enteric nervous system, my 'brain in the gut', which functions primarily without any direct input from the central nervous system. I simply am with what emerges.

And the mentioned in previous sections importance of feeling safe to engage with the living environment in movement plays a vital role here in the way I am able to express my sense of belonging to what I see, touch, smell or sense remotely.

It also becomes clear to me that the majority of my explorations in movement have been happening within the autonomic nervous system that collects information from the somatic system as well, and so it is important to pause here, and have a reminder about the 'towards and away from' relationality within the nervous system as a whole.

And so, thanks to the work of the afferent and efferent spinal nerves, the spinal cord is the link between the brain and the nerves in the rest of the body. The afferent spinal nerves are responsible for carrying information from the body to the brain, and the efferent nerves carry information from the brain to the body. The work of the central nervous system, of brain and spinal cord, is supported by the complexity of the peripheral nervous system, which subdivides into the somatic and autonomic systems (Cohen et al. 2012).

The peripheral nervous system, like the central system, functions thanks to the afferent and efferent neurons that translate information back and forth between the body and the external stimuli. Somatic nervous system operates on carrying and processing both motor and sensory information connected to skin, sensory organs (of hearing, touch and sight) and skeletal muscles. And, the automatic nervous system is then further divided into sympathetic and parasympathetic nervous systems, with the former one responsible for fright, fight, flight or freeze reactions, and the latter one responsible for the digestive functions, the repair and recuperation.

Going back to my practice, I am now able to breathe whole bodily, deepening the relaxed receptivity that supports more complex connections to be noticed and acknowledged, both physically and emotionally. I feel more and more integrated as a living continuation of everything around me, while being the centre of it all at the same time. I am becoming more and more aware of the layered-ness of experience and how it all belongs together, including myself within life's multiplicity, while the highly vascularized regions of my abdomen and the solar plexus feel very present in lowering my heart rate and integrating my often scattered breathing patterns. And, as my presence in felt thinking matures while sitting on the rocks caressed by the warmth of the sun, I now relate it to Andrea Olsen's explanatory comment, when she writes:

> Focusing attention on the brain can be foolish – even dangerous – if it is not rooted in autonomic connections. When the visceral body is ignored, we can find our stomachs queasy, moods irritable, heads aching, and vision disoriented. As we return

our attention to the needs of the organs and digestive tract through the autonomic nervous system, integration lets us move wholeheartedly through our lives.

(2002: 50)

And that following this restful process that allows recovery and integration for all the body systems, it is often during this parasympathetic state, and which for me includes also my intuitive art work taking shape, that 'things start to make sense, and that we have a clear insight or image about seemingly disparate thoughts and experiences' (Olsen 2002: 51).

Bergson too states, I rephrase, that to reach a higher level of intuition it is not necessary to transport ourselves outside the domain of the senses, but to admit that knowledge is not completely resolvable into the terms of intelligence, but to combine what can be achieved through both sensuous and intellectual intuition (Ansell-Pearson 2018b). For Bergson then, intuition denotes neither a vague feeling nor a disordered sympathy but a method that aims at precision in philosophy.

As explained already then, the enteric nervous system, or the 'brain in the gut' processes sensory information and maintains homeostasis with little interaction with the central nervous system, yet remains in constant communication with it. The ongoingly developing studies of the system, which is lined with more than 100 million nerve cells, show that attending to its unconscious functioning and its intuitive hints can affect mood, cognition and behaviour as well as improve quality of life. And that we can notice that, 'when we engage all the dimensions of our nervous system potential, we feel supported by, rather than in conflict with, our deepest motivations' (Olsen 2002: 53).

This dimensionality of experience of the self in time shared and co-created with the environment, which I call ontogenetic, and with all the sensed complexity of endless processes happening at the same time, is clearly communicated in my movement. And so, as often as time is associated with a form of order, it is becoming more and more feel-able to me that it can also divert creatively into differently experienced phases, loops, bypasses, etc., establishing thus specifically inclusive relationships to my ever changing image if it.

Following from the previously described phases, understanding of time as creative flow, consisting of succession of events, can now be easily expanded to its polychronic version, as a flow of multiple or endless perhaps successions and overlaps of events alongside the emerging from the data felt thinking about self as time, or time as self.

Ansell-Pearson too writes about the irreducibility of Nature, saying that 'we should not allow our need for unity of knowledge to impose itself upon the multiplicity of nature', or 'shrink nature to the measure of our ideas' (Ansell-Pearson

2018b: 95). And, that 'change, transformation, and evolution are bound up with living and open systems' (Ansell-Pearson 2018b: 93).

And, if time emerges here as relevant to the creative processes sensed both in Nature and within myself, it must be closer to its Bergsonian definition, who talked about more human (or humane, perhaps) notion of time than Einstein did. Time is action. It is the emergence of something new taking place. And, as Jimena Canales (2015) reminds, Bergson's favourite metaphor was about waiting for the cube of sugar to dissolve, or stir it to make the dissolving or disappearing of it faster, and which does say a lot about how one can influence the experience through creating its time-based possibility. Time is real, as Bergson would say.

And in contexts of return to the qualities of the parasympathetic system within my bodily experience which favours taking time for any recuperation and transformational change to happen, in his Tibetan teachings on the *Joy of Being*, Rinpoche Tarthang Tulku (2016) too reminds that it is only through relaxation obtained in the internal integration of the self that the true nature can come to forth.

Through the power of relaxation then, and I would add the inner trust in Life itself, I believe that our true nature can find its way to the foreground, cutting through habitual conditioning, clock-time pressures and cultural anxieties. And while we use the body and the breath as the main vehicles, it is the power of relaxation that heals our conditioning and discloses that we really are the light, radiant beings (Tulku 2016).

But let us follow the movement experience itself here, to speak for itself, after my reflective and reflexive modes of being with the experience have merged into a new, profound depth of being that experience.

22

Multi-dimensionality and Permeability in Movement

I'm sitting on the rocks …
With a grassy hill as my horizon,
Sitting by a barb-wired fence
Waiting for the sheep …
[…]
Looking at the birds, flying above
All those divisions, and walls
They couldn't bother less …
[…]
crossing that fence felt such a big thing to do …
but now that I'm here,
it feels like nothing
feels like just a little step
in getting me here, and that's
where I'm supposed to be.

(*Moving Thoughts Journal*, March 2017)

FIGURE 22.1: *Moving Thoughts Journal, On The Sheep Side*, September 2018.

Having already sensed the described depths within the nervous system, it is important to remember that movement, as we use the term in its singularity, is the movement of All (that is), the multidirectional and multidimensional movement(s) of various temporalities, some slower, some faster ... happening all at the same time. It is impossible to separate one movement from another, it/they coexist. I am also 'arriving' at deeper places within myself, crossing borders I never thought possible, as I describe above, and joining a herd of sheep again by jumping over fences.

Sinking deeper into my experience, I am now able to feel think alongside the simple yet always relational pulsing movements of a breath cell in its circular embrace, as a way of transcending dichotomies of relation and following the changeable dynamics of movement-based ontological creativity.

Relationality of such basic movements points me to the fact that at the core of my own sensitivity resides an inborn capacity for care, or better even, 'care for life'. And this systemic, within the bodily organs, care brings all the movement in constant relationship with itself and other. Coming into relationship gives a form to otherwise not visible, it is a process of materializing the feel-able.

My emotions become e-motions, the eternal motion, the guiding force of the archaic affect, and I stop having the need to understand where it all comes from. The connection I sense is self-explanatory. Like in the embracing it all breath of movement forward and backwards – on an inhale, it embraces me moving away from myself and towards the world, and, on an exhale, it embraces me moving towards myself and away from the world. One movement in its endless creativity and omnidirectionality of the in-between-ness.

And if our life is so relational and malleable, as I sense it is, again and again, it is the patterns of movement, perceived as constant entities that bring us support and comfort. How and why we obtain that support though is a matter of an open and cared for relationship. Sometimes it is just that warmth of a sun shine on my back that is enough to 'feel one with' the life around.

> Bare feet on the grass, aaahhh! Finally!
>
> How good is it to be reminded that the softness of this ground covered with thick layers of moss with grass is soft because of volumes of water it stores underneath ... the Scottish grounds, literally sinking into the soil ... as if you were giving every step to the Earth ... not owning it ...
>
> And so in moving forward, I add another layer of dimensionality, I go down-forward and sideways at the same time, and that makes it so much more difficult to do. Adding directions, open to all the possibilities of movement ... in water, with water.
>
> (*Moving Thoughts Journal*, April 2018)

And so sensing this multi-directionality in movement makes me feel think that control is possible only in simple, or limited to linear, patterns. Once the multi-dimensionality of movement is sensed, controlling the directional movement becomes very demanding and the only solution to that is surrender, and working with the playfulness of possibility ... Then, my curiosity kicks in.

And, as an integral part of functioning in multidimensional reality, moving becomes part of life as a creative process, somewhere between endless openness and directionality. I re-discover that later too, while playing with clay.

FIGURE 22.2: *Moving Thoughts Journal, A Living Thing*, May 2018.

Curiosity is always there, isn't it? What am I going to make? Out of the material that I have. Shape is changing every second, and I am shaping some sort of a hand, as I thought at first, but now it looks more like a texture-juicy star, with a lot of inside body, and looks like a starfish now as I expand its arms with some good imprint of my own fist tight squeeze.

> It is the starfish that I see, the shape that came up … but it also looks a lot like any living thing … be it a human or another animal, with the head being the fifth limb. The sensing limb that picks up directions, and the conditioning it fluid spine, which comes as a deep crack in my clay's shape.
>
> And it really feels feasible to me now that the head used to be a limb …
>
> After all, one of those limbs had to lead(!)
>
> And so the need for senses (on the head) could have come along as responding to that need for leadership, for giving some sort of unified movement to so many options of moving in different directions.
>
> (*Moving Thoughts Journal*, May 2018)

After that, I become more and more eager to connect with multiple modalities of materials, trusting the emerging shapes. The directionality will come along anyway, even if I keep expanding on its possibilities for 'anything else', or simply 'going nowhere' by creating chaos, or a mess. And indeed, it comes, alongside the melodies that come out of my mouth, as if guiding it, while having my hands engaged in crafting the shapes up.

> With cold hands …
>
> I would like to work with a cross-selection of drawing materials …
>
> I've just opened the water paints, as well as soft pastels, oil pastels, just to grab a pencil as well.
>
> I think I'm looking for warmth in the many, and in the colour choice …
>
> Helps me release my humming, singing voice …
>
> (drawing, singing)
>
> I feel like I'm voicing relationships …
>
> Earth, Water, Air, Sound, Feeling …
>
> And their creative process …
>
> Their melodies …
>
> (*Moving Thoughts Journal*, May 2018)

And the spiral, 'building upwards' imagery takes over, as in this pastel work in Figure 22.3.

By reading and reflecting on the above, it is interesting to notice that the experience of being with breath as movement, and in movement, enables new understandings of many opposite realities like the internal/external, hot/cold, silent/noticed, etc., as its flowful movement stretches wide in-between the physical and the metaphorical, or the metaphysical.

In my somatic experience, breath, as it seems, grows from its basic in and out exchange to movement exceeding the physical realm of association and connects

FIGURE 22.3: *Moving Thoughts Journal, Dizzy Voice Sprout,* June 2018.

me to the wider contexts of eternal flow which lies, surprisingly, within 'the bodily' as well.

In her book *Body and Earth*, Andrea Olsen (2002: 114) also writes about the multifacetedness of breath and that it can touch us deeply on the emotional level as much as it can be a soft massage to the organs through the workings of the diaphragm on the physical level at the same time.

And to expand further on its physical dimensions, the workings of the breath are ever more connected to the workings of the heart as well, which pumps the oxygenated blood to every cell of the body. Every cell, and human body, consists of trillions of them, breathes, and the exchange between air and blood happening in bronchioles, and the expel of the carbon dioxide from the lungs, as well as removal of waste materials through the semipermeable cell membranes in osmosis, continues throughout this process of intake and release all the time.

'Two crus muscles, or crura, of the diaphragm attach to the front of the spinal column through connective tissue extending to the tip of the coccyx' (Olsen 2002: 114). Thus, the tail and the pelvic floor are as much involved in the deeper breathing processes. And to initiate breath, a signal from the nervous system must be sent to the muscles of the diaphragm. Breathing then occurs multidimensionally and any change in its pattern results in a change of oxygen in the blood.

This multidimensionaly of breath translates too onto the movement of thoughts and emotions, being reflected in our breath instantaneously. As Olsen further writes, it increases the heart rate and tightens breathing muscles even before we realize that a thought has taken place. And she points to the fact that the ongoing exchange of 'interior and exterior landscapes', as she calls them, happens reflexively, without our attention, and yet it can also be observed and affected by conscious awareness (Olsen 2002: 115). And such merger of internal and external worlds, as present in somatic movement experience helps to release any tensions that mask sensations and helps to notice the 'sensitive interplay of breath' (Olsen 2002: 115).

And to connect back to the introductory relation of wit(h)nessing breath with the subjective 'I', in Ettinger's (2006) matrixial theory, and co-emerging in relation to the 'non-I', Olsen too writes that the patterns of breath can reflect rhythms that go beyond our current time/space engagements, like that of mother's breath in pregnancy, the birth process itself, or other impressionable events in life that become fixed in the neural circuitry (Ettinger 2006).

Rephrasing Bergson (1988) too, our actual existence then, while it unrolls in time, always duplicates itself along with its virtual existence. It is because the present does not simply follow the past but co-exists with it and every recollection is created alongside an actual perception.

'The double movement of contraction and expansion by which consciousness narrows or enlarges the development of its content' (Bergson 1988: 166) that Bergson talks about, definitely speaks through the somatic experience as one that suggests that in an open interaction of the two contradictory yet complementary ways there is always a form of potency of the third dimension of movement possible.

And by placing Life at the centre of the study of Nature as Bergson did too, such vital impetus can be conceived neither as pure unity or pure multiplicity, 'neither purely internal finality nor absolutely distinct individuality' (Bergson et al. 2007: 42). This is because 'within any actual perception it is the totality of recollections that are present in an undivided, intensive state' (Bergson 1988: 85) and which foreground future events as well.

Thus Bergson suggests that it is possible

> to cultivate, through intellectual effort, a perception of life where we experience something of the very impetus of creative life itself or what he describes as the push of life and that has led to the creation of divergent forms of life from a common impulsion, such as plant and animal.
>
> (Bergson 1988: 98)

In *Creative Evolution*, Bergson's conclusive thoughts are that 'life does not proceed by the association and addition of elements, but by dissociation and division' (Bergson et al. 2007: 89). To sum up my somatically sensed experiences in felt thinking though, and perhaps to expand on Bergson's suggestion, I feel that that the processes of dissociation and division are, nevertheless, always accompanied by those of synthesis and symbiosis, happening at the same time. Even though it seems too complex to comprehend in cognitive thought, it feels very natural in movement carried on the intuitive ontogenesis.

Further to that, thinking alongside Edward Hall's (1983) work in *The Dance of Life* again, and drawing on the fact that like my own body, the Earth's body follows its own biological timing, 'being with breath' can also connect me directly to the Earthy experience of this omnipresent activity.

The experiential exchange of in and out breath correlates then directly with Earth's cycles of movement in space, and day onto night or light into darkness transitioning. With Earth's activity during the day reflecting its proactive intensity for breath intake, and the night-time being a restful exhale turn in its enormous, time-wise scale. And being able to connect to that larger scale of earthy breathing in its rhythmic and periodic way through whole-bodily, cellular breathing, has an immediate influence on calming down my own, often disturbed by the daily load, breathing patterns, as much as it expands on the enriched felt sense of belonging within the Earthy life.

The Earth breaths in cycles as well, and Hall adds that: 'Sunspot cycles and the swelling and shrinking of the earth's primitive atmosphere like a huge beast breathing in its sleep all established a rhythmic change of environment that early life forms not only adapted to but eventually internalized' (1983: 16).

It is then worth adding, or correcting rather, that through the reflection on my somatic experiences so far, the change that Hall is referring to is not limited to early life forms on Earth but is a continuous and bodily sensed process that shapes ongoingly through every breath exchanged.

To sum up, our attention to the 'dances' of the breath can experientially bring one closer to both, what can be sensed when followed intuitively or imaginatively, and to what is cleansed and nourished in processes occurring through lung, diaphragm and cellular breathing throughout the whole body. Thus, somewhere between more traditionally understood anatomy and physiology transformed into the actual physical and emotional sensations, as Susan Aposhyan points out in her introduction to Bonnie Bainbridge-Cohen's book *Sensing, Feeling and Action*, a very intimate experience of the body arises, in which 'not only can we be aware *of* each part of our physical self, we can be aware *with* each part of our physical self' (2012: vvii).

And reflectively speaking, widening one's attention to breath in felt thinking has a strong potential for retrieving balance in important aspects of emotional, mental and physical wellbeing as well as for widening one's sense of belonging in all-encompassing contexts of earthy life. It can help moving beyond the limited frames of understanding that preclude life in materialistic terms as secluded selves and those that see breath as one's strife for life sustaining air, only.

In Ettinger's (2006) terms, it could be proposed to see the always alive and responsive exchange happening between the breath in and the breath out as a co-creative process that involves what she calls *self-fragilization*, as the 'I' meets the vulnerability of the 'non-I' in resonating transjectivity of the breath. And so, offering our witnessing attention to breathing in movement-guided way can be considered an unprecedented occasion for noticing its value not as a survival call only but as an aspect of shared and nourishing co-presence and ongoing co-emergence in life that is worth participating in, more consciously.

And I carry on felt thinking, while the process of 'movement becoming thoughts becoming words becoming movement' builds up its sweeping upswing again and again, leaving me feeling anew and refreshed. Then, while drawing again, I feel think:

[W]hat is the point of talking lines
when we live open shapes
what's the point of thinking lines
unless they can outgrow and expand
a line is just an abstraction
it's just an abstraction
of a multi-dimensional shape
of way more complicated movement
happening all the time
escaping all simplification
escaping contained understanding
possession
because it is open
and never-ending
and unless you agree to that
mobile nature of life
you can but comprehend it
while being with it
joining yourself while you live through life
with life of life within life
and perhaps if you want to make any sense of it
then you can always give it a temporal frame
as a container
allowing us to think:
'oh, i get it!'

(spinning around)
the very thought
is an abstraction
thought is a tool
and we have developed our toolbox amazingly ...
thought is a tool!
aren't we witty ...
aren't we the crafters!?
shapeshifters ...
drawing lines
making things make other things ...
by continuously contained movement ...
what do you think made us?
it is the Earth
the Earth's repetitious movement
we have been created by it
we have been created by the circular movement of the Earth around the Sun
while it lives and creates life in the same way
by repeating the pattern of night and day
by living the transformative power
of creation
closing the circle is after all also sharing
and so it shares life
it shares its own life
with creating anew
through constant reshaping
there is no escape
if the circle of day and night is closed,
there will always be life
and its safe-contained opposite
I wonder what would happen
to the shape of our thoughts
and our bodies
if the circle of night and day
was to be altered
or opened
what if a day could follow another day
without a night in between
would it still be two
feels like opening the circle

would not necessarily mean killing it
and so what if the Earth
was once following a different pattern around the Sun in space?
what new shapes would the life on Earth grow
I wonder
and perhaps one day it will happen
or perhaps one night ...
depending on who is talking
or who is doing the thinking
(drawing)
isn't that amazing how yellow and blue, the night and day colours make green?
it's not like the Earth had a choice becoming a blue planet with all its green.

(Moving Thoughts Journal, July 2018)

And looking back at the movement material shaping during such like enlightening moments, I see my body yearns for omnidirectional connections between all the living world elements, the elements that I embody as well. Air, water, earth and the fire-y emotional stir within myself permeate movement in its physical extensions and reaches between the ground and the above, and 'the emotional' joins in as wind, as visible in the stills below, both outdoor and indoor (see Figures 22.4 and 22.5).

Then, in the remainder of my movement process, I feel complete and satisfied. I say less and less, simply trying to embrace the awe for life I feel inspired by, and I feel more and more myself.

I also keep coming back to the spiralling imagery that has been with me all along, and in which I have found my own key to relationality of movement, and

FIGURE 22.4: *Moving Thoughts Journal*, *The Surge*, June 2018.

FIGURE 22.5: *Moving Thoughts Journal*, *Life Turns*, June 2018.

FIGURE 22.6: *Moving Thoughts Journal*, *The Spiral's Imprint*, May 2018.

where with the slightest change in intention while spiralling inwards I am able to redirect the movement and start spiralling out (see Figure 22.6). And which makes me feel that the ongoing change in life happens in most minute ways we carry on with in every breath, and anytime we care to pay attention.

And I am sensing that healing, like insightful contemplation of creative process, happens when I allow and commit myself, as in believing, to be healed, and that's what the process of self-care offers and what Nature, including my own, can support in achieving.

Looking back at my process of felt thinking, I can now conclude that intuitive guidance inspired by movement comes along trusting the existential depths we share with Nature. The irreducible complexity of relational dynamics of back and forth movement that we embody reveals itself in the healing or re-balancing processes of self-care, while caring is the life-sustaining relationship between the movement towards and the movement away from the self.

And although there is, so far, no way of equating the physical with the metaphysical, as Hall points out, 'the fact cannot be a basis for writing off the mass of human experience, in all cultures, with this extraordinary dimension' (1983: 19). And as a form of final exemplification that combines the elaborated on three dimensions of practice in felt thinking, I would like to ponder over this movement session that directed me to the experiential depths of the pelvic floor (see Figure 22.7) and translated itself into an environmentally inclusive and definitely enlightening comprehension of the self in my voicing session.

FIGURE 22.7: *Moving Thoughts Journal*, *The Fly Open*, May 2018.

I feel a strong tendency towards rest today,
  I've just been trying to tune into breath …
  And I'm not the only one breathing in here …

Settling into a restful position takes me straight to reflecting upon the quality of being at rest. And from that little exploration on the quality of being I arrive at that most common yet perhaps quite misinterpreted question of:

'How am I today?'

And yet I have not encountered anybody answering this question in any other way but 'good', 'so so', or 'bad', etc.

And I think it is a great way for me to start today, just being with that question and give it as much as I can.

How am I?

(loud bird noises)

I am with the warmth of a cushion under my back as I'm lying on the floor, my left side has been stretched out a little as if pulling towards the sounds of the birds ... the loud seagulls and some softer chirping.

I'm agitated a little by the sounds of a buzzing fly in the space ... and as I receive the sounds mainly from the right side of the space, I feel like my right shoulder wants to sink in a little bit toward the rest of the right side of the body in some sort of a twitchy, discomfort-y way and putting a frown on my face as well. Ok, that's better now, my shoulder got some comfort.

How else am I?

I am lighter, enjoying the warmth of the day, I feel the joy of the whole body cells ... sensing the spring time in bloom.

Cold fingertips remind me of the freshness in the air.

(yawning, sounding)

(background sound of an airplane)

And having been brought up by the field airport the sounds of the planes keep reminding me it is a sunny day – a good day to fly.

And there is this fly buzzing again flying around the space ...

How else am I?

I am soft and spongy, ready to belong to the space, yearning to feel the air in my fingers, in the palms of my hands ... inside my head ...

I feel quite airy today ...

And I want to invite air deeper into my bones, to both sides of my pelvis, with my right side of it experiencing some stubborn pain ...

(sighing)

And so my easiest guess about that question about the 'how' of the being is that it would take a lot of feeling qualities from weather conditioning, like today, I am airy, I feel sun-lit, light and spacious, because it is a warm sunny day with spring freshness felt in my breath and while I am moving with the temperature nuances between the fresh and cool, and the warmer I am developing some rocky movement in my pelvis.

The playful rocking with all my limbs up, massaging the lower back with the floor. And the swaying I give into helps me get up so lightly, and I thought it would be so difficult to do initially ... it gives me a lot of freedom ...

And from the rocking it is such an easy transition onto the fours ... and very easy to get up as I'm being drawn towards the warmth and light.

And it makes me wonder – where is the lightness inside?

Do we have the inner light? And where is the darkest and the deepest place in my body?

I am drawn to the deepest vastness under my tummy.

To the pelvic floor ... and, this is also the same place I would look for the light!

I feel it could be quite a centralized location where the light mixes with the dark, and where they both reside. I would not locate them anywhere separate, in any kind of polarized positions ... I would rather feel the light resides in the deepest dark, embraced and protected by it, nesting it ...

And so I have been deeply drawn today to the pelvic environment, the symmetrical bone structure shaped beautifully by its round circulatory spaciousness ...

(looking at hands stretched out open like the pelvic bones)

Being with that sense of embrace that provides both protection and a gate to the open, the airy chamber where the dark meets the light, and where the light rests within darkness.

This is where time is made

This is where time comes alive

As time is the play, the lived interplay

Between the darkness and the light

Creating this most amazing shape reaching out and sitting in at the same time, reminding me that such opposite movements are possible to be performed at the same time in slow motion.

Reminds me that the breath in starts already somewhere in the breath out, there is no border line.

And that we visualize movement too much, forgetting and losing its felt multi-dimensionality inherent in every glitch.

So how am I? ...

I am The How ...

(*Moving Thoughts Journal, Felt Thinking in Movement*
audio transcript, May 2018)

23

Feeling with the Land:
Stories in Insightful Responsibility

FIGURE 23.1: *In Insightful Intuiting*, Drumdollo, Aberdeenshire. Photograph by Anna Dako.

It is Sunday morning. I wake up to see that after yesterday's sun, the rain has finally arrived. And this additional humidity in the air intensifies the smells of the earth, the vast Scottish wetlands. I see water penetrating the spongy grounds. And I feel like I am also being rinsed, and cleansed, and so are the heavy thoughts I have been collecting and carrying within myself for a long time. They too start dissolving and flowing up to my widened awareness in lighter forms.

It is the third, final day of the shared residency time and I begin my morning session sobbing, as the awakened memories of visiting Cove Park for the first time come back to me. It was the time when I had my first close-up encounter with an awe inspiring bird, the heron, as she/he landed on a rock in the middle of a little pond and right in front of my face, having not noticed me at first, as I was sitting hidden from her/his sight. Yet, this majestic landing, which I could now describe as an amazingly graceful in its slow-motion delivery but very powerful in its spatial expression – vertical descent, has been followed by a moment of realization, the moment of recognizing my presence, and translated immediately into a single flap of wings, and an almost explosive, take off.

And I remember registering that moment as 'the past in the present in the future', as it happened so quick, and so unexpectedly, without any time to process. The heron took flight in less than a blink of an eye. And I know she/he was not expecting it herself/himself, yet her/his readiness to flee was astounding. She/he left me with a sense of 'loss', and my ongoing, since then, inner yearning for mastering active stillness, and which I felt had failed me on that day.

And indeed, in that very meeting, and to my own surprise as well, all my normally opposite associations of movement and stillness came together in the image of a heron, and its potent skill of stillness within a powerful thrust upwards. Movement within stillness and stillness within movement, as one being a continuous extension onto the other, not its opposite. And I find that realization both soothing and empowering, just like this place (see Figure 23.2).

Waking up with that memory, I then feel that our co-residing time, in its third day, is able to shape itself now. I suggest we let the day reveal itself, 'reveal the sense of place' (Seamon and Mugerauer 1989) and the sense of ourselves by allowing all responses to come forth as they will, shaping for us the deeper wonderings about 'How' and 'Why', in any form we sense relatable. In hope, we are able to offer insights about the non-physical, emotional implications of the place, and recognizing the existence of implicit (Gendlin 1993) characteristics of life that go beyond the many purely physical properties or forms, movement takes over in our studio space.

And we all start very slowly, from resting positions on the floor or carrying on from reflective work in the journals, which, for me, meant paying attention to the intangible qualities that might actually be essential attributes to the sense of wellbeing

FIGURE 23.2: *After the Take Off*, Cove Park, February 2018.

as well as releasing all the creative thinking in motion and its personalized interpretations. Today's depth of emotional relatedness to the earth, as I have felt from the start of the morning, reminds me that it certainly is not enough to generalize about the nature of being, as the differences in experiences are infinite, for everyone, and at any point in time, and yet the shared quality of co-presencing is always there too.

And indeed, this morning session feels like coming from so far away or from long ago without being elicited on purpose. I look around the space and I see everybody being together here and now, yet individually carrying on their own processes influenced by all, but following their consistent, individual paths.

Some are restful and some active, some work manually and some engage whole-bodily, some interact with the walls, some find comfort in others' backs, some hide under blankets and some jump over the collected throughout the space arts and crafts materials, some seek contact and some preferring to stay away (see Figure 23.3). We initiate, engage, merge, create and leave. We leave to seek other paths of connection, create, merge and initiate again. The session turns into a scene of co-existent multiplicity, full of individually meaningful moments to some while being observed or ignored by other, only to switch turns in another moment to come.

Experienced from my own perspective, I start in a long session of stillness and listening, while hearing a lot of activity taking place in the space already, my eyes are closed. I hear sounds of singing, humming, laughing. I also hear many sighs

FIGURE 23.3: Video stills, Cove Park, April 2018.

and moments of relief. I feel somebody lying down, like myself, close by, within my arm's reach, and I decide to stay with that sense of closeness on the floor for a long while, yet without doing anything physically.

With my eyes closed, all the auditory happenings in the studio spread amongst other movers in the group and grow in visual texture that I experience. I sense the air being filled with sound and movement, both intensive and restful and merging into a mesh of collected energy of many shapes. There is tapping on the floor, or humming, there are sounds of bare feet squeaking against the floor, there is a lot of breathing sounds, there is some slight hitting of elbows, heels or knees against different surfaces, and there is a lot of silence in between too.

I am lying down with my face on the floor now, picking up slightest nuances carried by the surface of the wooden floor and I feel that sensing through the contrasting differences is exactly what allows a deeper experience of connectivity to form within myself.

Movement permeates reflection, it permeates rest, then permeates finding comfort in whatever comes and it becomes movement again, abrupt or gentle, as it is the same and other at all times.

My session of lying in stillness while attending to the density of sound rising up in the space carries onto a slow creepy-crawly movement exchange with my lying in stillness mate. And after we find our separate ways again, I feel drawn to the light, and in crawling, I move across the space to meet the window glass with my face (see Figure 23.4). I start breathing on it and get joined by another mover in the presented below heartfelt exchange of 'breath and hand' dance. And the exchange engages others to watch, while letting that witnessing become a living process itself, translatable onto their own continuous reflection in movement, stillness or art-making as well, without any defined beginnings or ends.

Then, our exchange carries on into the middle of the space and picks up in playfulness and sharpness of movement until it reaches its dynamic peak in powerful pushes, pulls, lifts, tumbles and falls (see Figure 23.5). At this point, we are quite

FIGURE 23.4: Cove Park, April 2018.

FIGURE 23.5: Cove Park, April 2018.

aware of the shared space and how every development of movement influences others who are engaged in more stationary activities of resting, sleeping or artistic reflection work. And so, they appropriate their location as our exchange spreads out uncontrollably, causing a lot of laughter and heavy pounding from strenuous switches and shifts.

We all carry on, embracing the individual choices and following the intuitive developments of every moment in space. And at some point, slowly, the intensity changes its course too, as we get drawn to other happenings in the studio, while ever new constellations of interactions keep emerging.

And I now connect it to the fact that experience high in emotional content like that uses the wholeness of the environmental pattern of the place as a vehicle to sense its 'collective subconscious' (Jung 1960) in the power of the creative process and helps re-finding the shared roots while seeing the inclusivity of living environment around in rich unison.

I also experience that being pulled in and elevated by the creative dynamic of the lively exchange in improvised movement like this transforms a lot of internal stuck-ness and pain. It has been fascinating to feel how the letting go off control and any form of guidance is the guide itself, and how it builds its momentum in relational strengths and weakness of every shared moment. And I mean shared with everything and anything, as once I feel open to life around – there is no room for loneliness, or being alone within myself, unless framed or exposed as such in dedication. In my movement experience, the creative energy and active co-presence always translate itself onto something new, often unexpectable.

Visibly, this lifting and building up energy is also present for others and recognizable particularly in the art work of the day. As the image of a bird taking off comes along in my own clay work (see Figure 23.6) and gets accompanied by similar imagery of spinning upwards dynamics (see Figure 23.7), while sharing words like these:

So today I welcome everything.
I am meeting Whole.
The whole clay, not a piece
My hands are full
I think the ?
The 'How' is SPACE
To . . . .
. . . .
. . . .
So my question is …
What do I fill my space with and
How many layers of space do I have.

(*Cove Park Journals*, April 2018)

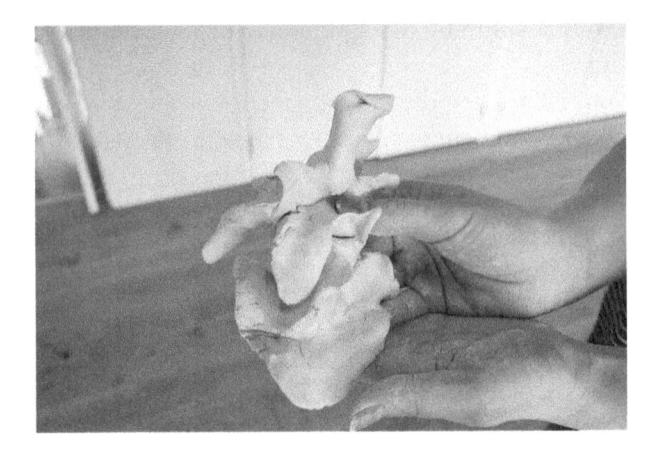

FIGURE 23.6: *Moving Thoughts Journal*, Cove Park, April 2018.

FIGURE 23.7: Cove Park, April 2018.

And the movement session continues with its multiplicity of flows and patterned engagements. My sudden need for spreading out an encountered shawl creates a base for another mover's invitation, as she lies down on it in contemplation. Her presence connects everybody around, as she seems dependent on the group's support. The shawl changes from a meaningless object to the centre of action, as in those shared moments we wrap her face in it and carry on with both conscious and intuitive touch-based assistance in what feels like in-depth and transformational renewal (see Figure 23.8).

Sharing movement in co-creative presence as this shifts emotional intensity and provides multiple openings for ongoing change. It comes with sense of relief while something new is being born. And the lifting energy takes over again, as the mover raises her arm up in a meaningful gesture.

FIGURES 23.8: Cove Park, April 2018.

Two other movers observing the shawl scene pick up tempos from there and begin to jump around the space creating a lot of stomping noise and versatile rhythms.

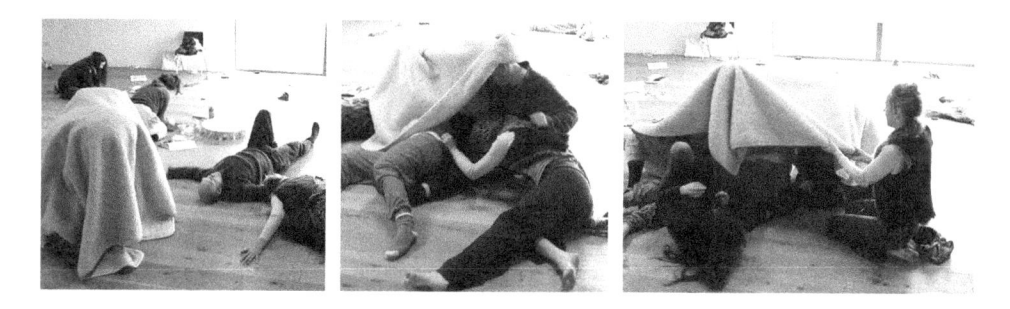

FIGURES 23.9: Cove Park, April 2018.

The sound permeates the space again. Through jumps, laughs, tapping and random drumming the released animal voices re-enter the space as we continue letting the movement engage with anything the space provides, on this occasion, it being a sheep skin-like blanket that gets twisted in the movement exchange (see Figure 23.9).

We become loud with sheep sounding, and wild with laughter and emotional discharge. The blanket creates a form of shelter, or skin almost, with the few of us, movers, becoming the animal's gut. The animal voice is very real in me, as if it has always been there, unheard and waiting for today to come, to unearth. And, in my personal experience, the transformational energies of the voice's final release reshape the whole time/space we are sharing as a group, as it feels malleable and moving together with us. I feel, we create each moment together and re-create ourselves in it as well.

Then, the slow takes over again. Moments of deep reflection in rest or supportive co-presence follow (see Figure 23.10), while the ongoingly meaningful little changes to what we offer to one another, including the presence of all the outdoor life we experience, carry on, on multiple creative paths, and for each of us, individually. The sense of spatial connectivity between the skies and the Earth and us in it fills my embodied sense of self. I feel both enriched and humbled at the same time.

FIGURES 23.10: Cove Park, April 2018.

By the end of the session, and despite the rain, one of the movers opens the glass door again, and the wet air enters the space carrying all its oxygenating support. The Shapeshifter too gets wet in the meantime and changes its aura (see Figure 23.11).

FIGURE 23.11: *Shapeshifter in the Rain*, Cove Park, April 2018.

And the supportive and the transformative experiences of the session find their place is one of the mover's words:

I want to be land for you sister
I want you to grow out of darkness and light,
out of stone and soil, out of roughness, wet, soft
and wet, juicy and dry. I am here for you,

I am serving. I am at your service. If you are
not here, I am not here.
I don't care. I give you ground to grow.
I am land for you sister ... I don't want anything.
(*Cove Park Journals*, April 2018)

This selfless offering of self and what Fraleigh (2004) calls 'self-surpassing' while becoming the true self in such a process and in not wanting anything in return becomes a very transformational experience that nourishes and grows in relational connection. And in the mover's journal, she is sharing that her felt thinking journey guided her towards the cited words from earth-listening, to earthing and finally to earthling. And that she has been experiencing the transitioning from being lost, as she did many times during her walking explorations outdoors, and feeling as if she is, now, entering the real nature of herself, the nature of possibility and new becoming(s).

Other sharings too reveal that the movers have touched upon the experiences they hold very dear to themselves and mention their personal meanings and the sacred, soulful dimensions.

For one of the movers, today has had an illuminating effect on seeing both grief and joy as extensions of one another, and which are blended in Nature as an animating force that 'doesn't give a damn' or 'has no sense of humour' (*Cove Park Journals*, April 2018). And so, in a way, they are the same, with one cry for everything, 'they are one revolving thread, the deepest dark and the brightest gold' (*Cove Park Journals*, April 2018). Then she writes how she feels today saying:

Everything unblocked, [...] The pressure is off both my womb, somehow, and my head. They are linked in some unique coordination of circuits I can't understand – but know how to intervene or live with. This is nature too, mine and not mine.
(*Cove Park Journals*, April 2018)

And what seems to be a connecting and re-emerging theme here is the one of being like a baby, who can switch from cry to joy in an instant, without any need for transitioning time indeed, and just like the heron's movement capabilities, confirming thus how close the opposite emotions, and their expressive qualities, reside with one another.

And the ongoing wondering about our relationship with life and its perversity continues, as I read along these eye-opening wonderings:

What are we exchanging with the earth?
All different sensual currencies.
How long will the exchange go on?

As long as it is beneficial to both parties …
[…]
Compromise and sacrifice
[…]
One leg forward
One leg backward
[…]
Freedom in containment
[…]
The dual womb
[…]
The spinal flute.

(*Cove Park Journals*, April 2018)

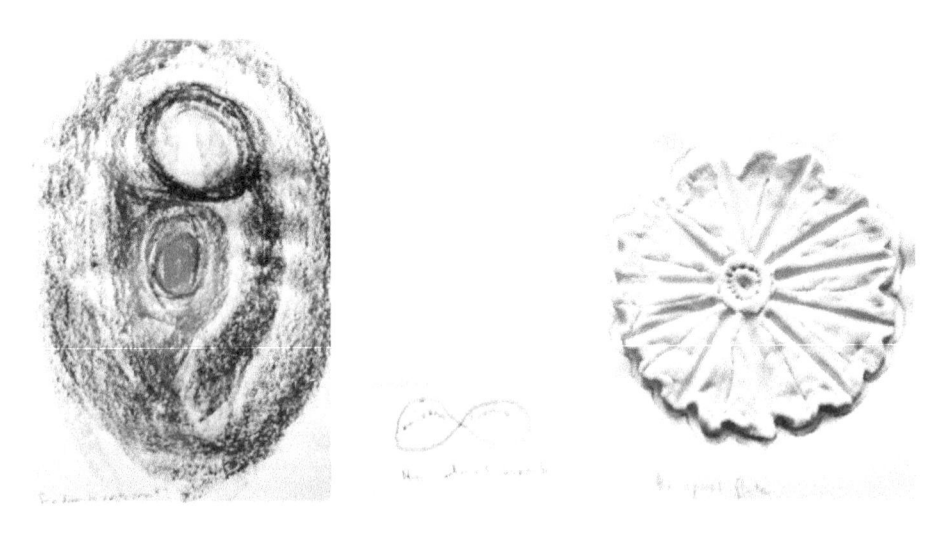

FIGURE 23.12: *Cove Park Journals*, 'Freedom in Containment' | 'The Dual Womb' | 'The Spinal Flute', Cove Park, April 2018.

Or these wonderings on belonging with the Earth:

How dare we pretend that we create?
[…]
Changing as the sun goes down, the earth turns and we don't know it. But we know it so we can 'knowfeel' it, or we can feel our knowing.
[…]
So bright in the darkness –

I don't need to own the land but the land
owns me, in 'not ownership' belonging.

(Cove Park Journals, April 2018)

Another mover mentions her sense of how unknowable many qualities of being are, and her own ability to tap into their territories, without grasping their totality but being familiar with aspects of landscapes only.

She carries the story of grieving within herself through re-lived memories about the loved ones, and the stories of the future of them not being there. She also mentions the beauty of 'this dance of life and death' (*Cove Park Journals*, April 2018), and the unknowable about what is happening on the Earth and with the earth. She senses ease connecting to other people with whom she shares sorrows through touch and being moved by touch, tending to all the experiences arising in response.

And she feels deeply grateful for the experiences of today, and the openness to honour what's arising through deep listening and shared processing within our hearts. She feels deeply nourished by the recognition she has received in 'resonating with other movers' (*Cove Park Journals*, April 2018).

In gratitude for this deeply cathartic experience, she says: 'I honour and welcome tears wherever they come from. And so I do welcome this, as a gift, and I now know that the earth has my back, and that's what I pray we all have' (audio transcript, Cove Park, April 2018). Then, in reference to the mentioned 'unknowable' in life, another mover reflects on how movement has always been a crucial help for her in creating the character , while working as an actor all her life. The mover shares from her professional experience that she never had a permission from the director to include the movement on stage, so after devising and embodying a role through movement backstage, she would have to carry on with the sensation of being the character, but cutting it off from the movement itself when performing on stage. As if the 'being' was possible for her only in movement.

The experiences of felt thinking in movement brought her to realize that she needs a tangible contact with everything around in Nature to feel it. She needs to be on her fours, in direct contact with the ground, trees, mud, etc. and only then she becomes herself. Simple looking at the landscape is not enough.

Yet experiencing that made her more and more curious about human nature, and about how she could possibly do the same with people. And, that only in that established contact in movement which she has shared with a few movers today she feels that she arrives at her real self. Only in contact with other, she experiences her own being. And the depth of such experiences with others makes her wanting to experience the darkness of such density further and further. And what stops her from carrying on is the fear for having permission to do so in such mutual exchange in movement, alongside her own fascination with death.

And she shares an example of her wish to experience water like that through lying on her back on the surface and carrying on submerging by arching her back backwards until her head is underwater and she cannot breathe anymore. 'How far can I experience the other and play with the danger of losing myself in it or hurting anyone?' (*Cove Park Journals*, April 2018 [translated]), she asks, wondering. And she keeps drawing flowers in her journal (see Figure 23.13). This time round, they also carry other movers names, together with sensed in movement personal qualities reflected in the shapes of the flowers.

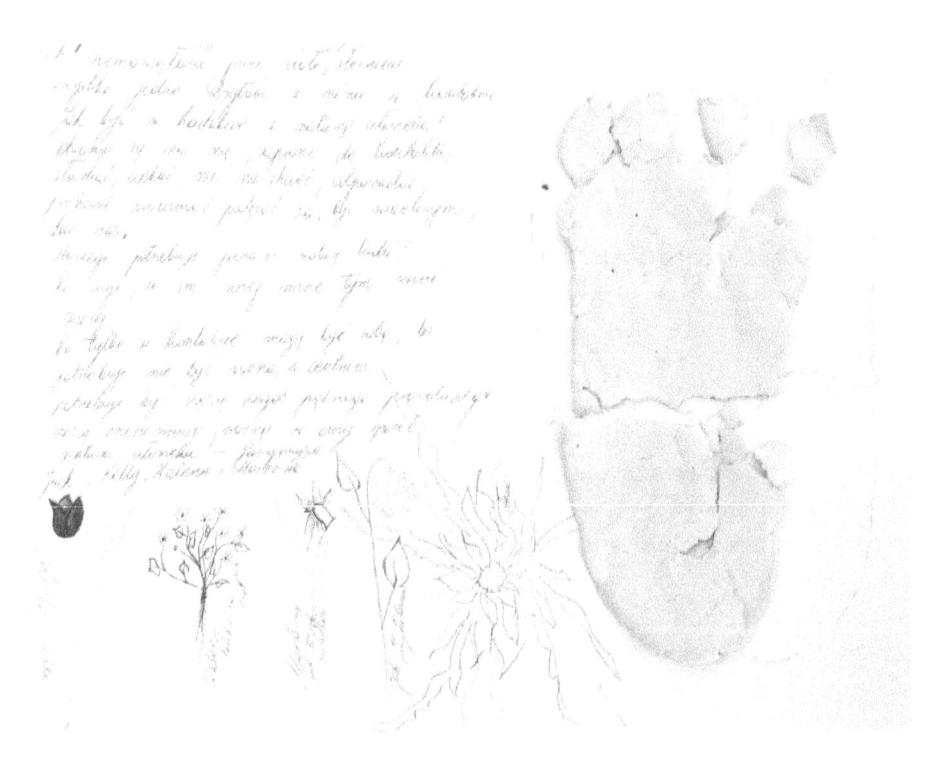

FIGURE 23.13: *Cove Park Journals*, April 2018.

By now, how the earth makes us feel, daily and ongoingly expresses us, as individuals, becomes another theme of wonder, for another mover (see Figure 23.14). And so are the sudden changes in weather conditions which has also been noticed to affect her on different levels.

And since it is about time for all of us to slowly part with the place, on this final day of residency, the aspects of time, its temporality as felt in the changeability of emotions and different heart beats have also been sensed.

Earth Day
Where When | What Who | How?
Rainy day
Just want to sit and pray
Rainy day
Then sunshine comes
A ray
Ray of light
Keep me warm
Hold me tight
Ray of light
Stay with me
Till the night
How?
Attending to time and temporality
Following the changes of the season
Getting inspired by humidity
Smell of the soil
Smell of the soil
Cuddle me

FIGURE 23.14: *Journal no. 7*, Cove Park, April 2018.

The mover mentions the fleeting sense of life, and the need for reflecting upon life passing, retrospectively but ongoingly, as well as finding ourselves in this constant loss and gain process. She has experienced a lot of 'relief in pausing today' (*Cove Park Journals*, April 2018), and she was accomplishing the pausing in art making and engaging with found objects, like the pieces of picked up sheep wool she was stitching together for half a day. She also mentions finding the wool entangled in different textures, as animal trails, stuck in grass or branches, and that she had experienced those findings as 'pieces of art' themselves.

And in this sensuous cosmos of movement, to use Abram's words, time 'is not separate from the circular life of the sun and the moon, from the cycling of the seasons, the death and rebirth of the animals – from the eternal return of the greening earth' (1996: 185).

Collecting of wool was like bringing the animal trails together with her own while she was walking and encountering them, 'so they can meet and stay together in a paused moment', in her artwork (see Figure 23.15). And she also points to how pleasant it is to smell the wool …

FIGURE 23.15: *Cove Park Journals*, April 2018.

And indeed, with all the sensed changes happening for all of us individually yet brought about as a group of friends, we now notice that the sun is out, yet still in a drizzly relationship with the rain.

With a few final sounds of a drum, which felt like another voice heard, we get pulled outside again to embrace in what we have all experienced as an amazing time together with our Nature/selves in ongoing wondering, and finding the essence of Nature in our own surrender to the flow of things … 'I close my eyes, I am a circle' (*Cove Park Journals*, April 2018).

FIGURE 23.16: Video still, Cove Park, April 2018.

And the open-ended questions of *How* and *Why* that brought so much depth on this last day of our movement explorations with Nature at Cove Park shape into these concluding felt thoughts:

Last snatches of the walks I didn't have – along the top and down with the mossy waterfall stream …

And came back with the conclusion – How? Like this – non-violent conditions of acceptance and growth – making them everywhere and for everybody.

Why? – because the earth can't take anymore abuse and neither can we.

I fell in love with it (the place) and falling in love with it made me cry

FIGURE 23.17: *Cove Park Journals*, April 2018.

FIGURE 23.18: Video still, Cove Park, April 2018.

And as we conclude this amazing journey together in shared hugs and thanks to one another, all I can hear around us is the loud presence of the sheep, and when I raise my eyes up to the skies, I can taste the wonderfully Scottish weather on my

FIGURE 23.19: *Moving Thoughts Journal*, video still, April 2018.

face too, a great blend of fresh wind, rain and sunshine fused all together. And so, in thankfulness, we part. And, and, and, and, and, and …

And, we open up the circle … in hope for ongoing renewals, again and again and again …

As I know now that in my felt thinking, I will keep coming back to this wonderous place, the grazing wetlands, where, thanks to the amazing friendships formed barefoot, I danced with the sheep for the first time. In movement, Scottish countryside feels to be the land of sheep.

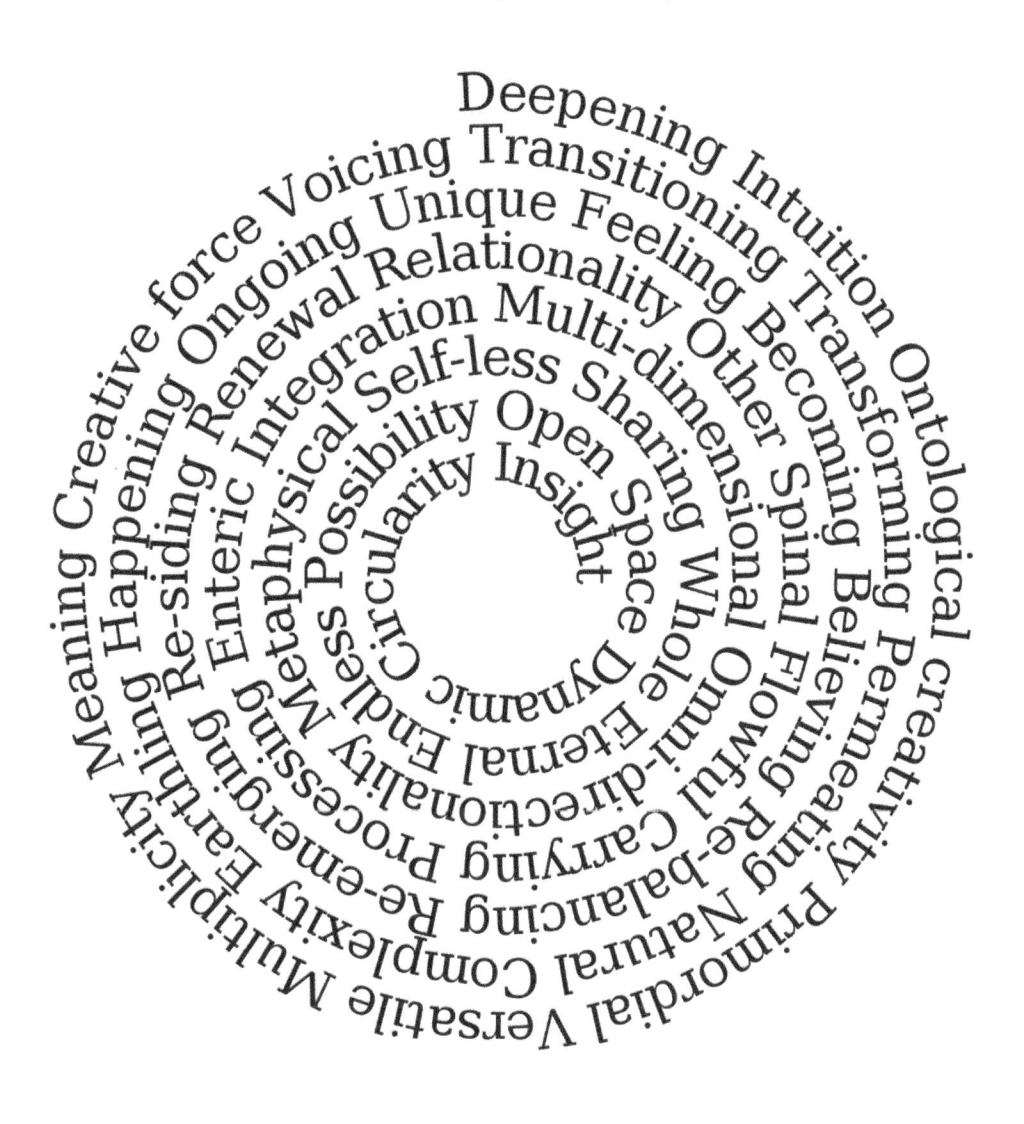

SECTION THREE

DISCUSSION AND DEVELOPMENTS

24

Felt Thinking and Moving towards Inclusive Wellbeing Practice

What happens to perception of our own nature when we engage with feeling it more instead of thinking about it?

How can somatic experience of the natural world help us in bringing up, embodying and comprehending the essence of 'being' human or more-than-human, and in restoring the ontological connection between the self and Nature?

How can our embodied focus on movement as the source of all experience redefine our comprehension of our creative Nature/Self and what effect can the proposed practices of felt thinking have on overall wellbeing?

To begin this discussion section properly, it is important to outline that the many years of the somatic practice-based process in felt thinking, reflecting upon the questions above, evolved and shaped into a form of contemplative practice that can function as a daily, or periodical, practice of reconnection with our real nature in its ongoingly changing multiplicity. The process helped me create a relatable form of both 'in-search' and sensorial 'out-search' grounded in somatic improvisation with the natural world around and within oneself which will hopefully bring movement closer to anybody, with or without any prior experience in expressive arts practices.

As a practitioner, speaking from various movement experience perspectives, I have hopefully shown that creativity resides not in specified talents but in every breath we exchange and every heartbeat we chose to pay attention to. Our attention to movement per se is the key to a new perception and a new consciousness as well. It is the presented here practice that reminds me of the living dynamic we embody which is not only productive but first and foremost receptive. And that both receptivity, i.e. our ability to listen whole-bodily, and productivity embrace each other in the living dynamic of life and co-create ongoingly. They feed one another ongoingly, and continue sharing the relational essence of Life, in its creative forms.

It is also important to underline that the described stages of practice of relating with receptivity, relating with responsiveness and relating with responsibility, as well as the embodied travelling through ectodermic, mesodermic and endodermic depths of our embodied experience of movement, happen all the time in Life as creative activity, with the third stage being closest to what creativity really brings about by being closest to the deepest self which is never separate from Nature as 'other' and which springs from the imaginative, shared unconscious.

And all those processes can be accessed within the presented here form of practice in felt thinking which reconnects, in creative contemplation, to the living dynamic that speaks for and guides at any chosen moment. Every stage of the described process is not separate from another, as they permeate and enable one another, but they can be given a specific focus and be practised with substantial amount of time offered, depending on the purpose of practice.

For everyday use, the practice, at least in my own version of it, lasts anything between a quarter to half an hour and rounds up with a thorough enlivenment of my psycho-somatic functioning that reconnects me to both myself, the environment around me and the deeper meaning of pursued livelihood I participate in with other living beings. In movement, I ongoingly feel that I both share and owe my life to them as much as I am both, self and other.

The practice itself also helps me realize that embarking on and talking about metaphysical relatedness of being human does not belong to the secluded parts of the society only, usually prescribed to philosophers or theologians, but starts within every breath that we take, as long as we pay attention and let it guide all the daily movement, be it at work, at play or doing the regular chores. As long as it means doing something that feels right in a bigger, all life-inclusive picture.

And that picture appears to be simpler than initially thought, as it takes the shape of a story. A story that any child wants to hear, the one with a beginning, middle and an end – a well-known 'three act structure' that we have all grown up with, which corresponds to Bateson's 'symmetry, play and metaphor' (Bateson 2000) as well, and where an end means a beginning to yet another story emerging, or multiple of them at the same time, as I continuously discover in my reflexive felt thinking.

The most important point here then and biggest realization of the work presented here, with crucial importance to any ontological inquiry and any philosophical thought in general I would suppose, is that movement is always one in its omni-directionality. And that the way we describe movement, in everyday language, in its instructive directionality comes from using simple, and often helpful, but limiting frames of reference like yesterday and tomorrow, or, left and right. In its living relationality, as the practice confirms, movement is better described by its *towards* or *away from* tendencies.

This ontological principle of open and creative relationality intrinsic to the 'towards and away from' movement, as described in previous chapters, is also where the natural circularity in Nature and Life comes forth as a grounding context to all experience.

Importantly too, I initially thought that in self-inquiry, to reconnect with more universal aspects of movement experience would mean moving from subjective to more objective (social) levels of reference first, and then opening it further from there. It initially seemed more logical to move from subjective to objective to primordial. In his essay 'Self realization: An ecological approach to being in the world', Arne Naess describes 'maturing' as moving from ego to social self and from social self to metaphysical self (Seed 1988: 20).

Nevertheless, as Naess admits as well, in such a process, our identification with the natural world is largely ignored. And indeed, in the presented here practice and its findings, the process of self-inquiry reveals itself as that beginning at the social level first, as the most superficial level of clock/physical time we live by every day, then traveling through the personal levels of psychological relatedness, only then to develop towards the ontologically primordial sense of Nature/Self that we naturally embody.

The process shows me that the bigger, eternal movement that guides any free improvisation with the natural world in Life is the one towards the deeper self. It is the movement that opens the social functioning up to the personal, i.e. subjective and psychological dimensions first, and, if followed through, guides us towards the ontogenetic/primordial one, which resides within ourselves and which connects all Life on Earth from inside out.

The most essential message here then is that movement itself indicates that we embody the deepest levels of relation to the widest sense of Life possible and that within that movement lies an opening to something beyond it all, the eternal and infinite creative force we all take part in, both consciously and unconsciously, human or more-than-human.

Another crucial realization of the presented work here is that a significant part of human nature resides in ongoing *wondering* and that we should also be open to wondering without, or beyond words, as in responsive listening and sound making. Wondering about the self and the world should then be understood and practised more as 'being with' and less as making sense of something external to ourselves for cognitive understanding only. And that doing research could potentially mean not only producing and analyzing data but also enriching our embodied comprehension of co-existence, as children learn about life in full engagement.

I thus agree here with Bateson that moving flexibility between the smallest and largest contexts of any question gives us an opportunity to grow alongside the work and comprehend its depths, not only understand or organize its contents for further use, utility or reproduction.

Arne Naess reminds that 2500 years of humankind's wondering about who we are and what kind of reality we are part of is a very short period of time in a lifetime of a species, not to mention in a lifetime of the Earth. Delving deeper into the nature of our intimate relationship with the Earth is the most revealing and most rewarding kind of wondering one could embark on, yet it is never easy or straightforward. The resulting from it expansion of our own idea of the self and our living nature always surprises and humbles. Human nature, as Naess describes, 'is such that with sufficient all-sided maturity we cannot avoid "identifying" ourselves with all living beings, beautiful and ugly, big or small, sentient or not' (Seed 1988: 20).

The path proposed here for reconnecting with oneself while reconnecting with Nature goes close to what Naess is also proposing. Our natural self is ontologically richer than living within our societal structures of modern world, and the core of our maturing realization is seeing ourselves in all other living beings as present in our consideration for living and letting live. Naess argues that 'the ecological self of a person is that with which this person identifies' (Seed 1988: 22), yet, to me as a practitioner, it is clear that what Naess is proposing is not quite enough, as our lack of identification with the natural world has been an ongoing phenomenon throughout the history of modern civilizations.

I would like to propose then that what is needed is the full, embodied, engagement in the felt dimension of our thinking as the creative process of movement and art making, and as more holistic method of understanding ourselves, and which can further support our processes of both human and humane identification.

I agree with Naess that the ultimate way for ecophilosophical growth is through the selfless love. And by selfless love Naess (Seed 1988) does not mean the neglected self but the love that goes beyond the narrow understanding of the self as ego and towards the wider, universal self within which every living being is intimately connected on an empathic level of Life's interdependence. And with his direct references to the Sanskrit word of *atman*, he concludes that 'to identify self-realization with ego indicates a vast underestimation of human self' (Seed 1988: 26). And that through cherishing the natural landscapes and the increased sensitivity towards the richness of life around, including ourselves in it, the joy of life will be found. And with it – a new ecological ontology, grounded in the intimate relationship with the Earth.

What he sees needed then is what he calls *community therapy* which can 'heal our relations with the widest community, that of all living beings' (Seed 1988: 29), thus the proposed here is embodied practice in creative exploration of the essence of the self. I would also add that it doesn't matter if we are seeking connection with Nature indoors or outdoors, as the point of the creative work conveyed in felt thinking has proven that our connection with Nature starts within ourselves, as wherever, whoever and however we are, we are Nature too.

Wondering about many mutually exclusive paradoxes, like day and night, in and out, or body and mind, that our conscious functioning often implies becomes quite erroneous once we engage with it whole-bodily. It would then be advisable to be cautious of deterministic reasoning without allowing ourselves enough time and space to get involved first.

Relating to William S. Condon's research within behavioural studies, Hall too writes that there is a genuine coherence between things we perceive and think about and that it is important to remember that by making or finding distinctions within the world, we do not break it into fragments which can never again be brought together. 'The temporal is basic and involves history. Processes have their histories. There are many histories, so that while history is pluralistic, it is not therefore discontinuous' and that 'all nature paradoxically is both discrete and continuous – simultaneously and without contradiction' (Hall 1983: 179). Nothing is excluded. And, reflectively speaking, a practitioner, as I became to understand in this process myself, also becomes a living part of the practised.

Some say: Time is all we have, yet, do we? Just like being oneself doesn't mean having control of what one's life is going to look like, time, as movement itself, is us. Thus 'having' time, as I have argued and exemplified throughout the previous section, creates a wrong idea of our intimate relation to it, to ourselves and to others. Ownership is but a harmful simplification of life's connection to and with time.

Our blind following of the clock creates a lot of separation and alienation from the natural rhythms of the Earth and thus time itself. My ongoing suggestion is that we should start paying more attention to the creative dynamics within the *lived time* and engage in felt nuances between what only seems like black and white reality. Our attention to the relational movement of everything can lead us *out* into the universe as much as *into* the immeasurable depths of a living cell.

Tuning into the rhythms and movement in Nature can help us create a healthy global culture of a mindful species in its life-long learning experience. Attending to movement in its most natural emergence and development, as I argue for and support with practice here, teaches us about our own life on Earth. And, there definitely is still a depth of unvoiced potential for positive change that people, as a species, share. It also feels like about time, now, to embrace and move towards that.

Based on life-long work detailed in *Body–Mind Centering* and experiential anatomy, Bonnie-Bainbridge Cohen reminds:

The interplay between our unconscious and conscious mind is fluid and flows in both directions all the time. The conscious and unconscious are a continuum of one mind. They are each the shadow or support of the movement and expression of the other. [...] It is in the shifting and alternating between the listening and expressing roles within the continuum that we know ourselves and feel strong and free in mind/emotion/spirit. [...] It is in the dialogue and weave between the two that creates the full fabric of our individual, creative, and cognizant self.

(Cohen et al. 2012: 13)

When allowed to express its natural strengths then, every bodily system supports and sustains the function of other systems and will automatically allow change and transformation to happen internally. And, to conclude here with Andrea Olsen's words on principles of wellbeing, 'a cyclic balance between silence and speaking, rest and activity, is fundamental to the healthy functioning of our internal organs' (2002: 52) and I would add, healthy Life in its personal dimensions too.

25

Felt Thinking and the Embodied Experience of Time/Space and Its Cultural Implications

The main issue to tackle when allowing ourselves to feel think is a form of detaching oneself from the dominating cultural environment in which we live and which 'dulls and conditions our perceptual capacities' (Seamon and Mugerauer 1989: 131). Engaging with creating the working material in the course of this project has definitely brought a lot of societal limitations we all carry to my attention. I realized a lot of my own limitations of needing to shift between roles of a researcher, a practitioner, a mover, a facilitator, a friend, a mother and a human being, and which I am all at the same time. I became aware that I am constantly bound by multiple time frames present in my daily, urban and social life which often function and impose themselves on artificially exaggerated scales of relevance or importance.

The developing, interdisciplinary research in environmental studies, as referred to on multiple occasions in this study, does provide a lot of support for the proposed here practice already. For example, in the phenomenologically grounded collective volume *Dwelling, Place and Environment*, one reads that

> by developing a greater sensitivity to the meaning of our environments through intuitive awareness, we might overcome some of the problems of conflict between the mechanized environmental processes of today and the human and participatory process of urban growth in the past.
>
> (Seamon and Mugerauer 1989: 134)

Indeed, to embark on a journey of self-discovery attending to movement in Nature, including movement within ourselves, we need to become responsive to the topographic character of the land we chose to reside in, its physical form, patterns and spatial feel. It is often helpful to ask oneself what is it in my living environment that makes me feel good and which positively influences my own wellbeing.

There will also be things we react to negatively and which communicate a lot of information about why it is so. Sustaining such living and mindful dialogue with everyday clues opens a new door to reactive changes we will decide to make for ourselves without influencing the environment negatively. After all, the same environment may have a very different effect on somebody else.

Reflecting back on the experiences gathered within the Scottish landscapes at Loch Lomond and the Trossachs National Park, as described in *Cove Park Journals*, it became apparent to me that even though the place influenced everybody in similar ways, the reflections reveal their very individual contexts and vary substantially in their experiential continuations.

By referring to holy wells of Ireland, with reference to wider Celtic cultures and how influential a site, a place or a living environment can be, L. Walter and J. R. Brenneman describe the sensed experience of the place, as 'loric'. And he further portrays it as the uniquely particular and the idiosyncratic that sets a person, a thing or an event involved with it apart, and that the sense of intimacy that resides in such places provides a key to the understanding of loric power. That is how he describes his experience with the holy wells:

> What we felt when we were surrounded by the wooded grove nestled in the watery bowl was a power that was drawing us inward toward a center. It was a power that was implosive rather than explosive and was connected exclusively to that place. This centering was the most outstanding sensation, an impression of being truly there within that place and responding to its power and its uniqueness.
>
> (Seamon and Mugerauer 1989: 142)

And then he adds that loric and the sacred, which he calls the opposite, share a participation in the archetypal, with the difference being that the sacred derives its power from the eternal, whereas the loric derives its primary power from differences manifested from repetition to repetition, like every story cannot be told twice in the same way. Underlining the experience of intimacy of the place, he sums up that as a power, intimacy is so self-contained that it is completely hidden to those who possess it and revealed only to those who chance to enter a place as a stranger, immediately aware of the otherness and intimate nature of the place, who through discomfort may wish to either flee, or be fascinated to participate and be influenced by its cosmological power.

And he refers here to the Celtic cosmology which, unlike the western or most eastern cosmologies organized around the sky, sources its power from the 'otherworld', beneath the Earth. The result is that the power and any form of enlightening wisdom radiate upward from below rather than downward from the sky. And, although the sky contains some powerful forces such as the Sun, within Celtic cultures, it is understood as a secondary or complementary power to the forces found in the otherworld and the earth under our feet.

The underworld in Celtic myths is generally prescribed with feminine qualities or even feminine identity, the Great Mother, and the first form of all life, with the surface world being a reflection of that archetype, containing the same structural components but lacking the power, except at critical times or in particular sacred places. 'The two worlds are like two electric circuits, one (the otherworld) alive and the other (the surface world) dead until a contact wire links the two' (Seamon and Mugerauer 1989: 144). The great mother is both, devouring and life giving.

In further development of this collective publication on phenomenologies of place, Bernd Jager too describes body as situated and forming a privileged unity of mutual implication.

> It is here that human life becomes situated and centered; from here it unfolds and comes to encompass a temporal and spatial world. It is only as situated life – as life arched by the sky, supported by a welcoming earth and sheltered by an environment – that the past, present and future can announce themselves. It is only as surrounded by a physiognomic world, by things and being attractive and repellent, by things to do and to avoid, that a primitive geography can first emerge, that a forward and a backward, a high and a low, an up and a down, a left and a right can first come into being.
>
> (Seamon and Mugerauer 1989: 215)

And my summing thought here is that we do not just occupy time and space, but we generate it.

26

Felt Thinking as 'Green Awakening' and Its Wider Philosophical Implications

In his article on Bergson's 'living philosophy' entitled 'Henri Bergson and the perception of time', fully relatable to the undertaken here discussion, John-Francis Phipps writes that over the past few decades, there has been an ever-increasing growth in demand for many varieties of alternative healing, including a psycho-somatic approach, and that he sees this growth as a revolt against reductionist, materialist, mechanistic fundamentalism.

Recent advances in the new physics and cosmology, he continues, have also led to a radical reappraisal of old ways of thinking about time and causality.

> The way we perceive time is surely a core perception, which affects all other percep-tions. It determines our philosophy of life, matters of war and peace, how we perceive work and the amount of quality time we devote to the people and things that really matter. (Yet) despite the recovery of a more vitalistic outlook in attitudes towards physical and mental wellbeing, the main underlying perception of our modern, urban-industrial society remains mechanistic and soulless.
>
> (Phipps 2004: n.pag.)

Have things developed in a more Bergsonian way, Phipps continues, 'perhaps we would have learned from this a greater respect for all expressions of the life force, including our own species' (2004: n.pag.).

At this stage in presenting and discussing the work on felt thinking, it is impor-tant to underline that even though, as summarized powerfully by Phipps, Bergson's philosophy aligns with objective of this embodied practice of being with the world as Nature/Self, the generated in felt thinking and presented in the previous section material, with its three stages of practice, has been done in full independence of, and unfamiliarity with, Bergson's work.

All the emergent themes and their storied developments happened exclusively within the facilitated by myself practice of felt thinking as based on somatic expe-riencing of the self as Nature and are considered by me as imminent in movement per se. Their contextual grounding and affiliation with Bergson's work has been attempted only in retrospection.

It is thus crucial for me, as a practitioner–researcher, to highlight the authenticity of the practice that sprung from somatic experiencing of the self in movement, and which, as I argue, goes beyond Bergson's work, especially in the philosophical value of the presented here ontological principle of relationality in 'towards and away from' movement, and its ongoing flow of change and exchange.

Having said that the essential analogy to Bergson's work on duration, affection and intuition discovered during interpreting the material has only invited me to revive and promote his work further. The work which has been visibly underappreciated and underacknowledged in respect to its influences on phenomenological thought of other philosophers including Maurice Merleau-Ponty, Jean-Paul Sartre, Emmanuel Levinas, Anna-Teresa Tymieniecka, Alfred Whitehead or Gilles Deleuze. And, the work which until today remains unanswered, yet undeniable in close reading, in respect to its influence on one of the most important works on philosophy of time i.e. *Being and Time* by his contemporary, Martin Heidegger, and which will be further discussed in the following chapter.

What strikes as the closest resemblance between Bergson's work and presented here findings is the unquestionable value of 'the intuitive' as the most authentic method in philosophical inquiry. Also, one of Bergson's strongest beliefs was that the failure to take into account the experience of time, which became an immediate, though entirely unplanned, theme in my own sessions in felt thinking, results in the failure to appreciate the uniqueness of life.

In *An Introduction to Metaphysics* (1912), Bergson expands on the central role of intuition when thinking about self as time and he concludes that the true purpose of knowledge is to know things deeply, to touch the inner essence of things via a form of empathy. A true empiricism, he writes, 'is that which proposes to get as near to the original itself as possible, to search deeply into its life, and so, by a kind of intellectual auscultation, to feel the throbbing of its soul; and this true empiricism is the true metaphysics' (Bergson and Hulme 1912: 22).

As an explanation to such comparison, auscultation means listening to the internal organs through a stethoscope. And Phipps writes that 'just as the physician does this to find out what is happening within the patient's body, so the metaphysician practises a mental equivalent of auscultation to apprehend the inner essence of things' (Phipps 2004: n.pag.).

In its subtle connection to breath, then felt thinking in movement (and art making) can be understood as a practical follow up to such 'internal listening' and to Bergsonian metaphysics of change. Nevertheless, it is a practice-based method which also underlines that we do not need any external tools to achieve such internal hearing as it resides within our embodied capacity we are all born with. It also reminds that both feeling and thinking are both movement-based experiences that foreground any conscious or conclusive reasoning.

Following movement and its ongoing dynamics of change, and which I simply call openings, shapes itself via qualitative integrations and differentiations which are in continuous dialogue with life and its both internal and external stimuli. It cultivates more fluid understanding of 'life frames' within established, language based, concepts. And, as in Bergson's philosophy, attending to movement calls for experience to be purified of intellectualism by, what I suggest means, trusting one's insightful intuiting.

Following free movement as it penetrates our embodied selves every single second is thus seen by me, like Bergson's philosophy, as introduction into life's own domain, and which can be described as a 'reciprocal interpenetration and endlessly continued creation' (Bergson 1983: 178), an intrinsic quality of being.

When Bergson speaks about a 'free self', this is the self that is outside automatism and social utility functioning and which is the expression of the 'fundamental self' and our 'whole personality'. But, as Ansell-Pearson points out too, he does not provide any clear conception of this active, authorizing self, and thus it is an issue that remains elusive in his writings.

What Bergson does recognize though is that not all elements of our being are so incorporated as to form a unitary and fully integrated self: not everything that forms us blends perfectly 'with the whole mass of the self' (Ansell-Pearson 2018a: 70).

Controversially perhaps, in his quest for the genuine selfhood, Bergson makes a decisive point: unless we act for ourselves we will lose our autonomy and be acted upon. Thus, while we live for the external world more than for our true self, we make our life unfold in space rather than in time.

Nevertheless, the findings of felt thinking processes point me to conclude that the two, external and internal worlds we live by become one in experience, and it is the depth to which we can let those two worlds communicate and co-create with each other that enriches our experience of the self and helps to live according to our true potential, always in binding connectivity with the natural world and where following the intuitive and losing oneself in movement springs with the emergence, or continuous re-emergence rather, of the authentic self.

And perhaps I can resort here to Bateson's words too when he says that 'major problems in the world are the result of the difference between how nature works and the way people think' (n.d.: n.pag.) and that the pathology of wrong thinking, or wrong doing, can only be corrected by discovering the relationships which make up the beauty of Nature.

To me though, it is important to add that discontinuity, like any fault or mistake, is immanent in movement experience as well, and it is equally important to acknowledge discontinuation as part of ongoing processes of life, in their multiplicity. And, as long as we don't lose touch with 'the feeling' in new movement developments to come, life processes keep shaping and transitioning onto new relationships ongoingly with or without our impact. Their positive or negative influences on our overall wellbeing though depend on our sensitivity to the balances between moving towards ourselves and away from the world, and the other way round too, just like in breath.

Bateson (2000) too said that it is dangerous or monstrous even to separate thought from emotion and that we live in a world that is only made of relationships; which is also why dance, as the most ephemeral artform embraces that essence of being, and human expression in art and movement prove to me to be the most authentic form of human communication in agreement with the Earth's natural movements and its life-giving capacity.

27

Felt Thinking and the
Concept of Temporality

As a brief reminder here, feeding into contexts of felt thinking as time/space-based experience within this compendious discussion, what Heidegger calls the ordinary or 'vulgar' comprehension of time is the one derived ultimately from Aristotle's *Physics*, where the future is the not-yet-now, the past is the no-longer-now, and the present is the now that flows from future to past at each passing moment.

Being and Time (Heidegger 1967) can primarily be seen then as Heidegger's criticism of the idea of time as a uniform, linear and infinite series of 'now' points. And, to avoid such standard comprehension of time, Heidegger is trying to avoid any conception of time that begins with a distinction between time and eternity, and which he prescribes to Augustine's model. In this model, temporality is derived from a higher non-temporal state of eternity which is 'co-extensive with the infinite and eternal now of God' (Critchley 2009: n.pag.).

At the same time, for Heidegger, the primary phenomenon of time, i.e. *Dasein*, as experienced in anticipation, is that future is revealed in being-towards-death. Thus, *Dasein*, projecting towards the future in anticipation, comes towards itself. Yet, what *Dasein* carries over into the future is its ontological indebtedness to the past. What comes out of the future then, is the past, or what Heidegger calls 'having-been-ness'.

This does not mean that we are either condemned to the past or stuck in the present moment of anticipation. For Heidegger, the present is something that one can seize hold of and resolutely make one's own. 'What is opened in the anticipation of the future is the fact of our having-been which releases itself into the present moment of action' (Critchley 2009: n.pag.), and this is what in *Being and Time* is called 'the moment of vision', the authentic *Dasein*.

With temporality being neither reducible to the vulgar experience of time as chronological, nor originating in distinction from eternity, time, to Heidegger, should be grasped in and of itself as the unity of the three dimensions, which he calls three ecstases, of past, present and future. This is what he calls 'primordial' time and he insists that it is finite, and points to human finitude. For Heidegger, we are time, and temporality is a process with three dimensions which form a unity.

A question arises then: if Heidegger says that we are time, and then he says that we, obviously are finite, as is the experience of time, the two statements do not match, or even exclude one another. Unless he means the time of the universe that we live in ... and which might be finite indeed, as dependent upon our solar system and other, larger contexts of life on Earth.

And, following this brief summary of Heidegger's philosophy, one of my summing up thoughts is that there are a plenty of theories of human nature in western tradition but there are no practices of human nature. Perhaps then, inspired by various traditions of the world, as it has been for me, somatic education in movement and expressive arts can be seen as one, and this is one of the reasons this study, on somatic felt thinking, should indicate such need even further.

Heidegger describes phenomenology as the process of letting things manifest themselves and to me, by delving into the realm of the experiential, felt thinking in movement expands on such motivations for phenomenological inquiry and builds on Husserl's 'to the things themselves'. Only 'things' in movement can mean anything like an ancient stone covered by moss sharing its coldness when touched and which shapes as the most ephemeral and fluid sensation, always changing, always transforming, and which can be comprehended by the intuitive insights only.

Stressing the intuitive dimension in furthering our comprehension of 'the self as time' brings me back to the value of Bergsonian work on the subject. It also relates again to a famous debate of 1922 during which Henri Bergson publicly debated on the nature of time with Albert Einstein. In her recent book *The Physicist and the Philosopher: Einstein, Bergson, and the Debate That Changed Our Understanding of Time*, historian of science Jimena Canales tells the story of how this remarkable meeting impacted fields from logical positivism to quantum mechanics and drove a rift between science and the humanities that persists today. She also explains how the many technologies of the last century, such as wristwatches, radio or film, helped to shape people's conceptions of time (Canales 2015).

She then concludes that in Einsteinian comprehension of time, the perception of temporality, suggests it is just an illusion. And that in reality, there is no distinction between past present and future.

Bergson (2001), on the contrary, said that if we didn't have a prior concept of time in human experience, time clock would not be used as a tool that serves us and points to the biological roots of such conception, those residing in the body and our embodied ability to experience the 'lived time', or 'real duration' as he called it.

The most important to the discussion presented here though is that there is a grounding agreement in this iconic debate between the two world views, the scientific and the philosophical, or the Einsteinian and the Bergsonian, and which is that: there is no time without movement. And so, if the universe went to zero motion/speed, there would be no time.

The difference in the worldviews lies then between asymmetry and the flow of time, Canales says. In one view, the flow of time has to do with the emergence or release of something new that wasn't there before into the scene of the universe (the making of time), and in the other view, the past and the future are obviously different, as in asymmetrical relation, but there is no flow of time as such.

In any case, movement as ontological principle of Life, as underlined throughout this work, prevails and as a mover in embodied thinking I can easily feel into the merger of both, the asymmetry and the flow as co-creative anyway, in the mentioned already implicit heterogeneity of movement which incorporates the opposite motions in its ongoing possibility.

28

Felt Thinking and
Nature as Wholeness

In her article 'Nature, water symbols, and the human quest for wholeness', Anne Buttimer summarizes four major conceptions of Nature as present in western thought. She lists: Nature as appropriate form, designed by the divine to fit the mankind; Nature as organism, demonstrated primarily in the analogy to human body; Nature as a machine, evidenced by scientific experiments; and Nature as a theatre of events, with its spontaneity and unpredictability included. Then she comments:

> From Greece, as well as from the Hellenic stream of the Judaeo-Christion tradition, has come a legacy of suspicion about the emotional, sensory, and intuitive features of our humanness. This distinction, and eventual separation, of intellectual and moral virtues in education is one which split Western approaches to thought and being, truth and goodness.
>
> (Seamon and Mugerauer 1989: 267)

In movement-based philosophy, embracing fully our human capacities of sensual connection with Life, and the implicit in it fragility, hclps to mature in appreciative mode of living and to forgo the action-obsessed reality which seems imperative to the current day an age. Zimmerman writes that 'as soon as we see that we are not separate substances but the openness in which phenomena appear, there is an end to the suffering that stems from clinging, grasping, and manipulating' (Seamon and Mugerauer 1989: 247) and that for Heidegger too, both alienation and the feeling of homelessness are symptoms of a lack of self-understanding.

Going back to the cultural outlook upon concepts of Nature and the differentiation between monochronic and polychronic comprehension of time Hall says that that 'polychronic cultures are by their very nature oriented to people' (1983: 53) and that the polychronic cultures and their people are individually more oriented towards intimate value of relationships, which then includes those of human–human as well as human–nonhuman nature. He also writes that 'one of the many paths to enlightenment is the discovery of ourselves, and this can be achieved whenever one truly knows others who are different' (Hall 1983: 8).

In her search for proper groundings and helpful metaphors in envisioning the mindful world, which supports diversity and the integrity of all things, Anne Buttimer boldly asks:

> Can we envision environmental and human sciences ready to be tamed of their managerial hybris and listening to a reading of the earth's surface in terms of the accumulated wisdom of civilizations – and thereby led to a sense of Creation as a whole?
>
> (Seamon and Mugerauer 1989: 277)

In listening to movement, there are no parts independent of the whole, every particle consists of all other particles and remains in consistent relationship. Implicit to the logic of reason assumption of linearity becomes a paradox.

> Logic is analytical, whereas meaning is evidently holistic and hence understanding cannot be reduced to logic. We understand meaning in the moment of coalescence when the whole is reflected in the parts so that together they disclose the whole.
>
> (Seamon and Mugerauer 1989: 285)

It is the hermeneutic circle, also called the *unfolding of enfolding*.

The whole imparts itself and is accomplished through the parts it fulfils. We cannot know the world or self in its whole/totality as we know only its thingness. And speaking reflectively again, I would like to connect that to the act of writing, where we do not have the meaning before us, as an object, but it exists in our relationship to it as performed in reading and informed by the whole life process.

Henri Bortold concludes his paper, 'Counterfeit and authentic wholes: Finding a means for dwelling in nature', referring to developmental psychology offerings in proposing a notion of the whole as 'nothing', as well as the notion that we can develop sensitivity to the whole as an active absence. He also says that there are two major modes of organization for human beings, action mode and receptive mode and that over the last few centuries, for survival reasons, I rephrase, and due to mastery of manipulation of physical objects, we definitely developed more in the realm of activity than receptive being.

The result of such development is that our consciousness has also attuned to experience with solid objects in analytical mode and got institutionalized through language. The receptive mode remains underdeveloped, it is the mode in which we allow events to happen, and instead of being verbal, analytical, sequential and logical, this mode of consciousness is non-verbal, holistic, non-linear and intuitive. It is based on taking the environment in rather than manipulating.

As a consequence, it is because we operate in the active mode of consciousness, we perceive 'the whole' as active absence. 'If we were re-educated in the receptive mode of consciousness, our encounter with wholeness would be considerably different, and we would see many different things about our world' (Seamon and Mugerauer 1989: 291). And that experience of authentic wholeness, as emergent in somatic felt thinking, requires a new style of education.

Education grounded less in intellectual faculty, analytical skills or verbal reasoning and more in concern, respect and responsibility, along with the skills of eco-phenomenological listening that guides towards perception of multiplicity within holistic perspective without harmful fragmentation. It is not enough, I argue again, to dwell in Nature sentimentally and aesthetically, what we need is an ongoing discovery of its authentic wholeness.

And, considering that the issue for humans is to somehow be able to perceive and open up to the transcendent nature of the world, Sondra Fraleigh too writes that:

> If existence is indeterminate, open-ended and not predictable, then we dance as unfinished metaphysical artifacts in much the same way as phenomenology and evolutionary science explain how life is ongoing. We are works in progress, in other words, and like works of art we live between content and progress. Our living metaphysical reality does not mount to heaven, but spreads into our everyday dances – of auspicious being and indeterminate becoming.
>
> (2004: 49)

Also, in relation to attention to breath, advised here as the ground for practices of felt thinking, and its educational value, Irigaray adds that 'cultivation of breathing allows us to assume the solitude of our singularity while venturing to share with another ontological destiny' (2017: viii). She criticizes the existing educational systems for not cultivating children as living beings, but merely helping to adapt them to norms of common existence.

She further writes:

> If the little human succeeded in coming into the world by breathing by itself, a culture of its own breathing is also what can enable it to pass constantly from the vital to the spiritual stage of existence. Taking charge of its breath and cultivating it is a means which can allow it to transcend itself here and now and to reach the beyond of a mere living state while being faithful to its earthy existence.
>
> (Irigaray 2017: ix)

And I appreciate Irigaray perspective on human development and natural belonging when she states that a human being has in itself the source of the motion which guides its development and which is endowed with an energy which is of its own kind, 'the source and motion of which lie in itself' (Irigaray 2017: 15). At the same time, to me, it rests upon anthropocentric history (or psychology) as we know it already and not enough upon ways of sensing it deeper in the bones as coming from the earth itself.

Cultivating the breath definitely starts the process of appreciating the natural self-inquiry in its capacity for life but it is the practice of letting go in movement as described in the previous section of this study that can take us into the more experiential depths of life while transforming energies that we embody. To me, real philosophy cannot lack comparison to all other forms of life we co-create this world with.

29

Felt Thinking and the Cycle of Life

In his evocative book *The Politics of Inner Experience*, John-Francis Phipps (1990) brings up the issue of modern day's politics being no longer appropriate to our global reality. Reality's conventional, historical time stopped together with the first nuclear bomb being dropped at Hiroshima in 1945, claims Phipps. Similar to many other authors that he quotes, he is proposing we are currently living out of our 'timeworld' when the culturally superimposed conception of time and reality have been finally identified as mere abstraction.

And he refers here to the Christian culture upon which the whole developed world is based, grounded in linear time, and comprehension of wars as those that come and go as part of 'normal' life. Since Hiroshima then, we have been living within the real possibility of omnicide, the global and apocalyptic extinction.

Initially celebrated as a success – the end of all wars – this unprecedented in its political, psychological and cultural consequences development of human kind changed the world irreversibly. It also demarcates, as Phipps says, the end line for the western culture and its devalued cosmology driven by consumeristic ambitions for progress, defence, technology, economic growth and prosperity. The cosmology grounded in linear time, causal relationships, monetarism and end-product mentality.

He also makes a strong point, which this work grounded in felt thinking has been addressing and resolving through practice, that the modern societies live in dualistic worlds, of one being the world of the individual, personal and intimate, and the other world being the exterior, public, social and political. And that we superimpose this split view onto our reality thinking that 'if something is personal it cannot by definition be political'.

In reality, there is no such dividing line. Phipps writes that 'inner and outer processes are in fact continuously interacting and affecting each other, the outside world being shaped by what goes on in our inner spaces both consciously and unconsciously' (1990: 3). And that whenever we focus unduly on one world to the exclusion of the other we obtain an unbalanced view of reality as well as feel powerless as individuals.

He then concludes that the more integrated our vision of the world is, the more responsible we feel for the planet as a whole and the more involved we become. There is also a timeless sense, Phipps says, in which 'a given individual at a given time represents all persons at all times' (1990: 4).

Most people, he further writes, consider themselves apolitical. Yet, 'in taking no action to change the status quo they are thereby prolonging its existence, which is a highly political thing to do' (Phipps 1990: 8). The western psyche has been traumatized by histories of wars and repression of human spirit. Yet, the cynical view of human nature can nevertheless change immensely, once allowed an authentic access to our inner richness and dimensionality of experience as present in embodied experience of free movement, where the subtle work of the psyche and the creative work of the imagination take over. And Phipps too, as one of the best known interpreters of Bergson's work, points in the direction of the higher values residing within the qualitative realms of experience.

It is then important to realize that as society, driven by linear concepts of time and productivity, we repress the value of anything intangible and felt. The quantitative efforts lack balance with the qualitative, and action seeks its repressed counterpart of stillness. The deeper cause to the currently experienced ecological crisis is then our repressed metaphysical belonging. And in Bergsonian terms, Phipps sums up that 'conflict and war are part of the traditional temporal pattern – they have causes and effects. Higher values, peace, compassion and creative inspiration all belong to a different aspect of time' (Phipps 1990: 39). And that the inner essence of life's interconnectedness, here facilitated in the experience of immanent creativity and the poetic spirit of movement, is in reality accessible to us all.

The horizontal time of everyday life and the vertical time of higher consciousness experienced when 'letting go' coexist within the different and presented here as eternally multitudinal, dimensions of time. And they are possible to be tuned into simply by following the transitional dynamics of Nature, be it in its daily, seasonal or yearly cycles.

They are all present within our bodily experience of the self, starting with the presence of breath. And just like processes of breath and its relational movement *towards* and *away from* the self or the world, the going and coming rhythms, the theme of belonging to this and other, eternal life is deeply present within ourselves.

Also, there is an enormous amount of trust present in us that allows each breath complete its ongoing cycle. And that trust in Life itself allows certain processes to pass so that more creative ones can come into being. The open cycle of ongoing exchange as present in processes of felt thinking speaks to the very essence of life as timelessness and a metaphor for deepened meaningfulness. Like in the highly suggestive saying that it is in learning how to die that one truly learns how to live.

And, Abram contextualizes that within Indigenous cosmologies of oral cultures by saying that:

> The individual experience of birth is thus related to the collective emergence of life from under the ground. Similarly, human death, for oral people, is not just a personal event but also a transformation in the land, a process whereby one's individual sensibility opens out-ward to rejoin the encompassing, more-than-human field of sensations.
>
> (Phipps 1990: 219)

And that thought on transitional relationship between life and after life carries on in my felt thinking when I rediscover that:

> When I submerge into movement the space opens up. There are no directions really, as what is up becomes the down, and the left is right. Making a step forward is as meaningful as a step back.
>
> And so 'no movement' is the same moving as the most expressive emotional act.
>
> I feel united with the universe, where yes is no and no can be yes at the same time.
>
> Living this universe with(in) the bodily palpable self, I know that the unity of the opposites gives infinite possibilities of time/space manoeuvres as time/space is becoming real through movement and movement enables time/space to shape.
>
> In such universe then, the past , the present and the future happen all at the same time enabling each and one another (as time/space events) to continue moving, and to continue the infinitely creative life force.
>
> And where death is a passage, a passage through time and space, as living universes we embody eternity like a continuous traveller ... that chooses his/her/its preferred speeds of relation to time/space.
>
> [...]
>
> Life is an eternal mover.
>
> (*Moving Thoughts Journal*, February 2018)

30

Felt Thinking as Living Philosophy

In further consideration of the relationship between humans and Nature, the processes of 'identifying' oneself with all the living beings and all life on Earth, as mentioned already in Naess's philosophy of Nature, become even more important when we consider the immanent role of feeling. In his *Introduction to Metaphysics*, Henri Bergson writes that 'out of that indivisible feeling, as from a spring, all the words, gestures, and actions of the man would appear to me to flow naturally' (Bergson and Hulme 1912: 2). And even though the main point of his introduction is to facilitate further understanding of intuition as a valid method in philosophical inquiry, he foregrounds intuition in attending to feeling first.

Bergson establishes a thorough argument in which he brings a complementary role of scientifically analytical outlook on life alongside the intuitive one and describes our relating to any philosophical issue in life, which we want to tackle in its essence, as first and foremost dependent on our capacity for *intellectual sympathy*, and *intuitive empathy* (Bergson and Hulme 1912).

Just like felt thinking in movement then, his method of philosophizing is an attempt to build bridges between the conscious and the unconscious thought, the logical and the intuitive-imaginative. And, as shown already in the previous section, by following the movement in practice, searching for life's meaningfulness resides in moving between inside-out and outside-in, or towards and away from. The closest I can ever agree and attune to Bergson's philosophy, while speaking primarily from practitioner's point of view, is that we both agree on the change-inducing role of 'tendency' (Bergson and Hulme 1912: 40) in movement, where, as I have shown, the slightest change in tendency, i.e. our intuitive intention to relate, changes movement's directionality.

That slightest change in tendencies of movement teaches us a lesson that to take an opposite view does not necessary mean to take a sharp turn. Or another lesson yet that the opposites are penetrating one another seamlessly in movement without any conflicting movement needing to take place. And these are the kinds of movements that shape the Earth as well, powerful in their subtlety and subtle in their powerful effects overtime.

The metaphysical realm of relating to the world, as argued in this study, is expressive beyond words, beyond translation or representation and finding ourselves within it. It has been very interesting to me to follow Bergson's attempts in exemplifying, by numerous comparisons, the way creative life force can be felt in experience. He does admit himself too that it is beyond comparison. And my hope is that I managed to simply 'seize' it in its creative unfoldings through presented in the previous section lived, personal stories in movement, connected by internal intention to attend to ourselves as Nature.

Bergson says:

> There is one reality, at least, which we all seize from within, by intuition and not by simple analysis. It is our own personality in its flowing through time – our self which endures. We may sympathize intellectually with nothing else, but we certainly sympathize with our own selves.
>
> (Bergson and Hulme 1912: 8)

And, as metaphorically connected here while describing the three dimensions of felt thinking, Bergson too believed that metaphysical wondering should penetrate the very heart of ourselves, as integral experience of self and other in constant movement and away from hermetic concepts and static judgements.

'The life force constitutes the unique nature of all that is animate' (Phipps 1990: 91), and intellect alone, unaided by intuition cannot possibly form an adequate idea of life for us. 'The inner life is all this at once: variety of qualities, continuity of progress, and unity of direction' (Bergson and Hulme 1912: 9) and it cannot be represented by images or concepts but lived, felt and experienced only.

Felt thinking in movement has opened up to me new ways of relating that go beyond the rigid and ready-made concepts. It creates new paths for more mobile reasoning that comes from the felt and which moulds my thoughts by intuition and guides onto flexibility and trust in myself as a living being alongside all other life.

The essence of philosophy, the way I understand it in movement, is that in order to understand the movement of life, instead of viewing it from a static position, we must move with it. Life is pure mobility in its creative flow.

> It is movement that we must accustom ourselves to look upon as simplest and clearest, immobility (of scientific analysis) being only the extreme limit of the slowing down of movement, a limit reached only, perhaps, in thought and never realized in nature.
>
> (Bergson and Hulme 1912: 31)

And, similar to Bergson's living philosophy then, felt thinking is a philosophy of ongoing change, available to all, where philosophizing means being with life, including life's most gentle movements, those of sensuous connectivity, experiential responsiveness and insightful intuition, and which we can tap into whole-bodily while following the possibilities of living our authentic selves.

Rounding Up, Open Thoughts

In this work, I have argued that having threatened the health and integrity of the world, we come to live and breathe in, human beings, including myself, have to now realize that otherness is part of ourselves and that it resides within us.

The following task is then to offer our best in re-pairing the damage which, to me, starts with realizing our human potential for being an integral part of the process of 'listening within' and re-pairing ourselves while letting the natural world live and repair itself in interconnected belonging. The process of re-covery through re-dis-covery, nevertheless, won't happen without maturity, humbleness, respect and an embodied comprehension of time as self, thus all Life on Earth.

Time, as it shapes itself in somatic experience of felt thinking, is not relative as much as it is relational.

The real artist in me/you/us is in movement that comes about as our experience of co-created time. We are movement/time/Nature/selves. And, being relational too, time offers itself in its immediate and all-embracing meaningfulness that radiates with its transformative, change inducive and creative potential we can connect to and become a mindful part of. Thus, while authentically connected with movement/time/Nature/Self – we are, like all life on Earth, the meaning of life, ourselves.

We are one and all in Nature, and I trust we are able to create more integrated ways of perceiving and living in the world full of intrinsic meaning in its life-giving dynamics of folding and unfolding while embracing the endless possibilities of change in between.

It is important to say now that in the presented here material, I decided to include as much personal stories as possible to let the reader experience the stories being told within a particular place as meaningful in themselves, and I argue for their larger validity in context of scholarly writing. In hopes for retrieving a bit from the oral, Indigenous cultures of the world, Abram says that 'stories of such cultures give evidence of the unique power of particular bioregions', here alluding to Scottish landscapes, in which 'unique ecologies call upon the human community' (1996: 182). And that each place has its own mind, personality and its own intelligence.

The singular magic of a place is evident from what happens there, from what befalls oneself or others when in its vicinity. To tell of such events is implicitly to tell of the particular power of that site, and indeed to participate in its expressive potency.

(Abram 1996: 182)

And so, by letting the stories sprouted in particular places, here the Scottish Highlands, be presented in their original, not edited or interpreted version, I am trying to resist what Abram describes as 'abstract notion of space as a homogeneous and placeless void' (1996: 182) and let them convey the sense of place in 'storied resonance' with their ecological depths of meaning. It is also because the very reading of those stories means participating in an ongoing creative process and the ongoing emergence of new meanings as 'the storied universe that continually retells itself'(Abram 1996: 187).

The sensed reciprocity in movement expressed in repeating certain patterns shares the naturally cyclical nature of time. And, in creating circular movement, its co-creative relationship to space can be felt as well. Circular movement demarcates spatial fields through defining, embracing and permeating. Movement exists in time/space while time/space exists in movement as well, and, as Abram describes, the 'cyclical mode of time does not readily distinguish itself from the spatial field' (1996: 190) as people, or all living beings rather, find themselves experientially immersed in it. The time/space thus, as a 'qualitative matrix', move(s) in, with, through and thanks to us, even in stillness.

The way that we, as all living beings on Earth, incorporate this dual nature sets the foundation for many aspects of human life, and so is our ability to create new realities from our imaginary or sensed futures, grounded in the past experience and connected to the present moment. As in my writing too perhaps, where

to write means among other things to transform a material writing instrument into a quasi-part of the body, to incorporate it into the general scheme of bodily existence, to make it a channel through which the currents of human life can flow out to other.

(Seamon and Mugerauer 1989: 219)

Yet for it to become a responsible act of creation, it has to be informed by, grounded and co-created through embodied listening to the movement inspired by Earth and its lived stories of others. Only when purposeful appropriation of the environment diminishes, can we start creating an intimately responsive and endlessly meaningful paradigm for living *with* the world.

It is also where alienation, which Berndt Jager calls 'a loss of access to the flesh of nature' and 'a forced, brooding selfishness' (Seamon and Mugerauer 1989: 219), can be transformed into 'ceaseless transubstantiation' (Seamon and Mugerauer 1989: 220), the sensually embodied and co-creative co-presence.

It is thus the proper intention of action that will provide us with directions in the continuous search for the miraculous origins, where celebration of those does not indicate possession but mindful participation.

It is my hope then that the presented here practice of felt thinking in movement with Nature is seen as an invitation to live in connection with life beyond one's own while looking within, to follow the currents of moving thoughts that permeate feelings and sensations, and to surrender in trust for life's guiding wisdom. A three-fold practice of somatic experiencing of being Nature/Self through awakened sensitivity, embodied responsiveness and insightful responsibility and the continuous wondering about our movement-evoked nature while wandering the wonderous Earth in restorative contemplation and mindful co-creation.

And although the subject of human nature in its innate relationship to the living world around seems inexhaustible, I hope I have touched upon some major themes worth considering in a wider debate on life's creative force embodied in movement and its deep ecological dimensions and which bring experiential *feeling* to the forefronts of being, human or other.

Attending to somatic movement experience helps us move away from habits of forcing the living into our rigid 'moulds of thinking' (Ansell-Pearson 2018b) and which life ultimately cracks open anyway and helps us understand the whole as universal mobility and creative interaction.

Following Bergson, who points us to the 'pre-human sense of the world' (Hanna and Bergson 1962) and urges that 'there is a need to break with sedimented habits of thoughts, including and especially spatializing habits, that prevent the adequate conception of ourselves as beings of time (duration)' (Ansell-Pearson 2018b: 3), Gregory Bateson (2000) too says that the most important task today is to think in a new way, and I suggest that the new way is in felt thinking in movement. The practice that lets time and space blend into individually felt 's-pacing', so we can 'rediscover the enveloping earth' (Abram 1996) and where the emergent *circular paradigm of relationality* helps to move fluidly between the smallest cellular life and the largest cosmological contexts of life experience in an all-inclusive way through connectivity, embrace and permeability of being alive together.

In *being* we are all one, human, animal, plants, etc. We are earthlings – beings of the Earth, experientially immersed in its cyclical modes of time. And yet, within our 'earthly being', there is an infinite number of ways that only movement can define for us in its individually shaping, yet always changing patterns, that make you, and me in the endlessly emerging cycles of relational be(come)ing, just like the emergent in this process – dances with sheep.

FIGURE R1.1: *Moving Thoughts Journal, Handprint*, November 2017.

Glossary

Authentic Movement: is one of somatic movement practices that incorporates expressive and improvisational movement exploration and is guided by witnessing as a base for reflective, non-judgmental exchange offered to the mover. It was started by Mary Starks Whitehouse in the 1950s as 'movement in depth' practice to explore the principles of Jungian active imagination while working with psychiatric patients and it is now widely practised not only in therapeutic sessions but also in groups moving for personal expression of the unconscious mind and a form of spiritual practice.

Ecopsychology: the developing field of ecopsychology extends beyond the conventional view of psychology traditionally considering the psyche to be a matter of relevance to humans alone. It examines why people continue environmentally damaging behaviour, as well as develops methods of positive motivation for adopting sustainable practices. Other names used to refer to ecopsychology include depth ecology, Gaia psychology, psychoecology, ecotherapy, environmental psychology, green psychology, transpersonal ecology, global therapy, green therapy, Earth-centered therapy, nature-based psychotherapy or ecosophy.

Natural movement:

1. Phenomenon of spontaneously occurring movement characterized by a natural continuity between perception and sensation and movement whether this movement is large and visible, or the micromovement of minute shifting in the joints, or internal physiological movement.
2. Practice of attending to sensations and allowing those sensations to move, breathe and sound in their own way (definition used in Body–Mind Psychotherapy developed by Susan Aposhyan [Aposhyan 1999]).

Somatic movement education: is a field within bodywork, movement studies and movement therapy which emphasizes internal perception and experience of mindful movement as principal tools for enhancing human function and body–mind integration. It incorporates practices like postural and movement evaluation, experiential anatomy, movement patterning and aims at refining perceptual, kinaesthetic and proprioceptive sensitivity through attending to all movement based and life sustaining bodily processes. Somatic movement education and therapy supports homeostasis, co-regulation and neuro-plasticity (definition by ISMETA: www.ismeta.org).

With Alexander technique, Feldenkrais Method, Rolfing and Authentic Movement being most widespread somatic practices, other pioneers whose work has shaped and developed somatic practices in therapy include Elsa Gindler and Charlotte Selver (Sensory Awareness), Irmgard Bartenieff (Bartenieff Fundamentals), Thomas Hanna (Hanna Somatic Education), Anna Halprin (The Tamalpa Life/Art Process), Bonnie Bainbridge Cohen (Body–Mind Centering), Emilie Conrad (Continuum Movement), Sondra Fraleigh (Eastwest Somatics Institute), to name just a few.

Also, with its earliest connections to the Eastern practices of yoga, somatic movement education in western culture can be traced to the turn of the twentieth century, alongside the increased popularity of phenomenology and existentialism in philosophy and education and with John Dewey and Rudolf Steiner as advocates of experiential learning as well as with choreographic work of Isadora Duncan, Rudolf Laban or Mary Wigman who introduced new movement paradigms to contemporary dance world (further reference: *Mindful Movement: The Evolution of the Somatic Arts and Conscious Action* by Martha Eddy [Moving for Life, Dynamic Embodiment], available at www.drmarthaeddy.com/book).

Somatic movement experience: is free, improvised movement created through mindful attending to internal perception, and kinaesthetic and proprioceptive sensitivity while relating to bodily experience as 'experienced from within' (Hanna 1986), extended inclusively onto embodied conscious awareness, the experience of body, self and otherness, and also body as nature in lived experience, i.e. 'the unity of soma and psyche' (Fraleigh 2015).

Somatic psychology: the field of somatic psychology focuses on somatic experience and holistic approaches to body. Susan Aposhyan introduces the field as centering 'psychological exploration in the body' (1999: x). It originates in the 1930s with Wilhelm Reich's work on the role of energy flow and physical defences in psychological health and since then developed into an array of somatic psychological approaches including Dance/Movement Therapy, Bioenergetics, Hakomi, Integrative Body Psychotherapy, Expressive Art Therapy, Focussing, Rolfing, BMC (Body–Mind Centering), Life/Art Process, Somatic Experiencing and other.

Somatics: International Somatic Movement Education and Therapy Association (ismeta.org) defines somatics as the study of the self from the perspective of one's lived experience, encompassing dimensions of body, psyche and spirit (definition coined in 1976 by Thomas Hanna, Director of the Graduate School at the Humanistic Psychology Institute in San Francisco, Founder of Novato Institute of Somatic Research and Clinical Somatic Education: www.hannasomatics.com). Somatics is a broad field that incorporates many distinct practical approaches with their own educational and therapeutic methods (see somatic movement education, p.245–46).

Wellbeing: the basic understanding of *wellbeing* within the somatic movement and creative arts education and therapy emerges from the primacy of life and personal engagement in contemplative practice. It is also through live experiences that one is able to reflect upon such practice. According to John Christopher (2016), this living practice-based perspective might be seen at odds with the conventional, more intellectual way of understanding *wellbeing* as one's skill or 'mastery in maximizing the positive life experiences and minimizing the negative ones'. Practising this open attitude towards the self, the world and life, which embraces a co-creative involvement in life as a larger, universal force, as Christopher describes, can only be achieved by one's active participation through being mindful, and which in return creates a strong sense of connection to ourselves, the environment and life that our wellbeing can rest upon, and which opens doors for continuous self-discovery.

The conditioning aspects in understanding the ongoing sense of wellbeing in somatic movement and creative arts education/therapy would then include the following: sense of connection and safety; discovering the deeper body-based experiential dimension of self and our wider meaning in life/world; being active in joining life in its co-creating flow instead of managing self/life; staying open to discovering and learning; being mindful in sharing presence and developing respect for 'other' life.

References

Abel, D. C. (1992), *Theories of Human Nature: Classical and Contemporary Readings*, London: McGraw-Hill.

Abram, D. (1996), *The Spell of the Sensuous: Perception and Language in a More-Than-Human World*, New York: Pantheon Books.

Abram, D. (2010), *Becoming Animal: An Earthly Cosmology*, New York: Pantheon Books.

Aizenstat, S. (2003), *Nature Dreaming: Depth Psychology and Ecology*, http://www.dream-tending.com/naturedreaming.pdf. Accessed 2 February 2018.

Allen, R. C. (1999), *David Hartley on Human Nature*, Albany: State University of New York Press.

Anderson, R. (2001), 'Embodied writing and reflections on embodiment', *Journal of Transpersonal Psychology*, 33:2, pp. 83–96.

Anderson, R. and Braud, W. (2011), *Transforming Self and Others Through Research: Transpersonal Research Methods and Skills for the Human Sciences and Humanities*, Albany: State University of New York Press.

Ansell-Pearson, K. A. (2018), *Bergson: Thinking Beyond the Human Condition*, New York: Bloomsbury Academic.

Aposhyan, S. M. (1999), *Natural Intelligence: Body–Mind Integration and Human Development*, Baltimore: Williams & Wilkins.

Aposhyan, S. M. (2004), *Body–Mind Psychotherapy: Principles, Techniques and Practical Applications*, London: W.W. Norton & Co.

Archer, G. J. (2015), 'Dancing the wild life – An exploration of embodied practice with women in nature', Master of Arts Practice-Based Research, Preston: University of Central Lancashire, UK.

Aristotle, Waterfield, R. and Bostock, D. (1996), *Physics*, Oxford: Oxford University Press.

Aron, E. N. (1997), *The Highly Sensitive Person: How To Thrive When the World Overwhelms You*, New York: Broadway Books.

Azara, N. J. (2002), *Spirit Taking Form: Making a Spiritual Practice of Making Art*, Boston: Red Wheel.

Bacon, J. (2010), 'The voice of her body: Somatic practices as a basis for creative research methodology', *Journal of Dance and Somatic Practices*, 2, pp. 63–74.

Badiou, A. (2010), *The Communist Hypothesis*, London, New York: Verso.

Bainbridge Cohen, B. (1993), *Sensing, Feeling, and Action: The Experiential Anatomy of Body–Mind Centering: The Collected Articles from Contact Quarterly Dance Journal 1980–1992*, Northhampton: Contact Editions.

Barratt, B. B. (2010), *The Emergence of Somatic Psychology and Bodymind Therapy*, Basingstoke: Palgrave Macmillan.

Barrett, E. and Bolt, B. (2007), *Practice as Research: Approaches to Creative Arts Enquiry*, London: I. B. Tauris.

Barrington, J. (2006), *Loch Lomond and The Trossachs: An A–Z of Loch Lomond and The Trossachs National Park and Surrounding Area*, Edinburgh: Luath Press.

Bateson, G. (2000), *Steps to an Ecology of Mind*, Chicago: University of Chicago Press.

Bateson, N. (n.d.), 'International Bateson Institute', http://www.anecologyofmind.com/. Accessed 7 October 2022.

Bergson, H. (1983), *Creative Evolution*, Lanham: University Press of America.

Bergson, H. (1988), *Matter and Memory*, New York, London: N.Y., Dover Publications (Distributed by MIT Press).

Bergson, H., Ansell-Pearson, K., Kolkman, M. and Vaughan, M. (2007), *Creative Evolution*, Basingstoke: Palgrave Macmillan.

Bergson, H. and Hulme, T. E. (1912), *An Introduction to Metaphysics*, New York, London: G. P. Putnam's Sons.

Bird, M. Y. (2014), 'Decolonizing the Mind: Healing through neurodecolonization and mindfulness', Vimeo, https://vimeo.com/86995336. Accessed 11 August 2022.

Blackburn, J. (2007), 'Implications of presence in manual therapy', *Journal of Bodywork and Movement Therapies*, 11, pp. 68–77.

Bohm, D. (2002), *Wholeness and the Implicate Order*, London, New York: Routledge.

Bohm, D. and Nichol, L. (2004), *On Creativity*, London, New York: Routledge.

Brandstätter, H. and Eliasz, A. (2001), *Persons, Situations, and Emotions: An Ecological Approach*, Oxford: Oxford University Press.

Brodie, J. A. and Lobel, E. E. (2012), *Dance and Somatics: Mind–Body Principles of Teaching and Performance*, Jefferson: McFarland & Co.

Brooke, R. (1991), *Jung and Phenomenology*, London: Routledge.

Brooke, R. (2000), *Pathways into the Jungian World: Phenomenology and Analytical Psychology*, London, New York: Routledge.

Brooks, C. V. W., Selver, C., Lowe, R. and Laeng-Gilliatt, S. (2007), *Reclaiming Vitality and Presence: Sensory Awareness as a Practice for Life*, Berkeley: North Atlantic Books; Enfield: Publishers Group UK (Distributor).

Brown, C. S. and Toadvine, T. (2003), *Eco-Phenomenology: Back to the Earth Itself*, Albany: State University of New York Press.

Brown, L. R. and Brown, L. R. P. B. (2008), *Plan B 3.0: Mobilizing to Save Civilization*, New York, London: W. W. Norton.

Brown, N. G., Crawley, M.-L., Kim, E. S., Hayward-Smith, L. (2009), *Journal of Dance & Somatic Practices*, Bristol: Intellect.

Buhler, C. M. and Allen, M. (1972), *Introduction to Humanistic Psychology*, Monterey: Brooks/Cole Pub. Co.

Cambrn, J. A. (ed.) (1996), *Journal of Bodywork and Movement Therapies*, Edinburgh: Churchill Livingstone.

Canales, J. (2015), *The Physicist & The Philosopher: Einstein, Bergson, and the Debate That Changed Our Understanding of Time*, Princeton: Princeton University Press.

Cantopher, T. (2012), *Depressive Illness: The Curse of the Strong*, New York: Sheldon Press.

Carel, H. E. and Meacham, D. E., *Phenomenology and Naturalism: Examining the Relationship between Human Experience and Nature*, Cambridge: Cambridge University Press.

Carr, H. W. (1914), *The Philosophy of Change: A Study of the Fundamental Principle of the Philosophy of Bergson*, London: MacMillan.

Chodorow, J. (1991), *Dance Therapy and Depth Psychology: The Moving Imagination*, London: Routledge.

Chomsky, N. (2009), 'The mysteries of nature: How deeply hidden?', *The Journal of Philosopy* CVI:4, pp. 167–200, https://www.scribd.com/doc/99485222/Chomsky-Noam-The-Mysteries-of-Nature-How-Deeply-Hidden-Journal-of-Philosophy-2009. Accessed 11 August 2022.

Chomsky, N., Belletti, A. and Rizzi, L. (2002), *On Nature and Language*, Cambridge: Cambridge University Press.

Christopher, J. (2016), 'On well-being', in *Relational Implicit*, https://relationalimplicit.com/zug/transcripts/Christopher-2016-07.pdf. Accessed 2 February 2018 [no longer available].

Christopher, J. C. (1999), 'Situating psychological well-being: Exploring the cultural roots of its theory and research', *Journal of Counselling and Development*, 77, pp. 141–52.

Clements, J. (2004), 'Organic inquiry: Toward research in partnership with spirit', *The Journal of Transpersonal Psychology*, 36:1, pp. 26–49.

Cohen, B. B., Nelson, L. and Smith, N. S. (2012), *Sensing, Feeling, and Action: The Experiential Anatomy of Body–Mind Centering®*, Northampton: Contact Editions.

Collins, P. and Gallinat, A. (2010), *The Ethnographic Self as Resource: Writing Memory and Experience into Ethnography*, New York: Berghahn Books.

Combs, A. W. (1999), *Being and Becoming: A Field Approach to Psychology*, New York: Springer Pub. Co.

Condon, W. S. (1978), 'An analysis of behavioural organization', *Sign Language Studies*, 13, pp. 285–318.

Conrad, E. ([2007] n.d.), 'The fluid self', Excerpt from *Life on Land*, https://continuummovement.com/life-land-excerpt/. Accessed 11 August 2022.

Conrad, E. (2007), *Life on Land: The Story of Continuum, The World Renowned Self-Discovery, and Movement Method*, foreword by V. Hunt, Berkeley: North Atlantic Books.

Creswell, J. W. (2009), *Research Design: Qualitative, Quantitative, and Mixed Methods Approaches*, Los Angeles and London: SAGE.

Creswell, J. W. and Plano Clark, V. L. (2011), *Designing and Conducting Mixed Methods Research*, Los Angeles: SAGE Publications.

Critchley, S. (2009), 'Heidegger's *Being and Time*, part 8: Temporality', *The Guardian*, www.theguardian.com/commentisfree/belief/2009/jul/27/heidegger-being-time-philosophy. Accessed 11 August 2022.

Curtis, E. (2011), *Bringing Stone Circles into Being: Practices in the Long 19th Century and Their Influence on Current Understandings of Stone Circles in North-East Scotland*, Aberdeen: University of Aberdeen.

Dako, A. (2002), 'The evolution of the image of the Native Americans as depicted in films', bachelor's degree PWSZ, Krosno: Krosno State College, https://aberdeen.academia.edu/AnnaPeszkeDako. Accessed 9 November 2022.

Dako, A. (2010), 'Dynamic composing – On choreographic processes of conceptualization as a way to artistic knowing', Master of Arts, Amsterdam: University of Amsterdam, https://aberdeen.academia.edu/AnnaPeszkeDako. Accessed 9 November 2022.

Dako, A. (2015), 'Night(s) and day(s) inspired by light | drawn toward darkness inspired by darkness | drawn toward light: A behind the scenes story of night(s)&day(s) short dance film production inspired by somatic adventures into the experience of inter-connectedness between "knowing" and "not knowing"', Master of Arts in Dance and Somatic Wellbeing, Preston: University of Central Lancashire, https://aberdeen.academia.edu/AnnaPeszkeDako. Accessed 9 November 2022.

Dako, A. (2021), 'On how to feel think in movement: A short introduction: Contemplating ecological belonging in somatic practice', *Journal of Dance & Somatic Practices*, 13:1&2, pp. 19–27, https://doi.org/10.1386/jdsp_00033_1. Accessed November 2022.

Damasio, A. R. (1994), *Descartes' Error: Emotion, Reason, and the Human Brain*, New York: G.P. Putnam.

Damasio, A. R. (2000), *The Feeling of What Happens: Body and Emotion in the Making of Consciousness*, London: W. Heinemann.

Damasio, A. R. (2001), *Unity of Knowledge: The Convergence of Natural and Human Science*, New York: New York Academy of Sciences.

Decesaro, E. A. S. A. G. D. (2015), 'Modelling innovative methodological practices in a dance/family studies transdisciplinary project', *Journal of Family Theory & Review*, https://doi.org/10.1111/jftr.12109. Accessed 11 August 2022.

Denzin, N. K. (2013), *Interpretive Autoethnography*, Thousand Oaks: SAGE.

Denzin, N. K. and Lincoln, Y. S. (1994), *Handbook of Qualitative Research*, Thousand Oaks: SAGE.

Denzin, N. K. E. and Giardina, M. D. E. ([2013] 2016), *Global Dimensions of Qualitative Inquiry*, New York: Routledge, https://doi.org/10.4324/9781315428093. Accessed 11 August 2022.

Descola, P. A. and Lloyd, J. T. (2005), *Beyond Nature and Culture*, Chicago: Chicago University Press.

Eddy, M. (2000), *Access to Somatic Theory and Applications: Socio-Political Concerns*, http://www.wellnesscke.net/downloadables/Access-to-Somatics.pdf. Accessed 11 August 2022.

Eddy, M. (2002), 'Somatic practices and dance: Global influences', *Dance Research Journal*, 34, pp. 46–62.

Eddy, M. (2009), 'A brief history of somatic practices and dance – Historical development of the field of somatic education and its relationship to dance', *Journal of Dance and Somatic Practices*, 1:1, pp. 5–27.

Eddy, M. A. (2016), *Mindful Movement: The Evolution of The Somatic Arts and Conscious Action*, Chicago: Chicago University Press.

Eisner, E. W. (1991), *The Enlightened Eye: Qualitative Inquiry and the Enhancement of Educational Practice*, Toronto: Macmillan Pub. Co.

Embree, L. (1997), *Encyclopedia of Phenomenology*, Dordrecht: Kluwer Academic Publishers.

Etherington, K. (2004), *Becoming a Reflexive Researcher: Using Our Selves in Research*, London: Jessica Kingsley Publishers.

Ettinger, B. (2006), *The Matrixial Borderspace*, Minneapolis: University of Minnesota Press; Bristol: University Presses Marketing (Distributor).

Eriksen, T. H. A. (2016), *Overheating: An Anthropology of Accelerated Change*, London: Pluto Press.

Farnell, B. (1999), 'Moving bodies, acting selves', *Annual Review of Anthropology*, 28, pp. 341–73.

Farnell, B. (2000), 'Getting out of the habitus: An alternative model of dynamically embodied social action', *Journal of Royal Anthropological Institute*, 6, pp. 397–418.

Feldenkrais, M. (1980), *Awareness Through Movement: Health Exercises for Personal Growth*, Harmondsworth: Penguin.

Feldenkrais, M. (1993), *Body Awareness as Healing Therapy: The Case of Nora*, Berkeley: North Atlantic Books/Frog.

Feldenkrais, M. and Kimmey, M. (1985), *The Potent Self: A Guide to Spontaneity*, San Francisco: Harper & Row.

Fink, E. and Husserl, E. (1995), *Sixth Cartesian Meditation: The Idea of a Transcendental Theory of Method*, Bloomington: Indiana University Press.

Finlay, L. (2002), '"Outing" the researcher: The provenance, process, and practice of reflexivity', *Sage Journals*, 12:4, http://journals.sagepub.com/doi/pdf/10.1177/104973202129120052. Accessed 11 August 2022.

Forrester, M. A. (2010), *Doing Qualitative Research in Psychology: A Practical Guide*, London: SAGE.

Fraleigh, S. (1987), *Dance and the Lived Body: A Descriptive Aesthetics*, Pittsburgh: University of Pittsburgh Press.

Fraleigh, S. (2004), *Dancing Identity: Metaphysics in Motion*, Pittsburgh: University of Pittsburgh Press.

Fraleigh, S. (2015), *Moving Consciously: Somatic Transformations Through Dance, Yoga, and Touch*, Urbana: University of Illinois Press.

Fraleigh, S. and Hanstein, P. (1999), *Researching Dance: Evolving Modes of Inquiry*, London: Dance Books.

Frankl, V. E. and Crumbaugh, J. C. (1967), *Psychotherapy and Existentialism; Selected Papers on Logotherapy*, New York: Washington Square Press.

Frodeman, R. (2010), 'Experiments in field philosophy', *New York Times*, https://archive.nytimes.com/opinionator.blogs.nytimes.com/2010/11/23/experiments-in-field-philosophy/. Accessed 11 August 2022.

Gendlin, E. T. (1962), *Experiencing and the Creation of Meaning: A Philosophical and Psychological Approach to the Subjective*, Evanston: Northwestern University Press.

Gendlin, E. T. (1993), 'Human nature and concepts', in J. Braun (ed.), *Psychological Concepts of Modernity*, Westport: Praeger/Greenwood, http://www.focusing.org/gendlin/docs/gol_2060.html. Accessed 11 August 2022 [no longer available].

Gendlin, E. T. (1996), *Focusing-Oriented Psychotherapy: A Manual of the Experiential Method*, New York, London: Guilford Press.

Gendlin, E. T. (2003), *Focusing*, London: Rider.

Germain, C. B. and Bloom, M. (1999), *Human Behavior in the Social Environment: An Ecological View*, Chichester: Columbia University Press.

Ghiselin, B. (1980), *The Creative Process: A Symposium*, Berkeley: University of California Press.

Gibbs, A. (2007), 'Writing as method: Attunement, resonance, and rhythm', in B. T. Knudsen and C. Stage (eds), *Affective Methodologies*, London: Palgrave Macmillan.

Gilbert, P. J. A. (2017), *Human Nature and Suffering*, London: Routlege.

Gintis, B. (2007), *Engaging the Movement of Life: Exploring Health and Embodiment Through Osteopathy and Continuum*, Berkeley: North Atlantic; Enfield: Publishers Group UK [distributor].

Goodridge, J. (1999), *Rhythm and Timing of Movement in Performance: Drama, Dance, and Ceremony*, Philadelphia: J. Kingsley Publishers.

Green, J. (2015), 'Somatic sensitivity and reflexivity as validity tools in qualitative research', *Research in Dance Education*, 16:1, pp. 67–79.

Grosz, E. A. (1995), *Space, Time, and Perversion: Essays on the Politics of Bodies*, New York: Routledge.

Grosz, E. A. (1999), *Becomings: Explorations in Time, Memory, and Futures*, Ithaca: Cornell University Press.

Guattari, F. L. (2000), *The Three Ecologies*, London, New Brunswick: Athlone Press.

Gustafson, F. (1997), *Dancing Between Two Worlds: Jung and the Native American Soul*, New York: Paulist Press.

Hall, E. T. (1983), *The Dance of Life: The Other Dimension of Time*, Garden City: Anchor Press/Doubleday.

Halprin, A. (2012a), 'Ken Dychtwald Interviews Anna Halprin', YouTube, 'https://www.youtube.com/watch?v=SiUE0-NveZo [link no longer available].

Halprin, A. (2012b), 'Returning Home – Trailer', YouTube, https://www.youtube.com/watch?v=EvyI2MXzy4c&list=PLngclCawgWhiiTh1gT0Pa099Skg0RZ82O. Accessed 11 August 2022.

Halprin, A. and Kaplan, R. (1995), *Moving Toward Life: Five Decades of Transformational Dance*, Hanover, London: Wesleyan University Press.

Halprin, D. A. (2002), *The Expressive Body in Life, Art, and Therapy: Working with Movement, Metaphor and Meaning*, London: Jessica Kingsley Publishers.

Hanna, T. (1962), *The Bergsonian Heritage*, New York: Columbia University Press.

Hanna, T. (1970), *Bodies in Revolt; A Primer in Somatic Thinking*, New York: Holt, Rinehart and Winston.

Hanna, T. (1979), *Explorers of Humankind*, New York, London: Harper & Row.

Hanna, T. (1983), *Body of Life*, New York: Knopf.

Hanna, T. (1986a), 'Clinical somatic education: A new discipline in the field of health care', *SOMATICS: Magazine-Journal of the Bodily Arts and Sciences*, V, Spring–Summer, https://somatics.org/library/htl-wis1. Accessed 11 August 2022.

Hanna, T. (1986b), 'What is somatics? Part II', *Journal of the Bodily Arts and Sciences*, V, Spring–Summer, https://somatics.org/library/htl-wis2. Accessed 11 August 2022.

Hanna, T. (1987), 'What is somatics? Part III', *Journal of the Bodily Arts and Sciences*, VI, Spring/Summer, https://somatics.org/library/htl-wis3. Accessed 11 August 2022.

Hanna, T. (1988), *Somatics: Reawakening the Mind's Control of Movement, Flexibility, and Health*, Cambridge: Da Capo Life Long.

Hartley, L. (2001), *Servants of the Sacred Dream: Rebirthing the Deep Feminine: Psycho-spiritual Crisis and Healing*, Essex: Elmdon.

Hartley, L. (2004), *Somatic Psychology: Body, Mind and Meaning*, London: Whurr.

Hartley, L. (2009), *Contemporary Body Psychotherapy: The Chiron Approach*, London: Routledge.

Hartmann, T. (1999), *The Last Hours of Ancient Sunlight: Waking up to Personal and Global Transformation*, New York: Harmony Books (2001).

Harvey, S. R. (2009), *Heidegger and Eco-phenomenology:* Gelassenheit *as Practice*, Saarbrücken: Verlag Dr. Müller.

Heelas, P. and Lock, A. (1981), *Indigenous Psychologies: The Anthropology of the Self*, London, New York: Academic Press.

Heidegger, M. and Krell, D. F. (2008), *Basic Writings: From* Being and Time *(1927) to* The Task of Thinking *(1964)*, New York: Harper Perennial Modern Thought.

Heidegger, M., Macquarrie, J. P. U. T. S. N. Y. and Robinson, E. S. (1967), *Being and Time* (trans. J. Macquarrie and E. Robinson [reprinted]), Oxford: Blackwell.

Heraclitus and Kirk, G. S. (1954), *The Cosmic Fragments*, Cambridge: Cambridge University Press.

Herrigel, E. (1989), *Zen in the Art of Archery*, New York: Vintage Books.

Hervey, L. W. (2000), *Artistic Inquiry in Dance/Movement Therapy: Creative Research Alternatives*, Springfield: Charles C. Thomas.

Hibbs, T. and Aquinas, T. (1999), *On Human Nature*, Indianapolis: Hackett Pub.

Hillman, J. (1992), *The Thought of the Heart & the Soul of the World*, Dallas: Spring Publications.

Husserl, E. (1965), *Cartesian Meditations*, The Hague: M. Nijhoff.

Ingold, T. (2000), *The Perception of the Environment: Essays on Livelihood, Dwelling and Skill*, London: Routledge.

Ingold, T. (2011), *Being Alive: Essays on Movement, Knowledge and Description*, London: Routledge.

Ingold, T. (2013), *Making: Anthropology, Archaeology, Art and Architecture*, London: Routledge.

Ingold, T. (2016a), *Changing Epistemologies and Life* at the symposium on the *Expression of Difference and the Language of Similarity*, 7 October, Uppsala University, 'Tim Ingold, University of Aberdeen', YouTube, https://www.youtube.com/watch?v=Wh4BKSVSYyI. Accessed 11 August 2022.

Ingold, T. (2016b), 'From science to art and back again: The pendulum of an anthropologist', *ANUAC*, 5:1 pp. 5–23, http://aura.abdn.ac.uk/bitstream/handle/2164/7688/FROM_SCIENCE_TO_ART_AND_BACK_AGAIN.pdf;jsessionid=E19E16C922591769B2B8D93F5F95BF7D?sequence=1. Accessed 11 August 2022.

Ingold, T. (2017), *Anthropology and/as Education: Anthropology, Art, Architecture and Design*, Abingdon, New York: Routledge,.

Ings, W. (2014), 'The authored voice: Emerging approaches to exegesis design in creative practice PhDs', *Educational Philosophy and Theory*, 47:12, pp. 1277–90, [ACCESS: Supervising practice: perspectives on the supervision of creative practice higher degrees by research], http://www.tandfonline.com/doi/pdf/10.1080/00131857.2014.974017?needAccess=true. Accessed 11 August 2022.

Irigaray, L. (2017), *To Be Born – Genesis of a New Human Being*, London: Palgrave Macmillan.

Jaeger, R. M. (ed.) (1997), *Complementary Methods for Research in Education*, Washington DC: American Educational Research Association.

Jahoda, G. (1992), *Crossroads Between Culture and Mind: Continuities and Change in Theories of Human Nature*, London: Harvester Wheatsheaf.

James, A. (2012), 'Seeking the analytic imagination: Reflections on the process of interpreting qualitative data', *Qualitative Research*, 13:5, pp. 562–77.

Johnson, D. (1995), *Bone, Breath and Gesture: Practices of Embodiment*, Berkeley: North Atlantic Books.

Johnson, D. and California Institute of Integral Studies (1997), *Groundworks: Narratives of Embodiment*, Berkeley, San Francisco, Emeryville: North Atlantic Books: California Institute of Integral Studies (Distributed to the trade by Publisher's Group West).

Johnson, D. and Grand, I. J. (1998), *The Body in Psychotherapy: Inquiries in Somatic Psychology*, Berkeley: North Atlantic Books.

Johnson, D. H. E. (2018), *Diverse Bodies, Diverse Practices: Toward an Inclusive Somatics*, Berkeley: North Atlantic Books.

Johnson, R. (2000), *Elemental Movement – A Somatic Approach to Movement Education*, Boca Raton: Dissertation.com, https://www.academia.edu/3736040/Elemental_Movement_A_Somatic_Approach_to_Movement_Education. Accessed 11 August 2022.

Johnston, M. S. (2016), 'Men can change: Transformation, agency, ethics and closure during critical dialogue in interviews', *Qualitative Research*, 16:2, pp. 131–50.

Joseph, S. A. (2015), *Positive Therapy: Building Bridges Between Positive Psychology and Person-Centred Therapy*, London: Routledge.

Joseph, S. A. M. D. (2013), 'Person-centered approach, positive psychology and relational helping: Building bridges', *Journal of Humanistic Psychology*, 53:1, pp. 26–51.

Jung, C. G. ([1958] 2002), *The Undiscovered Self*, London: Routledge.

Jung, C. G. ([1960] 2001), *On the Nature of the Psyche*, London: Routledge Classics.

Jung, C. G. (1963), *Memories, Dreams, Reflections*, New York: Pantheon Books.

Jung, C. G. (1973), *Synchronicity: An Acausal Connecting Principle*, Princeton: Princeton University Press.

Jung, C. G. and Chodorow, J. (1997), *Jung on Active Imagination: Key Readings Selected and Introduced by Joan Chodorow*, London: Routledge.

Jung, C. G. and Sabini, M. (2002), *The Earth Has a Soul: The Nature Writings of C.G. Jung*, Berkeley: North Atlantic Books.

Kahn, C. H. and Heraclitus (1979), *The Art and Thought of Heraclitus: An Edition of the Fragments with Translation and Commentary*, Cambridge and New York: Cambridge University Press.

Kapitan, L. (2017), *Introduction to Art Therapy Research*, London: Routledge

Karkou, V. (2010), *Arts Therapies in Schools: Research and Practice*, London: Jessica Kingsley.

Karkou, V. and Sanderson, P. (2006), *Arts Therapies: A Research-Based Map of the Field*, Edinburgh: Elsevier Churchill Livingstone.

Kelly, J. G. (2006), *Becoming Ecological: An Expedition into Community Psychology*, New York, Oxford: Oxford University Press.

Kidner, D. W. (2000), *Nature and Psyche: Radical Environmentalism and the Politics of Subjectivity*, Albany: State University of New York Press.

Knox, R. (2013), *Relational Depth: New Perspectives and Developments*, Basingstoke: Palgrave Macmillan.

Kohn, E. (2013), *How Forests Think: Toward an Anthropology Beyond the Human*, Berkeley: University of California Press.

Kołakowski, L. (2001), *Bergson*, South Bend: St. Augustine's Press.

Kozel, S. (2007), *Closer: Performance, Technologies, Phenomenology*, Cambridge: MIT Press.

Kroll, J. (2005), 'The exegesis and the gentle reader/writer', *Text: Illuminating the Exegesis*, http://www.textjournal.com.au/speciss/issue3/kroll.htm. Accessed 11 August 2022.

Kupperman, J. (2010), *Theories of Human Nature*, Indianapolis: Hackett Pub. Co.

Lakoff, G. and Johnson, M. (1999), *Philosophy in the Flesh: The Embodied Mind and Its Challenge to Western Thought*, New York: Basic Books.

Lamothe, K. L. (2015), *Why We Dance: A Philosophy of Bodily Becoming*, New York: New York Columbia University Press.

Lars Petter Torjussen, J. S. A. S. A. O. (2008), *An interview with Anna-Teresa Tymieniecka*, https://www.phenomenology.org/images/Interview-A-T-Tymieniecka-27-August-2008.pdf. Accessed 2 February 2018 [no longer available].

Levine, P. A. (1997), *Waking the Tiger: Healing Trauma: The Innate Capacity to Transform Overwhelming Experiences*, Berkeley: North Atlantic Books.

Levine, P. A. (2005), *Healing Trauma: A Pioneering Program to Restore the Wisdom of Your Body*, Boulder: Sounds True.

Lewin, D. (2015), 'Heidegger east and west: Philosophy as educative contemplation', *Journal of Philosophy of Education*, 49:2, pp. 221–39.

Loizou, A. (2000), *Time, Embodiment and the Self*, Aldershot, Hants, England, Burlington: Vt., Ashgate.

Loomis, M. E. (1991), *Dancing: The Wheel of Psychological Types*, Wilmette: Chiron Publications.

Lopez, B. (2014), 'Nature and human nature by Barry Lopez – A Singapore writers festival 2014 lecture', Singapore Writers Festival, YouTube, https://www.youtube.com/watch?v=JQ63BC5iZHg. Accessed 11 August 2022.

Lou, L. I. T. A., Xiang, B. D. S. and Lora-Wainwright, A. D. S. (2016), 'Healing nature: Green living and the politics of hope in Hong Kong', Ph.D. thesis, Oxford: University of Oxford.

Loukes, R. (2003), *Psychological Awareness in Training and Performance: Elsa Gindler and Her Legacy*, Exeter: University of Exeter.

Louv, R. (2008), *Last Child in the Woods: Saving Our Children from Nature-Deficit Disorder*, Chapel Hill: Algonquin Books of Chapel Hill.

Luczaj, S. A. (2015), 'Felt senses of self and no-self in therapy', Ph.D. thesis, East Anglia: University of East Anglia.

Lyons, S. A. and Karkou, V. D. S. (2019), 'Arts therapies for dementia: A systematic review and community-based case study on the value of music therapy and dance movement therapy', Ph.D. thesis, Ormskirk: Edge Hill University.

Macnaughton, I. (2004), *Body, Breath & Consciousness: A Somatics Anthology: A Collection of Articles on Family Systems, Self-Psychology, the Bodynamics Model of Somatic Developmental Psychology, Shock Trauma, and Breathwork*, Berkeley: North Atlantic.

Macy, J. and Brown, M. Y. (2014), *Coming Back to Life: The Updated Guide to the Work that Reconnects*, Gabriola Island: New Society Publishers.

Macy, J. and Johnstone, C. (2012), *Active Hope: How to Face the Mess We're in Without Going Crazy*, Novato: New World Library.

Madill, A., Jordan, A. and Shirley, C. (2000), 'Objectivity and reliability in qualitative analysis: Realist, contextualist and radical constructionist epistemologies', *British Journal of Psychology*, 91, pp. 1–20.

Mafe, B. H. A. D. (2009), 'Acquiring know-how: Research training for practice-led researchers', in H. Smith and R. Dean (eds), *Practice-Led Research, Research-Led Practice in the Creative Arts*, Edinburgh: Edinburgh University Press.

Main, J. (1990), *The Way of Unknowing: Expanding Spiritual Horizons Through Meditation*, New York: Crossroad.

Malchiodi, C. A. (2007), *The Art Therapy Sourcebook*, New York: McGraw-Hill.

Malins, J. and Gray, C. (1995), 'Appropriate research methodologies for artists, designers & craftspersons: Research as a learning', http://carolegray.net/Papers%20PDFs/cc.pdf. Accessed 11 August 2022.

Manen, M. V. (2007), 'Phenomenology of practice', *Phenomenology & Practice*, 1, pp. 11–30, http://www.maxvanmanen.com/files/2011/04/2007-Phenomenology-of-Practice.pdf. Accessed 11 August 2022.

Mann, J. F. A. A. (2004), 'Illuminating the exegesis', *Text: Illuminating the Exegesis*, 3, http://www.textjournal.com.au/speciss/issue3/content.htm. Accessed 7 October 2021.

Manning, E. (2009), *Relationscapes: Movement, Art, Philosophy*, Cambridge: MIT Press.

Margitay, T. (2010), *Knowing and Being: Perspectives on the Philosophy of Michael Polanyi*, Cambridge: Cambridge Scholars Publishing.

Marlock, G., Weiss, H., Young, C., Soth, M. and Society For The Study Of Native Arts And Sciences (2015), *The Handbook of Body Psychotherapy and Somatic Psychology*, Berkeley: North Atlantic Books.

Massey, H. (2015), *The Origin of Time: Heidegger and Bergson*, Albany: State University of New York Press.

Masterson, J. F. (1988), *The Search for the Real Self: Unmasking the Personality Disorders of Our Age*, New York: Free Press.

Mathews, F. (1991), *The Ecological Self*, Savage: Barnes & Noble Books.

Mcgrane, B. (1989), *Beyond Anthropology: Society and the Other*, New York: Columbia University Press.

Mchose, C., Frank, K. and Society For The Study of Native Arts and Sciences (2006), *How Life Moves: Explorations in Meaning and Body Awareness*, Berkeley: North Atlantic Books.

Mchugh, J. (2016), interview with T. Carter, *Embodying Nature*, http://www.somaticexpression.com/articles/EmbodyingNature.html. Accessed 11 August 2022.

Mcniff, S. (1993), 'The authority of experience', *The Arts in Psychotherapy*, 20:1, pp. 3–9.

Mcniff, S. (1998), *Art-Based Research Shaun McNiff*, London, Philadelphia: Jessica Kingsley.

Mcniff, S. (2004), *Art Heals: How Creativity Cures the Soul*, Boston: Shambhala.

Meacham, H. C. A. D. (2013), *Phenomenology and Naturalism: Examining the Relationship Between Human Experience and Nature* (ed. H. C. A. D. Meacham), Cambridge: Cambridge University Press.

Mearns, D. and Cooper, M. (2005), *Working at Relational Depth in Counselling and Psycho-therapy*, London: SAGE.

Menzies, H. (2014), *Reclaiming the Commons for the Common Good: A Memoir & Manifesto*, Gabriola Island: New Society Publishers.

Merkur, D. and Mills, J. (2017), *Jung's Ethics: Moral Psychology and His Cure of Souls*, London and New York: Routledge, Taylor & Francis Group.

Merleau-Ponty, M. ([1962] 1986), *Phenomenology of Perception*, London: Routledge & Kegan Paul.

Merleau-Ponty, M. and Edie, J. M. (1964), *The Primacy of Perception, and Other Essays on Phenomenological Psychology, the Philosophy of Art, History and Politics* (ed. J. M. Edie), Evanston: Northwestern University Press.

Merleau-Ponty, M. and Lefort, C. (1968), *The Visible and the Invisible; Followed by Working Notes*, Evanston: Northwestern University Press.

Mills, J. (2019), *Jung and Philosophy*, New York: Routledge.

Mindell, A. (2002), *Working on Yourself Alone: Inner Dreambody Work*, Portland, Oakland: Lao Tse Press (Distributed by words distributing).

Mindell, A. (2007), *Earth-Based Psychology: Path Awareness from the Teachings of Don Juan, Richard Feynman, and Lao Tse*, Portland: Lao Tse Press (Distributed by independent publishers group).

Modeen, M. (2014), 'Breaking the boundaries of "Self": Representations of spatial indeterminacy', *Architecture and Culture*, 2, pp. 337–59.

Moffett, L. W. A. A.-T. (2017), 'Building bridges for dance through arts-based research', *Research in Dance Education*, 18:2, pp. 135–49.

Mooney, T. and Moran, D. (2002), *The Phenomenology Reader*, London: Routledge.

Moore, F. C. T. (1996), *Bergson: Thinking Backwards*, Cambridge: Cambridge University Press.

Mori, B. B. D. (2016), 'What makes Natives unique? Overview of knowledge systems among the world's Indigenous people', in *Past-Future-2016: Seminar on the Protection of Aboriginal Wisdom Creation; Proceedings*, Hualien: National Dong Hwa University, pp. 78–85, https://www.academia.edu/28266945/What_makes_Natives_Unique_2016_proceedings_preliminary_version_. Accessed 11 August 2022.

Moustakas, C. (1986), 'Being in, being for, and being with', *The Humanistic Psychologist*, 14:2, Summer, pp. 100–04.

Moustakas, C. E. (1990), *Heuristic Research: Design, Methodology, and Applications*, Newbury Park: SAGE.

Moustakas, C. E. (1994), *Phenomenological Research Methods*, Thousand Oaks: SAGE.

Moustakas, C. E. (1995), *Being-in, Being-for, Being-with*, Northvale: Jason Aronson.

Murphy, D. (2014), 'Psychotherapy, ontology and therapist positioning: Why simplistic integrationist approaches don't work', https://personcentredpsych.wordpress.com/2014/05/14/psychotherapy-ontology-and-therapist-positioning-why-simplistic-integrationist-approaches-dont-work/. Accessed 11 August 2022.

Næss, A., Rothenberg, D. and Næss, A. (1989), *Ecology, Community, and Lifestyle: Outline of an Ecosophy*, Cambridge, New York: Cambridge University Press.

Næss, A. and Haukeland, P. I. (2002), *Life's Philosophy: Reason & Feeling in a Deeper World*, Athens: University of Georgia Press.

Næss, A., Drengson, A. R. and Devall, B. (2008), *Ecology of Wisdom: Writings by Arne Naess*, Berkeley: Counterpoint (Distributed by Publishers Group West).

Neisser, U. and Jopling, D. A. (1997), *The Conceptual Self in Context: Culture, Experience, Self-Understanding*, Cambridge: Cambridge University Press.

Nelson, R. (2013), *Practice as Research in the Arts: Principles, Protocols, Pedagogies, Resistances*, Houndmills, Basingstoke, Hampshire, New York: Palgrave Macmillan.

News, G. (2019), 'David Attenborough speaks in parliament about climate change', YouTube, https://www.youtube.com/watch?v=rv3DPaMaS2g&feature=youtu.be. Accessed 11 August 2022.

Noë, A. (2004), *Action in Perception*, Cambridge, London: MIT Press.

Noë, A. (2012), *Varieties of Presence*, Cambridge: Harvard University Press.

Olsen, A. (2002), *Body and Earth: An Experiential Guide*, Hanover: Middlebury College Press: University Press of New England.

Olsen, A. (2014), 'The place of dance: A somatic guide to dancing and dance making', *Journal of Dance Education*, 15, pp. 164–65.

Olsen, A. and Mchose, C. (1998), *Bodystories: A Guide to Experiential Anatomy*, Barrytown: Barrytown, Ltd.

Papadopoulos, R. K. (2006), *The Handbook of Jungian Psychology: Theory, Practice and Applications*, London: Routledge.

Parviainen, J. (1998), 'Bodies moving and moved: A phenomenological analysis of the dancing subject and the cognitive and ethical values of dance art', Ph.D. thesis, Tampere: University of Tampere, Tampere University Press.

Payne, H. (1992), *Creative Movement & Dance in Groupwork*, Bicester: Winslow.

Payne, H. (2006), *Dance Movement Therapy: Theory, Research and Practice*, London: Routledge.

Phipps, J.-F. (1990), *The Politics of Inner Experience: Dynamics of a Green Spirituality*, London: Green Print.

Phipps, J.-F. (2004), 'Henri Bergson and the perception of time', Philosophy Now, https://philosophynow.org/issues/48/Henri_Bergson_and_the_Perception_of_Time. Accessed 11 August 2022.

Piaget, J. ([1929] 1997), *The Child's Conception of the World*, London: Routledge.

Plotkin, B. (2008), *Nature and the Human Soul: Cultivating Wholeness and Community in a Fragmented World*, Novato: New World Library; Enfield: Publishers Group UK (Distributor).

Poetdox (2015), 'Nora Bateson – An Ecology of Mind – 7th CPH Open Dialogue Meeting', YouTube, https://www.youtube.com/watch?v=y8lA8jsQkNw. Accessed 11 August 2022.

Polanyi, M. and Sen, A. (2009), *The Tacit Dimension*, Chicago: University of Chicago Press; Bristol: University Presses Marketing (Distributor).

Politsky, R. H. (1995), 'Toward a typology of research in the creative arts', *The Arts in Psychotherapy*, 22:4, pp. 307–14.

Prentice, H. (2003), 'Cosmic walk; Awakening the ecological self', *Psychotherapy and Politics International*, 1, pp. 32–46, http://www.hilaryprenticepsychotherapy.net/article%203%20 cosmic%20walk.htm. Accessed 2 February 2018 [no longer available].

Prinz, J. J. (2012), *Beyond Human Nature: How Culture and Experience Shape the Human Mind*, New York: W.W. Norton.

Reddekop, J. (2014), 'Thinking across worlds: Indigenous thought, relational ontology, and the politics of nature; Or, if only Nietzsche could meet a Yachaj', *Electronic Thesis and Dissertation Repository*, http://ir.lib.uwo.ca/etd/2082. Accessed 11 August 2022.

Reed, E. S. (1996), *Encountering the World: Toward an Ecological Psychology*, New York, Oxford: Oxford University Press.

Richards, J. R. (2000), *Human Nature After Darwin: A Philosophical Introduction*, London: Routledge.

Richardson, K. (2000), *Developmental Psychology: How Nature and Nurture Interact*, Basingstoke: Macmillan.

Richardson, W. J. (2003), *Heidegger: Through Phenomenology to Thought*, New York: Fordham University Press.

Robèrt, K.-H. (1996), 'Educating a nation: The natural step, Langley: Context Institute', http://www.context.org/iclib/ic28/robert/. Accessed 11 August 2022.

Rogers, C. R. (1961), *On Becoming a Person; A Therapist's View of Psychotherapy*, Boston: Houghton Mifflin.

Rogers, C. R. (1969), *Freedom to Learn: A View of What Education Might Become*, Columbus: C. E. Merrill Pub. Co.

Rogers, C. R. and Stevens, B. (1967), *Person to Person: The Problem of Being Human; A New Trend in Psychology*, Walnut Creek: Real People Press.

Roly Russell, A. D. G., Balvanera, P., Gould, R. K., Xavier, B., Chan, K. M. A., Klain, S., Levine, J. and Jordan, T. (2013), 'Humans and nature: How knowing and experiencing nature affect well-being', *Annual Review of Environment and Resources*, 38, pp. 473–502, https://www.annualreviews.org https://www.annualreviews.org/doi/full/10.1146/annurev-environ-012312-110838. Accessed 11 August 2022.

Romanyshyn, R. D. (n.d.), Robert Romanyshyn, http://robertromanyshyn.com/works-in-progress. Accessed 11 October 2022.

Romanyshyn, R. D. (1982), *Psychological Life: From Science to Metaphor*, Milton Keynes: Open University Press.

Romanyshyn, R. D. (2002), *Ways of the Heart: Essays Toward an Imaginal Psychology*, Pittsburgh: Trivium.

Romanyshyn, R. D. (2007), *The Wounded Researcher: Research with Soul in Mind*, New Orleans: Spring Journal Books.

Rorty, A. L. (1980), *Explaining Emotions*, Berkeley: University of California Press.

Roszak, T. (1992), *The Voice of the Earth*, New York: Simon & Schuster.

Roszak, T. (2010), 'Towards an eco-psychology (excerpt)', Thinking Allowed, YouTube, https://www.youtube.com/watch?v=83VHiA2HhkM&t=212s. Accessed 11 August 2022.

Roszak, T., Gomes, M. E. and Kanner, A. D. (1995), *Ecopsychology – Restoring the Earth, Healing the Mind*, San Francisco: Sierra Club Books.

Rowan, P. R. A. J. (1981), 'Issues of validity in a new paradigm research', in P. Reason and J. Rowan (eds), *Human Inquiry*, Chichester: J. Wiley, pp. 239–50.

Reason, P. and Rowan, J. (1981), *Human Inquiry: A Sourcebook of New Paradigm Research*, Chichester: Wiley.

Rowland, S. (2012), *The Ecocritical Psyche: Literature, Evolutionary Complexity and Jung*, Hove, New York: Routledge.

Russell, P. (1982), *The Awakening Earth: Our Next Evolutionary Leap*, London: Routledge & Kegan Paul.

Russell, P. (2007), *The Global Brain: The Awakening Earth in a New Century*, Edinburgh: Floris Books.

Rytz, T. (2009), *Centered and Connected: A Therapeutic Approach to Mind–Body Awareness*, Berkeley: North Atlantic Books.

Sarco-Thomas, M. (2010), 'Twig dances: Improvisation performance as ecological practice', Ph.D. thesis, Dartington: University of Plymouth.

Seamon, D. and Buttimer, A. (1980), *The Human Experience of Space and Place*, London: Croom Helm.

Seamon, D. and Mugerauer, R. (1989), *Dwelling, Place, and Environment: Towards a Phenomenology of Person and World*, New York: Columbia University Press.

Seamon, D. and Zajonc, A. (1998), *Goethe's Way of Science: A Phenomenology of Nature*, Albany: State University of New York Press.

Seed, J. (1988), *Thinking Like a Mountain: Towards a Council of All Beings*, Philadelphia: New Society Publishers.

Sheets-Johnstone, M. (1979), *The Phenomenology of Dance*, London: Dance Books.

Sheets-Johnstone, M. (1984), *Illuminating Dance: Philosophical Explorations*, Lewisburg: Bucknell University Press; London: Associated University Presses.

Sheets-Johnstone, M. (1990), *The Roots of Thinking*, Philadelphia: Temple University Press.

Sheets-Johnstone, M. (2009), *The Corporeal Turn: An Interdisciplinary Reader*, Exeter: Imprint Academic.

Sheets-Johnstone, M. (2011), *The Primacy of Movement*, Amsterdam, Philadelphia: John Benjamins Pub. Co.

Silverman, D. (2004), *Qualitative Research: Theory, Method and Practice*, London: SAGE.

Singer, J. E. A. (2018), 'Being and becoming: The creative balance of the artist teacher', Ph.D. thesis, Aberdeen: University of Aberdeen.

Smith, H. and Dean, R. T. (2009), *Practice-Led Research, Research-Led Practice in the Creative Arts*, Edinburgh: Edinburgh University Press.

Smith, J. A., Larkin, M. H. and Flowers, P. (2009), *Interpretative Phenomenological Analysis: Theory, Method and Research*, Los Angeles, London: SAGE.

Smith, T. E. and Knapp, C. E. (2011), *Sourcebook of Experiential Education: Key Thinkers and Their Contributions*, London: Routledge.

Spiro, M. E. (1954), 'Human nature in its psychological dimensions', *American Anthropologist*, 56, pp. 19–30, http://onlinelibrary.wiley.com/store/10.1525/aa.1954.56.1.02a00030/asset/aa.1954.56.1.02a00030.pdf?v=1&t=j78tqqfr&s=aa4ce02845ac78d4e354f0b-0caff349385654e24. Accessed 2 February 2022 [no longer available].

Stevenson, L. F., Haberman, D. L., Wright, P. M. and Stevenson, L. F. T. T. O. H. N. (2013), *Twelve Theories of Human Nature*, New York: Oxford University Press.

Stewart, D. and Mickunas, A. (1990), *Exploring Phenomenology: A Guide to the Field and Its Literature*, Athens: Ohio University Press.

Stoller, P. (1997), *Sensuous Scholarship*, Philadelphia: University of Pennsylvania Press.

Stromsted, T. (2007), 'The dancing body in psychotherapy: Reflections on somatic pychotherapy and Authentic Movement', *Authentic Movement: Moving the Body, Moving the Self, Being Moved*, London: Jessica Kingsley Publishers, pp. 202–20.

Swimme, B. (2016), 'Journey of the Universe | Talks at Google, Talks at Google', YouTube, https://www.youtube.com/watch?v=YOlkkMxAhj4. Accessed 11 August 2022.

Tarnas, R. (1991), *The Passion of the Western Mind: Understanding the Ideas that have Shaped Our World View*, New York: Harmony Books.

The Journal of Transpersonal Psychology (1969–) Palo Alto: The Association for Transpersonal Psychology (ATP).

Tilley, C. Y. (1994), *A Phenomenology of Landscape: Places, Paths, and Monuments*, Oxford, Providence: Berg.

Toadvine, T. (2009), *Merleau-Ponty's Philosophy of Nature*, Evanston: Northwestern University Press.

Todd, M. E. (1968), *The Thinking Body: A Study of the Balancing Forces of Dynamic Man*, Brooklyn: Dance Horizons.

Todres, L. (2007), *Embodied Enquiry: Phenomenological Touchstones for Research, Psychotherapy, and Spirituality*, Houndmills, Basingstoke, New York: Palgrave Macmillan.

Torres, M. and Reyes, L. V. (2011), *Research as Praxis: Democratizing Education Epistemologies*, New York: Peter Lang.

Tougas, C. T. (2013), *The Phenomena of Awareness: Husserl, Cantor, Jung*, London: Routledge.

Tufnell, M. (2010), *Dance, Health and Wellbeing: Pathway to Practice for Dance Leaders Working in Health and Care Settings*, Leicester: Foundation for Community Dance.

Tufnell, M. and Crickmay, C. (1990), *Body, Space, Image: Notes Towards Improvisation and Performance*, London: Virago.

Tufnell, M. and Crickmay, C. L. (2004), *A Widening Field: Journeys in Body and Imagination*, Alton: Dance.

Tulku, T. (1977), *Time, Space, and Knowledge: A New Vision of Reality*, Emeryville: Dharma Pub.

Tulku, T. (2016), *The Joy of Being: Advanced Kum Nye Practices for Relaxation, Integration, Concentration*, Cazadero: Dharma Pub.

Tymieniecka, A.-T. E. (1986), *The Phenomenology of Man and of the Human Condition. [Part] 2. The Meeting Point Between Occidental and Oriental Philosophies*, London: Kluwer.

Tymieniecka, A.-T. E. (1991), *Phenomenology in the World Fifty Years After the Death of Husserl: 1st World Congress of Phenomenology: Selected Papers*, Dordrecht, Boston: Kluwer Academic Publishers.

Tymieniecka, A.-T. (2001), *Passions of the Earth in Human Existence, Creativity, and Literature*, Boston: Kluwer Academic Publishers.

Vakoch, D. A. and Castrillón, F. (2014), *Ecopsychology, Phenomenology, and the Environment: The Experience of Nature*, New York: Springer.

Van Manen, M. (1990), *Researching Lived Experience: Human Science for an Action Sensitive Pedagogy*, Albany: State University of New York Press.

Van Manen, M. A. (2007), 'Phenomenology of practice: Meaning-giving methods in phenomenological research and writing', *Phenomenology & Practice*, 1, pp. 11–30, http://www.maxvanmanen.com/files/2014/03/Max-Phenomenology-of-Practice1.pdf. Accessed 11 August 2022.

Varela, F. J., Thompson, E. and Rosch, E. (1991), *The Embodied Mind: Cognitive Science and Human Experience*, Cambridge: MIT Press.

Varley, M. (2009), *Discover Loch Lomond & the Trossachs National Park*, Edinburgh: Birlinn (in association with) Friends of Loch Lomond & the Trossachs, Edinburgh: Birlinn Ltd.

Von Eckartsberg, R. (1986), *Life-World Experience: Existential-Phenomenological Research Approaches in Psychology*, Pittsburgh: Center for Advanced Research in Phenomenology.

Whatley, S. E., Brown, N. G. E. and Alexander, K. E. (2015), *Attending to Movement: Somatic Perspectives on Living in this World*, Axminster: Triarchy.

Whitehead, A. N., Griffin, D. R. and Sherburne, D. W. (1978), *Process and Reality: An Essay in Cosmology*, New York: Free Press.

Whitehouse, M. S., Adler, J., Chodorow, J. and Pallaro, P. (1999), *Authentic Movement*, London: Jessica Kingsley.

Wildman, W. J. (2006), 'An introduction to relational ontology', in J. Polkinghorne (ed.), *The Trinity and an Entangled World: Relationality in Physical Science and Theology*, London: Wm. B. Eerdmans Publishing, pp. 55–73, http://people.bu.edu/wwildman/images/docs/(72)%202010%20-%20Wildman%20-%20Introduction%20to%20Relational%20Ontology%20(final%20author%20version)%20-%20Polkinghorne%20ed.pdf. Accessed 11 August 2022.

Williamson, A. E., Batson, G. E. and Whatley, S. E., *Dance, Somatics and Spiritualities: Contemporary Sacred Narratives*, Bristol: Intellect.

Wilson, E. O. (1978), *On Human Nature*, Cambridge, London: Harvard University Press.

Winter, D. D. N. (1996), *Ecological Psychology: Healing the Split Between Planet and Self*, New York: HarperCollins College Publishers.

Winter, D. D. N., Koger, S. M. and Winter, D. D. N. E. P. (2003), *The Psychology of Environmental Problems*, Mahwah, London: Lawrence Erlbaum.

Witt, C. (2003), *Ways of Being: Potentiality and Actuality in Aristotle's Metaphysics*, Ithaca: Cornell University Press.

Wittmann, G. A., Oppenheimer, A. T., Schorn, U. A., Lippe, R. Z. A. O. I. E., Land, R. A. and Halprin, A. A. O. I. E. (2015), *Anna Halprin: Dance, Process, Form*, London and Philadelphia: Jessica Kingsley.

Wood, D. (2007), *Time after Time*, Bloomington: Indiana University Press.

Woodman, M. and Mellick, J. (1998), *Coming Home to Myself: Daily Reflections for a Woman's Body and Soul*, Berkeley, Emeryville: Conari Press (Distributed by Publishers Group West).

Wrightsman, L. S. (1992), *Assumptions About Human Nature: Implications for Researchers and Practitioners*, London: SAGE.

Young, J. (2001), *Heidegger's Philosophy of Art*, Cambridge: Cambridge University Press.

Zwart, P. J. (1976), *About Time: A Philosophical Inquiry into the Origin and Nature of Time*, Amsterdam: North-Holland Publ. Co.

About the Author

Dr Anna Dako, RSME/T, UKSMDT

Anna is an interdisciplinary movement artists, and a Registered Somatic Movement Educator and Therapist with nearly 20 years of experience working with dance, movement and creative arts. Anna's experience stretches from dance research, dramaturgy and on-screen productions. She collaborates internationally and has lived and worked in Poland, the Netherlands and now in Scotland, UK.

Anna is the founder of Dunami – Movement, Arts, Wellbeing, a platform for ecologically mindful growth, psycho-somatic health, intercultural dialogue and artistic development.

As a writer, she specialises in practice-based research, ecopsychology and environmental philosophy perspectives. In her doctoral research on art-based therapeutic education she has been developing movement-based approaches toward more embodied ways for 'being well' with the natural environment guided by processes of creative felt thinking. Felt thinking opens up a whole new realm of philosophical contemplation on what it means to be human and on experiential movement as the basic ontology of relating to the living world. As a grounding methodology of reflexive and expressive self-inquiry, it is now offered as a training course in eco-somatic movement education by Dunami.

Following her interests in building bridges between movement arts practice, environmental psychologies of personal development and intercultural dialogue inspired by embodied reflection upon life experience in all-inclusive ways, Anna is now developing her movement productions with In The Open – Outdoor Arts Theatre, as well as offers regular workshops with the Spring Seedling annual event. She is also a board member of Somatic Movement Dance Therapies Association UK.

In her private practice Anna specializes in supporting and working through versatile psycho-somatic imbalances. She also loves guiding experiential walks, and working with children, both in therapy and creative education.

For more information, visit: www.dunami-somatics.com